THE GUINNESS BOOK OF
BUSINESS
RECORDS

Tom Cannon

with additional research by Karen Smith

GUINNESS PUBLISHING

THE GUINNESS BOOK OF
BUSINESS RECORDS

Design: Sarah Silvé

Layout: Rob and Rhoda Burns

Cover artwork: Peter Harper

Picture research: Image Select

First published 1996
Reprint 10 9 8 7 6 5 4 3 2 1 0

ISBN 0-85112-794-0

A catalogue record for this book is available from the British Library

Printed and bound in Great Britain by The Bath Press, Bath

Business
Records

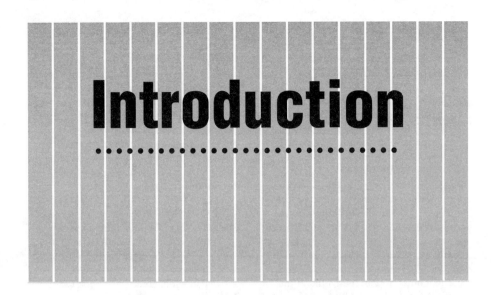

Introduction

The world of superlatives and the world of modern business are inseparable. The tallest buildings, the largest ships and many of the greatest endeavours are now developed and built for commercial gain or advantage. A hundred or more years ago, the largest buildings were often initiated to demonstrate the power of rulers. They were frequently designed to put the population in awe of the greatness of others or their power over them.

From the Great Wall of China to the Capitol in Washington DC, the message was clear – stand in awe of those who build this vast edifice. The greatest ships were designed for military or political ends. The largest organizations were the armies of conquerors from Darius the Great to Napoleon or the bureaucracies established to rule cities, countries or empires.

The emergence and success of modern industry changed all this. The largest organizations now have commercial ends. The Indian Railway system might have been built to serve the goals of the Raj but it is now a commercial venture. Its size, viability and survival ultimately depend on the willingness of its customers to use its services.

The largest purely commercial ventures – firms like General Motors and National Telegraph and Telephone of Japan – have far more permanent employees than the armies of their respective countries. Only in countries where the business edge is blunted by authoritarian regimes does the military machine continue to involve more people then the largest commercial ventures.

The greatest modern constructions are commercial rather than political or imperial. Even when the name, like the Empire State Building, conjures up the old images – the purpose is unashamedly commercial, and the recent financial difficulties surrounding this vast building showed that its viability depends on its profitability. Across the world, the greatest contemporary buildings such as the Sears Tower in Chicago, the Lloyds Building in London, the Hong Kong and Shanghai Bank in Hong Kong show the clarity of the link between scale, record, achievement and business.

The world of business is massive, exciting, dynamic and sometimes controversial. Record breakers vary in size, age, growth and performance. Sometimes, business distorts the image. The riches created by businesses, the wealth controlled by individuals, families and groups far exceeds that available to most other groups.

The collapse of businesses and the disappearance of wealth can be equally dramatic.

5

All these aspects of business are described in the *Guinness Book of Business Records*.

(S) The primary, social role of business activity is economic. It is little wonder that most business records centre on the economic performance of businesses and the ability of firms to grow, achieve economies of scale, mobilize resources and generate wealth, jobs and other economic outputs. Chapter 1 details the scale and range of business. The largest firms are identified, although business has developed various ways to measure and, hence, assess the scale and performance of organizations. The number of employees is an important measure, but the nature of the commercial activity largely determines the number of employees.

Manufacturing and retailing generally employ more people than sectors like telecommunications and banking. The small staff of a specialist financial institution might handle far more money and have a far greater economic impact than a medium-sized manufacturer.

(S) The turnover of a firm – the sum of its sales and other disposals is another important indicator but, again, this only gives part of the picture. Some enterprises have built up an asset base – the sum of its properties, goods, equipment etc. – which is far greater than its rivals with comparable turnover. Market capitalization, i.e. the value of all the shares in the firm, draws out another aspect of the venture.

The first chapter of the *Guinness Book of Business Records* draws these different strands together: it provides a picture of the range and scale of business activity across the world, in Europe, North America and other regions. The analysis extends beyond the current environment to the history of commercial activity.

(S) Many of humanity's earliest social activities were economic. People came together to trade, learn and compete. The earliest businesses are described in Chapter 2 – The First

Businesses. This highlights not only the antiquity of commerce but the proliferation of business activities around the world. Across the globe, surpluses led to trade and the benefits of trade prompted some people to look for ways to improve their output and gain even more benefits. Some activities which seem very modern, such as banking, have a history going back thousands of years.

(S) The wealth that commerce produces is vulnerable to the ambitions and attacks of others. Relatively few businesses survive from historical times, but their ideas and achievements are often better remembered. Some have persisted: their stories are often testaments to the strength of their enterprise and the resilience and innovativeness of their proprietors. Enterprising or creative individuals would either spot opportunities or would grasp the chance to build a business to tap an opportunity. Often, this involves creative solutions to old problems. Whitney was not the first person to be asked to mass produce guns. He was, however, the first person to do this successfully by breaking the product into its key components, letting workers specialize and assembling the parts.

The tool-using ability of human beings was long seen as a major difference between people and animals: that was, until some apes were shown how to use tools. The ability to build tools and invent new tools is probably a more important difference. Inventiveness is an age old characteristic of mankind. It is over the last two centuries that business has converted this ability into the major driving force of change. Chapter 3 examines these inventions and innovations.

The most important inventions are described and are placed in the context of the related changes which made invention and innovation more practical and productive. Some of the most important shifts were in the wider body of knowledge especially the growth of scientific knowledge. It is, however, the determination to use knowledge to innovate and meet market needs that distinguishes the business of innovation from the pursuit of science and invention.

Some of the greatest innovators amassed great fortunes. These were not only the inventors of new products and services but also people who found new ways to make existing products. Commodore Vanderbilt and J. D. Rockerfeller did not invent railways or the means to process or find oil, but they were masters of the process of finding new ways to reach markets. Henry Ford did not invent the motor car – he found ways to build more reliable and cheaper cars than anyone else.

The wealth of business people from Croesus to Perot is described in Chapter 4. The extent of these fortunes is often best understood in terms of comparisons. Commodore Vanderbilt, when he died, left more money than existed in the US Treasury. The Commodore argued that the trick with money was not acquiring wealth but holding on to it. Fortunes can be lost as quickly as they are made, and the spectacular collapses of personal and corporate fortunes are also described in Chapter 4.

 The distribution of wealth remains a major issue in industrial society. In the post-industrial world, in particular, great wealth often stands alongside great deprivation. The contrasts are especially sharp between the owners and controllers of enterprises and those who work in or serve these organizations. The growth of organized labour and other ways to defend workers' rights is charted in Chapter 5. This is not just a catalogue of exploitation and dispute. It highlights the sacrifices that were often needed to get a minimum of protection and the dedication of some people to the needs of others.

Trades unionism is only part of this picture. Some employers were major innovators in developing ways to give their employees a fairer share. Important developments such as the growth of the co-operative movement, which took workers into the marketplace as active members, are also described. In many countries, co-operative retailers and producers successfully compete with their more conventional rivals.

Chapter 6 describes the extent, scale and range of marketing activity. It, also, explores the different ways in which competition and conflict have been expressed. This competition often extends beyond the commercial sphere into wider political and international interest.

Competition and conflict are inseparable from risk. In Chapter 7, the different dimensions of risk and the chances people and groups take in pursuit of their business ambitions are described. A feature of the business world is the tendency of groups to follow each other in taking or avoiding risks. The most spectacular examples of this are the great bull and bear markets which have characterized stock markets since their first creation. The great surges and crashes in markets include the massive increases in values seen with the South Seas Company and during the 1920s, and the equally dramatic collapses. The same phenomenon is seen in some specific commodity markets, for example the attempt of the Hunts to control the silver market, which is described in this section.

The diversity of business activity is vividly illustrated in the range of industries and commercial activities. Chapter 8 highlights some of the more significant industrial sectors and why they are so important. The history of the major industries highlights the pace of change which characterizes business.

This means that the story of business is never ending. Today's records will be broken tomorrow. Even the issues that must be measured change. There is a growing preoccupation with responsibility and the conservation of assets. Chapter 9 looks at some of the new preoccupations and explores the ways they will set new standards which mean new records, benchmarks and achievements.

1

The Biggest Companies

What is the largest company in the world? How do we measure scale when there are so many possible indicators? When was the biggest takeover and how was it put together? These are just some of the issues we need to address in deciding which are the biggest companies in the world. There are many options. The most basic is the number of employees, but in this chapter the analysis goes beyond this single measure to other indicators which can give a more full definitive indicator of the biggest firms in the world, specific regions and areas of commerce.

The largest company in the world is probably still General Motors of Detroit, Michigan, USA, with total assets of over $188Bn in 1994, sales of just over $133Bn and a workforce which, despite a sharp contraction recently, still comprises about 700,000 people. It covers a wide range of industrial sectors from its core business of car production, to defence and aerospace to computers and communications. Alongside these positive features, it managed to post the **greatest annual loss** in corporate history in 1992 when it announced a deficit of $23Bn.

General Motors was founded in 1908 by William Crapo Durant (1861–1947) as General Motors Company of New Jersey. The firm was incorporated in Delaware as General Motors Corporation 1916, and has acquired many other auto-

mobile and accessory companies. General Motors makes not only Buick, Cadillac, Chevrolet, Oldsmobile, and Pontiac cars, accessories and trucks, but also Frigidaire appliances. It has worldwide operations. In its early years, it struggled to compete with Henry Ford's innovative Model T Ford, but under the leadership of Pierre S. Du Pont and Alfred P. Sloan, General Motors eventually wrested dominance of the US car industry from Ford.

General Motors wedded dominance of the US car industry with a widening portfolio of activities until it became recognized as the largest corporation in the world. It was probably at its zenith in the early 1950s when Charles E. Wilson – Company President – commented to the US Senate Armed Forces committee "What is good for the country is good for General Motors and what's good for General Motors is good for the country".

Another US giant, General Electric with business interests ranging from financial services through TV broadcasting (NBC) to consumer electrical products (Hotpoint), sometimes called 'white goods', has a valid claim to be the largest corporation if assets, profits and stockholders equity is given comparable weighting to payroll and sales. Analysis of the largest industrial and service corporations in the world which gives equal weight to the five indicators identified above – assets, sales,

9

William C. Durant – unacknowledged genius

If Henry Ford is one of the heroic figures of industry, William C. Durant can claim to be one of the clearest symbols of industrial leadership this century. Durant founded General Motors. Perhaps more important, he introduced a whole series of innovations which are at least as important as Ford's system of mass production.

He introduced the notion of the product range. While Ford offered one major product, Durant offered a full range. He pioneered decentralized management and integrated operations through a mixture of

acquisition and development which produced everything from Champion Spark Plugs to GM Trucks. Innovation and change were his life blood.

The fluctuations in Durant's fortunes also represented an increasingly familiar characteristic of competition. He established GM in 1908. By the end of 1909 he had added Buick, Oldsmobile, Oakland (now Pontiac) and Cadillac – producing sales of $7.5M and profits of $1.7M. Within two years, he had lost control of the company and was forced by his bankers to step down from the post of chief executive.

The Chevrolet Impala Custom Coupe,
an American advert of 1969. The Chevrolet has been one of
the most prestigious cars manufactured by General Motors,
probably the largest company in the world.
(Peter Newark's American Pictures).

A year later he was backing Louis Chevrolet in the formation of the Chevrolet Motor Company. By 1915 this was a nationwide enterprise, surging forward in sales and value.

A year later he used his influence at Chevrolet to regain control of GM. The acquisition of Chevrolet in 1918, and Fisher Bodies and Frigidaire in 1919, produced the core GM structure which can still be seen today. A year later he was forced to resign – once again – and finally to resign as President of GM. His personal and financial position never recovered. It is said that Harold Robins used his story as the basis for one of the characters in his book *The Carpetbaggers*.

The biggest companies in the world

Rank	Company	Country
1	General Motors	USA
2	Ford Motor	USA
3	Royal Dutch/Shell Group	UK/Netherlands
4	General Electric	USA
5	Exxon	USA
6	Nippon Telegraph & Telephone	Japan
7	Hitachi	Japan
8	Toyota Motor	Japan
9	Mitsubishi	Japan
10	Sears Roebuck	USA

profits, equity and payroll – makes General Motors the largest company in the world. In 1995 *Fortune* declared that Mitsubishi had overtaken GM as the largest corporation measured by income.

 General Electric's roots go back to the invention by Thomas Edison of

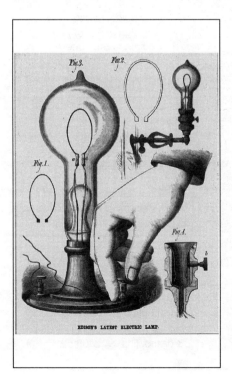

EDISON'S LATEST ELECTRIC LAMP.

the light bulb. It was created by the merger of Charles Coffin's Thomas-Houston company and Thomas Edison's Edison General Electric Company. For most of its history, it managed to combine steady growth in its portfolio of activities with excellent profits. It responded to the recession of the 1990s by disposing of several large activities, most notably its aerospace division which it sold to Martin Marietta for $3Bn. This was the latest in a series of acquisitions and disposals which totalled $21Bn of purchases and $11Bn of sales. General Motors and General Electric's market capitalization of $30Bn and $82Bn in 1992 are dwarfed by Nippon Telegraph and Telephone (NT&T) with a capitalization of $123Bn.

NT&T took part in the **largest privatization** exercise in history with an initial public offering of $12.4Bn in 1986. Privatizations have raised massive sums for sponsoring governments across the world. The gross revenues to date were estimated by *The Economist* in 1993 at $60Bn. Britain's biggest privatization

Edison's carbon filament lamp, an illustration from Scientific American (published in New York on 10 January 1880). The roots of General Electric, one of the five largest companies in the world, go back to the invention of the light bulb by Thomas Edison. (Ann Ronan Picture Library).

Market capitalization

Ranking	Company	Capitalization ($Bn)
1	NT&T	139
2	General Electric	82
3	Toyota	77
4	AT&T	73
5	Mitsubishi Bank	72
6	Exxon Corp.	71
7	Industrial Bank of Japan	71
8	Coca-Cola Co.	63
9	Fuji Bank Ltd.	62
10	Sumitomo Bank Ltd.	60
(22)	General Motors	35

Source: *Financial Times*

Biggest privatizations

Company	Date	Value ($Bn)
NT&T	1986	12.4
BP (Britain)	1987	9.5
British Gas	1986	7.8
BT (Britain)	1984	4.9
British Steel	1988	4.5
Scottish Power	1991	3.7
Société General (France)	1987	3.7
Yacimienytos Petroliferos Fiscales (Argentina)	1993	3.0
National Power (Britain)	1991	2.3
Telefonos de Mexico	1991	2.2

Industrial companies with the largest sales

Rank	Company	Headquarters	Sector	$Sales (M)
1	Mitsui & Co. Ltd	Japan	Sogo shosha	163.453
2	Mitsubishi Corp.	Japan	Sogo shosha	160.109
3	Sumitomo Corp.	Japan	Sogo shosha	157.551
4	Itochu Corp.	Japan	Sogo shosha	155.161
5	Marubeni Corp.	Japan	Sogo shosha	144.502
6	General Motors Corp.	USA	Transport manufacture & distribution	133.621
7	Ford Motor Co.	USA	Transport – manufacture & distribution	108.521

8	Exxon Corp.	USA	Oil, gas & nuclear fuels	97.825
9	Nissho Iwai Corp.	Japan	Sogo shosha	95.462
10	Royal Dutch /Shell Group	UK/ Netherlands	Oil, gas & nuclear fuels	95.134
11	Toyota Motor Corp.	Japan	Transport – manufacture & distribution	85.283
12	Hitachi Ltd	Japan	Electronics	68.581
13	Wal-Mart	USA	Retail	67.345
14	American Telephone & Telegraph	USA	Communications	67.156
15	Tomen Corp.	Japan	Sogo shosha	64.631
16	International Business Machines	USA	Communications	62.716
17	Nippon Telegraph and Telephone	Japan	Communications	61.651
18	Matsushita	Japan	Electronics, engineering	61.384
19	General Electric	USA	Electronics, communications, finance	60.823
20	Daimler-Benz	Germany	Transport – manufacture & distribution	59.102

Source: *Fortune* **NB** Banks, insurance and saving companies are excluded from this analysis because of the difficulty of comparing their tradable services e.g. deposit taking with sales income.because of the difficulty of comparing their tradable services e.g. deposit taking with sales income.

was BP which raised $7.8Bn. NT&T has over 230,000 employees and its turnover was $60Bn in 1994.

Mitsui and Co, the Japanese trading company or Sogo shosha , has the greatest sales of an industrial or trading company with sales of $163,453,200.

Sogo shosha are a distinctively Japanese form of general trading company. They usually cover a wide range of trading activities from banking to research and development. Their intimate links with many manufacturers and their powerful financial resources allow them to open up and develop markets effectively. At their peak the Sogo shosha handled roughly 60 per cent of all Japanese internal and external trade. More recently, this share has declined as some Japanese manufacturers have asserted their autonomy while the Sogo shosha have developed their links with producers from other countries. Many Sogo shosha had their origins in the Zaibatsu. These were 'wealthy cliques' of industrial enterprises that dominated Japanese industry between the Meiji Restoration (1868) and the end of World War II. Their involvement with the Japanese war machine and the use of slave labour prompted McArthur to try to suppress them during the US occupation. This failed as, after their shares were put up for sale, ownership and control scarcely changed. Many of the names of the Zaibatsu are familiar today, for example Mitsui, Mitsubishi, Sumitomo.

The **world's largest employer** is Indian Railways with 1,646,704 staff at the end of March 1990. This figure dwarfs the num-

Largest commercial employers

Rank	Company	Country	Employees (000's)
1	US Postal Service	USA	729
2	General Motors	USA	693
3	Wal-Mart Stores	USA	600
4	Pepsi-Co	USA	471
5	Siemens	Germany	382
6	Sears Roebuck	USA	360
7	Ford Motor	USA	338
8	KMart	USA	335
9	Hitachi	Japan	332
10	Daimler-Benz	Germany	331
11	AT&T	USA	305
12	Unilever	UK/Netherlands	304
13	IRI	Italy	293
14	Matsushita Electric Industrial	Japan	265
15	Philips Electronics	Netherlands	253
16	Fiat	Italy	249
17	International Business Machines	USA	243
18	Volkswagen	Germany	242
19	Deutsche Bundespost Telecom	Germany	223
20	General Electric	USA	221

bers employed in the largest industrial concerns. Between them, the three largest industrial employers have a total workforce of just over 1.5m (see the accompanying table).

General Motors is the **largest industrial employer** with just under 700,000 employees. After General Motors, the US retailer Wal-Mart is the largest employer. Wal-Mart was founded and built up by Sam Walton who was probably the richest person in the USA on his death in 1992. It is hard to compare employment in services like retailing with manufacturing because of the preponderance of part-time and temporary employees in many services.

Europe's largest employer is the British National Health Service with 1,250,000 employees excluding general practitioners.

Biggest UK employers

Rank	Company	Employees
1	Unilever	294,000
2	Post Office	193,163
3	BAT Industries	190,308
4	British Telecom	165,700
5	BTR	129,814

Source: *Financial Times*

Seimens, the German electronics and electronic equipment group is **Europe's largest industrial employer** with a total workforce of over 391,000 in 1994.

The **UK's largest business employer** is Unilever with 294,000 employees worldwide.

Largest companies by total assets

Rank	Company	Assets ($M)
1	Fuji Bank	507,218.6
2	Dai-Ichi Kangyo Bank	506,563.3
3	Sumitomo Bank	497,780.9
4	Sakura Bank	495,974.8
5	Sanwa Bank	493,588.0
6	Mitsubishi Bank	458,906.4
7	Norinchukin Bank	429,258.4
8	Industrial Bank of Japan	386,916.1
9	Nippon Life	339,052.8
10	Credit Lyonnais	338,848.3
11	Industrial and Commercial Bank of China	337,768.6
12	Deutsche Bank	317,240.9
13	Tokai Bank	311,451.3
14	Hongkong & Shanghai Banking Corporation Holdings	305,205.0
15	Long Term Credit Bank of Japan	302,185.2
16	Credit Agricole	282,866.8
17	Bank of China	262,879.8
18	Asahi Bank	261,963.2
19	Société General	259,793.7
20	ABN – Amro Holding	252,986.2
(21)	General Electric	251,506.0

Source: *Financial Times, Fortune.*

Although employment is a powerful indicator of the scale of an industrial enterprise, many commentators argue that the asset base of a company, i.e. the total property or resources as shown in the balance sheet, is a better indicator of size especially in service industries.

These resources are usually said to be of two types: physical assets such as plant or

Total assets (British companies)

Company	Assets ($M)
Hongkong & Shanghai Banking Corporation Holdings	305,205.0
Barclays	241,610.4
Natwest Bank	225,604.3
Abbey National	123,820.9
Halifax	100,776.0

Top 10 banks in Russia

Rank	Bank	Capital ($M)
1	Promstroibank of Russia	722
2	International Moscow Bank	653
3	Mosbusinessbank	367
4	Rossiyskiy Kredit Bank	257
5	Commercial Bank Imperial	212
6	United Export Import Bank	205
7	Inkom Bank	173
8	Stolichny Bank	154
9	Tokobank	127
10	Agroprombank	122

William Hesketh Lever (1851–1925)

The father of Unilever first observed the intricacies of consumer demand in his father's grocery shop in Bolton, Greater Manchester, England. Lever went into the family business but captured a more discerning market with careful packaging of his 'Sunlight' soap and guarantees of quality. Innovative 1994.marketing and aggressive deal making was a constant feature of the phenomenal growth of Lever Bros.

The very model of the benign dictator or 'philanthropic despot', Lever built his model worker's village Port Sunlight, near Ellesmere Port (Cheshire) on the River Mersey. Lever's company diversified into other household products, all of reliable quality and modest price.

Wanting his own oilseed supply, Lever satisfied a commercial need and romantic urge by creating from 1911, model palm oil estates, along the lines of Port Sunlight, in the Belgian Congo (now Zaïre).

By 1924, Lever had become Viscount Leverhulme and his business, which had been founded on a bar of soap, had a capitalization of over $200m and was the largest industrial conglomerate in the world. He became increasingly obsessed with his capacity for transforming Africa, and disastrous speculation led to the board taking control out of his hands. His death, when Lever employed 20,000 people worldwide, came four years before the merger with the Margarine Union to form Unilever.

equipment; and financial assets such as currency, bank deposits, stocks and shares. Fuji Bank of Japan has **the most assets of any commercial concern.** Among industrial producers, General Electric has the largest asset base.

BAT has the greatest total assets of UK registered companies excluding banks and financial services with assets of $46Bn. BAT was the subject of the **largest take over bid in British business history** when a consortium led by Sir James Goldsmith, and including Jacob Rothschild and Kerry Packer, unsuccessfully bid $20Bn for the company. The largest successful bid in Britain occurred when Hanson Group won control of Consolidated Gold Fields with a bid of $5Bn.

The largest company in the UK in terms of market capitalization is Shell Transport and Trading with a total capitalization of $23Bn. Unilever is **Britain's largest manufacturing company**.

*The headquarters of the Hongkong &
Shanghai Banking Corporation in Hong Kong.
The Corporation is the British company with the
greatest total assets.
(HSBC Holdings plc).*

Besides being the largest industrial
employer, it had assets valued at $24.7Bn
in 1993, had a turnover of $43.6Bn and
made almost $3Bn in profits in

Royal Dutch Shell is **Europe's largest
company** in terms of both turnover and
market capitalization. Its capitalization is
twice that of its nearest rival – $94.0Bn
versus $45.0Bn for Roche Holding. Its total

turnover was $99.1Bn in 1994. The compa
ny was created by Sir Marcus Samuel and
named in recognition of his father's early
trade in sea shells – an image revived, perhaps accidentally, in a comment by Tony
Curtis to Marilyn Monroe in the film Some
Like it Hot (see below).

Some Like It Hot

In the film Some Like It Hot a conversation
between Tony Curtis and Marilyn Monroe
harks back to the origins of Shell Oil.

Curtis has abandoned his disguise as a
member of an all-girl band to meet Monroe

on the beach. His latest disguise is as a millionaire waiting on the beach to be summoned back to his yacht. His problem is to explain to Monroe why he cannot take up her invitation to come and hear her band (in which he is playing in his other disguise as a female jazz musician).

Curtis: "I only come ashore twice a day, when the tide goes out".

Monroe: "Oh!"

Curtis: "It's on account of these shells – that's my hobby".

Monroe: "You collect shells?"

"Curtis: "Yes, so did my father and grand-father – you might say we had a passion for shells – that's why we named the oil company after them".

Monroe: "Shell Oil!"

Curtis: "Please, no names – just call me Junior".

The merger of Samuel's Shell Transport and Trading with Henri Detering's Royal Dutch Company created Royal Dutch Shell

on the basis of a handwritten note drafted in December 1901, and eventually finalized in 1907.

 Daimler Benz, with interests ranging from motors to aerospace, is **Europe's largest manufacturer** with a turnover of $63.1Bn, 371,107 employees and a market capitalization of $24.5Bn. The largest European companies are not distributed evenly across Europe but are concentrated in the larger European economies like the UK, Germany and France (see accompanying diagram).

Distribution of the top 20 largest firms

NL 5%
France 10%
Germany 20%
Italy 5%
Swiss 15%
UK 45%

The Fortune 500

Each year *Fortune* magazine publishes the most authoritative ranking of the world's largest firms: it provides a ranking of the world's 500 largest industrial and service corporation's besides ranking the 500 largest US corporations. Typically, the *Fortune* rankings cover profits, assets, stockholders' equity and the number of employees. It extends its analysis to identify the firms that have lost the most money during the year.

The rankings are aggregated in the main *Fortune* tables, but are subdivided by country and industrial sector. The industry analysis extends to give totals for revenues, prof-

its, assets, stockholder's equity and employees. Follow-up is made easier by *Fortune*'s policy of including the address, telephone number and name of the chief executive officer for each business in the rankings.

The *Fortune* analysis identifies those firms with the biggest increases in revenues, highest profits, greatest increases in profits, highest returns on revenues and assets as well as the largest business employers. The quality of the data and the related analysis makes the *Fortune* ranking an invaluable tool for examining business performance.

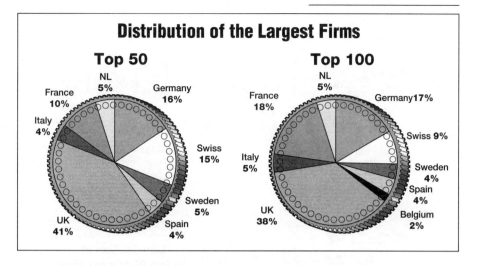

Distribution of the Largest Firms

Top 50

NL 5%
France 10%
Germany 16%
Italy 4%
Swiss 15%
Sweden 5%
UK 41%
Spain 4%

Top 100

NL 5%
France 18%
Germany 17%
Swiss 9%
Italy 5%
Sweden 4%
Spain 4%
UK 38%
Belgium 2%

Size: an asset or liability?

Commodore Vanderbilt – in his day, the richest man in the world – once said that accumulating wealth and assets was easy, the difficulty lay in holding on to wealth. The history of the largest corporations during this century attest to this notion. Of the 25 largest US corporations in 1900 only two remained in the top 25 by the mid-1960s. By the 1990s only one remained. Even if a hard measure like asset value is used, change is the norm.

The largest US industrial corporations by asset values over time

Rank	1917 Company	Assets ($M)	1948 Company	Assets ($M)	1994 (Company	Assets ($M)
1	US Steel Corp.	2450	Standard Oil of New Jersey	3526	Ford Motor Co.	219,350
2	Standard Oil of New Jersey	547	General Motors	2958	General Electric	194,484
3	Bethlehem Steel Corp.	381	US Steel	2535	General Motors	193,871
4	Armour & Co.	314	Standard Oil of New York	1500	ITT	100,900
5	Swift & Co.	306	Socony-I Vacuum Oil	1443	Exxon	87,790
6	Midvale Steel	270	Texaco	1277	IBM	81,091
7	International Harvester Co.	265	Gulf	1191	AT&T	79,262
8	E I du Pont Nemours	263	E I du Pont Nemours	1189	Philip Morris	52,649
9	US Rubber	258	General Electric	1177	Chrysler	49,539
10	Phelps Dodge	232	Ford Motor Co	1149	GTE	42,500
11	General Electric of California	236	Standard Oil	1075	Mobil	41,760
12	Anaconda Copper	225	Bethlehem Steel	1029	Xerox	38,999

13	American Smelting	222	Cities Service	992	Du Pont	37,914
14	Standard Oil of New York	204	Western Electric	786	Chevron	34,994
15	Singer	193	Union Carbide	723	Bell South	34,297
16	Ford Motor Co.	166	Sinclair Oil	710	RJR Nabisco	31,408
17	Westinghouse	165	Westinghouse	694	NYNEX	30,078
18	American Tobacco	164	American Tobacco	687	Amoco	28,811
19	Jones & Laughlin	160	International Harvester	671	Viacom	27,956
20	Union Carbide & Carbon	156	Anaconda Copper	660	Procter & Gamble	27,337

Source: *Scale & Scope: The Dynamics of Industrial Capitalism by Alfred D. Chandler, Jr.*

Eleven companies survive from the 1917 list in the 1948 list and only five of these survive to 1994, albeit in some cases under different names.

Even during the twenty years between 1972 and 1992, a similar pattern of change can be discerned. Of the top twenty US corporations in 1972 – measured by stock market valuation – only seven, retained their position in 1992.

Twenty years of change

Rank 1972		Value ($Bn)	Rank 1992		Value ($Bn)
1	IBM	46.8	1	EXXON	75.8
2	AT&T	29.2	2	General Electric	73.9
3	Eastman Kodak	23.9	3	Wal-Mart	73.5
4	General Motors	23.2	4	Royal Dutch Shell	71.8
5	EXXON	19.6	5	NT&T	71.4
6	Sears Roebuck	18.2	6	Philip Morris	69.3
7	General Electric	13.3	7	AT&T	68.0
8	Xerox	11.8	8	Coca-Cola	55.7
9	Texaco	10.2	9	Mitsubishi Bank	53.5
10	Minnesota Mining & Mft	9.7	10	Merck	50.3
11	Procter & Gamble	9.1	11	Industrial Bank of Japan	46.5
12	Royal Dutch Shell	9.1	12	Sumitomo Bank	45.6
13	Coca-Cola	8.9	13	Toyota Motor	44.1
14	Du Pont	8.4	14	Fuji Bank	41.8
15	Ford	8.0	15	Dai-Ichi Kangyo Bank	41.8
16	Avon	7.9	16	Sanwa Bank	37.9
17	Mobil	7.5	17	British Telecom	37.8
18	Johnson & Johnson	7.4	18	Procter & Gamble	36.4

| 19 | Chevron . . . . 6.8 | | 19 | Glaxo Holdings . . . . 36.1 |
| 20 | Merck . . . . 6.6 | | 20 | Bristol-Myers Squibb . . . 35.1 |

Source: *Fortune*

In the UK, a similar pattern of turbulence over the last century exists. Using market capitalization as an indicator, only five of the largest UK firms in 1917 survive in the top twenty of 1994.

The largest UK industrial corporations by market capitalization (Cap)

	1919		1948		1994	
Rank	Company	Cap (£M)	Company	Cap (£M)	Company	Cap (£M)
1	Burmah Oil Co. . .	63	Imperial Tobacco .	258	Shell	23,152
2	J & P Coats Ltd. .	49	Anglo Iranian Oil . .	204	BT	22,670
3	Anglo Persian Oil	29	ICI	198	BP	21,928
4	Lever Bros	24	Unilever	184	Glaxo	17,864
5	Imperial Tobacco	23	Shell	173	British Gas	12,944
6	United Steel	23	Distillers Co.	128	Hanson.	11,745
7	Vickers	20	Guinness	67	BTR	11,091
8	Guinness	19	Courtaulds	57	SmithKline Beecham	10,996
9	Brunner Mond . . .	19	Burmah Oil Co.	56	RTZ	9,371
10	Shell Transport . . . & Trading	18	Dunlop Rubber . . .	56	Guinness	9,210
11	Nobel Explosives .	16	J & P Coats Ltd. . .	54	Unilever	9,138
12	Courtaulds Ltd. . .	16	Vickers Ltd	39	Cable & Wireless	8,753
13	Metropolitan . . . . . Carriage	14	Guest, Keen . . . . . . & Nettlefolds	35	GEC	7,993
14	Armstrong, ... Whitworth	12	Reckitts & Son	34	Reuters	7,920
15	Fine Cotton . . . . . Spinners & Doublers	10	Stewart & Lloyds . . .	32	Zeneca	7,634
16	Portland Cement . .	9	Kemsley . . . . Newspapers	32	ICI	6,012
17	Dunlop Rubber . . .	9	Tate & Lyle	30	Vodafone	6,010
18	Reckitt & Sons . . .	9	AEI	29	National Power	5,895
19	Guest, Keen . . . . . & Nettlefolds	8	J Lyons	28	Wellcome	5,640
20	Levinstein	8	GEC	28	Reed International . . .	4,303

BAT is larger with a market capitalization of £13,458M but is excluded from the accompanying table as it did not have UK based manufacturing prior to the 1940s.

The **world's largest quoted firm based on market capitalization** as a per cent of total market is Royal Dutch Petroleum with 39 per cent of its total market in 1991.

The largest UK industrial corporations by market
Where are they now?

Original company name

Associated Portland Cement	Changed name to Blue Circle in 1978
Coats (J & P)	Merged with Patons and Baldwins in 1960 to form Coats Patons and Baldwins. Merged with Vantona Viyella in 1986 to form Coats Viyella.
Courtaulds Ltd.	Survives, demerged (Courtaulds & Courtaulds Textiles)
Distillers Co.	Bought by Guinness in 1986
Dunlop Rubber	Sold tyre interests to Japan in 1983; remainder is owned by BTR
Fine Cotton Spinners & Doublers Associated	Taken over by Courtaulds in 1964
Guest, Keen & Nettlefolds	Survives intact, but changed name to GKN in 1986
Imperial Tobacco	Bought by Hanson in 1986
Lever Bros	Merged with the Margarine Union to form Unilever
Tate & Lyle	Survives intact
United Steel	Nationalized in 1951, denationalized in 1960, renationalized in 1966 and became part of British Steel. Privatized in 1988.

Source: *Financial Times*

Demerger

Companies are demerged when they decide to put their component parts for sale or to get separate stock market listings. Sometimes, 'demergers' occur when firms that were previously merged are broken into their former parts. A notable example of this was the 'demerger' of Imperial Tobacco and Courage Breweries by the Hanson Group after the acquisition of Imperial Group.

Imperial had previously acquired Courage and merged it with Imperial Tobacco. 'Demergers' can occur also when a company is broken into component parts that had organically developed within a larger enterprise. This took place when the British chemicals giant, ICI, was split into two parts – Zeneca and ICI.

King Oil

Both the US and British tables on market size (see above) highlight the scale and power of the oil industry. No other industrial sector is as well represented in measures of the largest companies. King Oil has replaced King Coal during the 20th century. Few industries have exercised either the political and economic power or produced as many fascinating and mercurial personalities.

The century has seen power used repeatedly to protect oil interests. The Middle East, in particular, has witnessed a series of military interventions. The first direct military intervention in the Middle East to protect oil interests was probably the despatch of troops by Britain in 1907 'to the maintenance of British enterprise in South West Persia'. It started a tradition which continues with the retention of a garrison of significant forces in Kuwait since the Gulf War of 1991.

The history of the oil industry is rich in personalities. Some of the names are almost as familiar today as they were a hundred years ago. John D Rockefeller remains the archetypal 'robber baron'. He could be ruthless in building up his monopoly power and protecting his business interests, but he was a committed

Petroleum refining

Rank	Company	Global 500 rank	Country	1994 Revenues ($M)	Profits ($M)
1	Exxon	8	United States	101,459	5100
2	Royal Dutch Shell	10	UK/Netherlands	94,881	6236
3	Mobil	22	United States	59,621	1079
4	British Petroleum	31	Britain	50,737	2416
5	Elf Aquataine	46	France	39,459	(981)
6	Texaco	57	United States	33,768	910
7	ENI	63	Italy	32,556	1993
8	Chevron	63	United States	31,064	1693
9	RWE Group	81	Germany	28,628	547
10	PEMEX	83	Mexico	28,195	986
11	AMOCO	86	United States	26,953	1789
12	Total	98	France	24,653	610
13	PDVSA	113	Venezuela	22,157	2013
14	Nippon Oil	115	Japan	21,988	210
15	Sunkyong	156	South Korea	18,196	93
16	Repsol	163	Spain	17,717	723
17	Petrobras	169	Brazil	17,353	1432
18	USX	178	United States	16,799	501
19	Atlantic Richfield	196	United States	15,682	919
20	Japan Energy	203	Japan	15,434	(167)

Source: *Fortune*

churchgoer and eventually gave almost $500 million to charity. Others like Henri Deterding, the creator of Royal Dutch Shell, wanted the power but shunned publicity. Yet others entered the oil industry almost by accident. William Knox D'Arcy, the man who opened up the Iran oilfields to British influence, was semi-retired when he was offered the first Iranian (Persian) oil concession. In contrast, many like Calouste Gulbenkian decided early that they wanted to be in the biggest game in town – oil.

Today, 50 of the Fortune top 500 industrial companies are draw from the oil industry – the largest representation of any sector. Their combined turn over is $867,782M. Although this is slightly smaller than the total sales of the motor vehicle and parts industry ($931,931M), it excludes the massive, nationally-owned oil companies.

The Global Market

In the USA, the **largest sales of a specific company** were earned by General Motors with total sales of $154,951M in 1994, followed by Ford at $128,439M and Exxon with $101,092M. In Europe, the greatest sales were earned by Royal Dutch Shell with $99,170M, then Daimler Benz and BP with $63,101M and $54,712M respectively. BP's turnover in Britain of $34,950M is more than twice that achieved by the second and third companies – BAT, with

$17,879M, and BT, with $13,675M. These figures are dwarfed by Sumitomo Corporation's turnover of $172,154M. All five of the top Japanese corporations achieved a turnover of over $150,000M.

 The 1980s and early 1990s saw the emergence of giant corporations from newly emerging countries. Probably the **largest corporation in the developing world** is the Bank of China with assets of $334,752M. Thirteen industrial or trading companies from the developing world have achieved sales of over $10,000M. The largest industrial company among these firms is Samsung of South Korea.

Giants from the emerging economies

Rank	Corporation	Turnover 1994 ($M)
1	Samsung (S. Korea)	51,345
2	Daewoo (S. Korea)	30,839
3	Saudi Arabian Oil . . . . . . (Saudi Arabia)	26,621
4	Pemex (Mexico)	26,572
5	PDVSA (Venezuela).	21,275
6	Sunkyong (S. Korea)	15,912
7	Petrobras (Brazil)	15,029
8	Ssangyong (S. Korea) . . .	14,479
9	KOC Holdings (Turkey) . .	14,409
10	Hyundai (S. Korea)	!3,738
11	SinoChem (S. Korea)	13,241
12	Sonatrach (Algeria)	12,300
13	Barlow Rand (S.Africa) . .	11,467

One of the most popular management sayings asserts that "turnover is vanity, profits reality and cash reality". American Telephone and Telegraph earned **the greatest net profit** ever by a corporation when it reported profits of £7.6Bn from 1 Oct 1981 to 30 Sept 1982. BP came close to matching this in cash terms five years

Top Japanese corporations by turnover

Rank	Corporation	Turnover 1994 ($M)
1	Sumitomo	172,154
2	Marubeni	170,771
3	Itochu	163,392
4	Mitsui	156,920
5	Mitsubishi	151,863

Source: *Financial Times*

Europe's largest corporations, 1994 ($M)

Rank	Corporation	Market capitalization	Turnover	Profits
1	Royal Dutch Shell	94,069	99,170	9095
2	Roche Holding	44,990	11,102	2430
3	BT	35,488	21,407	4314
4	Nestlé	35,387	44,584	3602
5	BP	34,326	54,712	2038

Source: *Financial Times*

later when it reported **the greatest profits ever for a UK firm** with net profits of £7.053Bn in the year 1985/86. That year's gross profit of $9.059Bn for Royal Dutch Shell was **the greatest profit made by a European company.** The challenge of defining size is well illustrated by the analysis of Europe's top five companies. Royal Dutch Shell has the greatest market capitalization and sales. Roche Holdings has a much greater market capitalization than Nestlé but a smaller turnover.

 A firm's market capitalization is the sum of the value of each individual share times the number of shares. Turnover broadly equates with sales although it can include disposals of property and other transfers. Measuring profits has become even more complex in recent years as regulatory authorities have imposed specific requirements on the kinds of provision that firms must make to arrive at a picture of the true profit. The variety of European requirements partly explains why it is more common to see gross profits identified in analysis of European data but net profit in analysis of US data.

Gross profit

The term 'gross' profit is usually employed to describe the profit on a firm's trading activities before any interest payments, taxes or exceptional items. The 'net' profit is calculated after these deductions. In a highly simplified form, this produces figures along the lines below:

Item	Amount
Income	£3,000,000
Expenditure	£2,500,000
Gross profit	£500,000
Interest charges	(£100,000)
Taxes	(£200,000)
Net profit	£200,000

Figures in brackets are negative amounts so are deducted from the total sum.

Top 50 UK companies by market capitalization

Rank	Company	Market capitalization (£M)
1	Glaxo Holdings	23,503.6
2	Shell Transport & Trading	23,151.8
3	BT	22,669.9
4	British Petroleum	21,927.5
5	HSBC Holdings	18,179.4
6	BAT Industries	13,450.1
7	British Gas	12,943.8
8	Hanson	11,745.1
9	Marks & Spencer	11,218.8
10	BTR	11,090.6
11	Smithkline Beecham	10,995.7
12	Lloyds TSB	10,393.3
13	RTZ Corporation	9,371.2
14	Barclays	9280.9
15	Guinness	9209.9
16	Unilever	9138.1

17	Cable & Wireless . .	8753.0
18	Grand Metropolitan	8513.1
19	National . . . . Westminster Bank	8113.4
20	General Electric . . . Company	7993.3
21	Reuters Holdings . .	7920.3
22	Zeneca	7634.8
23	Sainsbury J	7210.0
24	Imperial Chemical . Industries	6012.4
25	Vodafone	6010.7
26	National Power . . .	5895.3
27	Allied Domecq	5832.7
28	Great Universal . . . Stores	5722.8
29	Prudential . . . . . . Corporation	5644.0
30	Boots Company . .	5488.3
31	Abbey National . . .	5103.3
32	BAA	4978.4
33	Tesco	4882.4
34	Bass	4498.3
35	Reed International .	4302.8
36	Thorn Emi	4199.5
37	Powergen	4139.1
38	P & O Steam . . . . Navigation	3754.4
39	Cadbury . . . . Schweppes	3739.4
40	British Steel	3480.4
41	Vendome	3480.2
42	British Airways . . .	3448.8
43	Rank Organisation	3331.2
44	Royal Bank	3324.2

40	British Steel	3480.4
41	Vendome	3480.2
42	British Airways . . .	3448.8
43	Rank Organisation	3331.2
44	Royal Bank . . . . . . of Scotland Grp	3324.2
45	BOC Group	3301.7
46	Kingfisher	3261.6
47	Commercial Union	3259.4
48	Pearson	3210.3
49	Land Securities	3182.7
50	Argyll Group	3090.4

Source: *Financial Times*.

Market capitalization or total assets are relatively stable measures of company size. Sales and, especially, profits can be volatile. One of **the greatest positive profit turnarounds** in history occurred when Ford moved from a deficit of $7.385Bn in 1993 to a surplus of $2.529Bn in 1994. The reverse of this occurred for General Motors when it moved from a profit of $4.224Bn in 1989 to a deficit of $23.498Bn in 1992. In fact, General Motors' move from a deficit of $23.5Bn in 1992 to a profit of $2.5Bn in 1993 is a profit turnaround of nearly $26Bn – even larger than Ford's improvement. These figures are a little misleading as many factors which contributed to the turnaround were technical rather than real.

The most profitable industries $M

Rank	Industry	Profits	Number of firms
1	Commercial banks	31,979	59
2	Petroleum refining	30,593	30
3	Telecommunications	26,977	21
4	Electronics	20,813	31
5	Motor vehicles and parts	20,433	26
6	Insurance (mutual)	17,925	24
7	Pharmaceuticals	16,609	10
8	Insurance (stock)	11,567	28
9	Food	11,373	12
10	Beverages	5474	6

General Motors' turbulent years

Year	Profit/loss ($USM)
1989	4,224.3
1990	-1,985.7
1991	-4,452.8
1992	-23,498.3
1993	2,465.8
Source: *Fortune.*	

The oil industry is **the most profitable industry** with those firms in the *Fortune* 500 earning total profits of $27,466M in 1993.

Among service industries, the greatest profits are earned by commercial banks. The total profits of the top 50 commercial banks in 1994 were $23,838M.

Private ownership

The majority of the firms defined as giants are state owned or publicly quoted. There are, however, giant corporations that remain in the hands of private individuals. Cargill Group of Minnesota (USA) with sales of $49,100M is **the USA's largest private company.**

 The different ownership structures around the world make it hard to compare companies. The largest privately owned companies outside the USA compare in size with their US counterparts. **The largest privately owned company outside the USA** is probably the Samsung Group of South Korea with a turnover of $54,345M in 1994. **The largest privately owned UK corporation** is Tetra-Pak with a turnover in the region of $4,500M, followed by Virgin and Littlewoods.

Largest private companies in the USA

Rank	Corporation	Sales 1991 ($M)
1	Cargill Group	49,100
2	Koch Industries	18,000
3	United Parcel Service	15,000
4	Continental Grain	14,100
5	Carlson Group	9300
6	M&M Mars	7500
7	NWA	7500
8	Bechtel Group	7500
9	Goldman Sachs	7000
10	R.H. Macy	6800

Source: *Fortune*

Largest private companies outside the USA (excluding mutual funds)

Rank	Corporation	Sales 1994 ($M)
1	Samsung Group (S. Korea)	54,345
2	Tengelman Group (Germany)	35,256
3	Daewoo (S. Korea)	30,839

Largest private companies in the UK (excluding mutual funds)

Rank	Corporation	Areas of Activity	Sales 1994($Bn)
1	Tetra-Laval	Packaging	4.5
2	Virgin	Retailing, travel, communications, entertainment	3.0
3	Littlewoods	Retailing, pools	2.6

Checking the football pools at Littlewoods.
The Merseyside-based Littlewoods organization is one the three largest privately-owned companies in Britain. The company's interests include its chain of department stores as well as football pools. The Moores family, who own Littlewoods, are well-known for sponsorship and charitable donations: Liverpool's John Moores University is named after its principal benefactor.
(Image Select).

Asia's biggest businesses

One of the most striking features of the modern business world is the growth and power of Asian business. Asian firms are now among the largest in the world. Initially, they were overwhelmingly of Japanese origin, but now South Korean, Indonesian, Taiwanese, Hong Kong, and Singaporean firms are vying for international leadership. The Asian firm with the largest market capitalization is the Japanese telecommunications giant Nippon Telegraph and Cable.

The largest sales are earned by ITOCHU Corporation, the Japanese general trading company with $155.9Bn in sales during 1994/95.

Asian companies with the largest turnover

Company	Main Business	Sales ($Bn)
ITOCHU	General trading	155.9
Mitsui	General trading	147.6
Sumitomo	General trading	143.1
Marubeni	General trading	140.6
Misubishi	General trading	135.1
Source: *Asia Week*		

Samsung has **the largest turnover of any Asian company outside Japan** with total revenues from trading and investment of $49.3Bn in 1994/95.

China Petrochemical is the largest employer among the unified, commercial Asian firms. Its payroll of 700,000 is lower than

Asia's largest business employers

Company	Main business	Employees
ChinaPetro Chemical	Chemicals	700,000
Coal India	Coal mining	641,000
Daqing Petrol	Oil production	270,853
China State Construction Co.	Construction	250,752
Jardine Matheson	General trading	220,770

Asia's largest corporations using a composite measure

Nippon Telegraph and Telephone

Toyota

Hitachi

Tokyo Electrical Power

Matsushita Electrical Industries

that of the Indian Railway System. The latter's looser organizational structure and public enterprise status excludes it from this analysis.

Analysis of Asia's largest companies which gives composite measure giving equal weight to sales, shareholder's equity, market capitalization, assets values and employees identifies Nippon Telegraph and Telephone as the largest company.

The professions and business services

Giant corporations buy in a host of business services. The accountancy profession has grown to service the needs of the largest industrial and commercial concern. **The largest accountancy practice in the world** is Ernst and Young with an estimated income of over $5Bn followed by KPMG and Arthur Anderson with revenues of over $4Bn and $3Bn respectively.

The scale of modern business losses has increased the interest and involvement of the legal profession. This is especially true in the United States where a tradition of litigiousness and allied specific legislation,

The largest Asian/Oceanian companies by country (based on sales)

Company	Country	Sales $Bn
Broken Hill Property	Australia	12.9
China Petrochemical	China	17.7
Jardine Matheson	Hong Kong	9.6
Indian Coal	India	9.0
Pertamina	Indonesia	13.1
Petroliam Nasional	Malaysia	6.5
Fletcher Challenge	New Zealand	5.0
San Miguel Corp	Philippines	2.6
Sony International (Singapore)	Singapore	7.7
Samsung Co	South Korea	19.4
Chinese Petroleum Corp	Taiwan	11.0
Petroleum Authority	Thailand	3.5

such as that on product liability, makes business legal costs the highest in the world. The tort system, i.e. the rules governing product liability, medical malpractice and other personal injuries, costs US business $180Bn a year, which represents a 30% increase over the last decade.

It is common to measure law firms in terms of partners, and on this basis Clifford Chance, who as based in London, is **the largest law firm in the world** with 1649 partners in 1992.

The largest law firms

Rank	Practice	Number of Partners (1992)
1	Clifford Chance (London)	1649
2	Baker & McKenzie (Chicago)	1249
3	Linklaters (London)	1250
4	Lovell, White, Durrant (London)	1076
5	Slaughter & May (London)	972
6	Skadden, Arps, Slate, Meager & Flom (NY)	958
7	Jones, Day, Reavis and Pogue (Cleveland)	945
8	Denton, Hall, Burger and Warrens (London)	854
9	Allen & Overy	787
10	Freshfield	762

World's top 10 insurance companies

Rank	Company	Country	Assets ($M)
1	Nippon Life	Japan	339,053
2	Dai-Ichi Mutual Life	Japan	239,205
3	Sumitomo Life	Japan	208,964
4	Prudential of America	United States	165,742
5	Meiji Mutual Life	Japan	144,773
6	Metropolitan Life	United States	128,225
7	Asahi Mutual Life	Japan	109,074
8	Prudential	Britain	95,785
9	Mitsui Mutual Life	Japan	90,384
10	Yasuda Mutual Life	Japan	79,898

Source: *Fortune*

World's top 20 contractors

Rank	Company	Country	Turnover
1	Mitsubishi Heavy Industries	Japan	20,170.7
2	Kajama	Japan	14,906.8
3	Shimizu	Japan	14,796.7

4	Taisei	Japan	14,685.0
5	Bouygues	France	12,893.0
6	Obayashi	Japan	10,604.0
7	Kumagai	Japan	9897.5
8	Bechtel	United States	7526.0
9	Brown & Root	United States	7018.8
10	Fluor Daniel	United States	6741.7
11	Skanska	Sweden	6253.3
12	Trafalgar House	UK	6162.0
13	ABB Lummus Crest	United States	5470.0
14	GTM-Entrepose	France	5393.2
15	Ansaldo S.p.A	Italy	5089.9
16	M.W. Kellogg	United States	4670.0
17	Spie Batignolles	France	4569.0
18	Hochtief	Germany	4360.4
19	Bilfinger & Berger	Germany	3590.7
20	McDermott	United States	3135.9

Source: Achievement

The largest corporate legal fees for one deal were probably those earned during the takeover of RJR Nabisco by Kohlberg, Kravis, Roberts and Co. This was **the largest corporate buyout** in history.

Largest takeovers

Rank	Deal	Value ($M)
1	RJR Nabisco by KKR	24,562
2	SmithKline Beckman by Beecham Group	16,082
3	Gulf by Chevron	13,205
4	Kraft by Philip Morris	13,100
5	Squibb by Bristol Myers	12,002
6	Warner Communications by Time	11,650
7	Getty Oil by Texaco	10,128
8	Conoco by Du Pont	8040
9	Standard Oil of Ohio by BP	7672
10	Marathon Oil by US Steel	6618

The First Businesses

Commercial activities in some mode go back to the earliest forms of social living by people. The production of the first flint tools and weapons was probably **the first industry** and can be dated back over two million years. It is, however, production for exchange that truly marks business or commercial activity. **The oldest commerce** of this kind is associated with raw materials production of either minerals or foods. There is evidence that exotic stones and amber were exchanged as far back as 25,000 BC while organized agriculture dates back to about 11,000 BC.

Business in the ancient world

The advent of urban living, or civilization, usually indicates the existence of the two primary pre-conditions for sustained business activity. These conditions are social or economic stability and surpluses. Jericho can be identified as a stable village or town beyond 9000 BC when it was an established agricultural community capable of producing surpluses, some craft work notably pottery and trade. There is similar evidence for craft activity especially pottery production in Japan at about the same time.

The expansion of civilization notably in the Eastern Mediterranean,

Mesopotamia, India and China over the next seven thousand years was linked with the same preconditions – political stability and agricultural surpluses – leading to the creation of urban societies which produced crafts and other 'luxuries', undertook trade and generally provided additional security in some form for agricultural communities. In the last millennium BC, the concentration of people in villages, towns and cities led to the emergence of a wider range of tradable commodities.

The oldest coins are the electrum staters of King Gyges of Lydia (Turkey) about 630 BC. The earliest dated coin is the Samian silver tetradrachm from Zankle (now Messina), Sicily. Chinese coins of the Zhou (or Chou) Dynasty can be dated to around 550 BC although a cowry shell based currency can be found in China well before 1000 BC.

Tools were probably first used for large-scale manufacture to make pottery by the Sumerians in the third millennium BC. **The first pottery products**, however, can be dated to around 10,000 BC in the Odai-Yamomoto region of Japan. **The earliest potter's wheel** was found at Ur (modern Iraq) and dates from circa 3000 BC. The same era saw the first use of the wheel, writing, early glass production, bronze casting and evidence of trade between the Mesopotomian region and India. Around the same time, there is evidence of the parallel invention of the wheel, writing and bronze casting in China. In the Yellow River (Huang He) region in China, the plough and spun silk were developed during the same period. Alongside these innovations in agriculture and production emerged the first societies based on trade.

The Harappan civilization in modern Pakistan traded with the civilizations of the Near and Far East. The great dockyard at Lothal (in Gujarat, India) was over 213 m (700 feet) long, and was connected by perhaps **the first navigation canal in the world** which stretched 1.5 km (a mile) to connect the docks to the sea. The Grand Canal of China is **the oldest and largest surviving canal in the world**. It was started around the 7th century BC and eventually completed in AD 1280 by Kublai Khan. It stretches 1600 km (1000 miles) between Hangzhou (Hangchow) to Beijing.

Two key inventions were made in the middle of the second millennium. The discovery of how to extract iron by smelting provided a metal with far greater durability and a wider range of uses than copper or bronze. Demand for iron led to **the first, large-scale commercial mining** around 1500 BC. This coincided with the collapse of the greatest period of Egyptian civilization – the Middle Kingdom – and the turbulence that eventually led to the final period of Egyptian greatness – the New Kingdom. The Egyptian invention of papyrus around 2000 BC led to **the first books**. Much of our knowledge about the ancient world is based on the records kept on papyrus. There is even some evidence from these records of the early sub-division of labour for factories in Egypt at the time of the Middle Kingdom (2052–1786 BC). Apart from one or two specific areas, the Egyptians had little interest in technology for large-scale commerce. It is possible that **the first steam driven machine** was built in Ancient Egypt by the engineer 'Hero' sometime between 100–50 BC. It was used to open and close a heavy temple door.

The growth of cities and the expansion of trade was linked with the emergence of insurance and banking. There is evidence of a form of insurance in Babylon around 4000 BC. This consisted of the insured person borrowing funds for a venture. These were then deposited as a surety with a third party as a guarantee of good faith. This primitive form of liability insurance was common across the ancient world. **The first recorded bank** was the house of Egibi & Son of Babylon around 700 BC. The British Museum has several hundred cuneiform tables dealing with a familiar array of products and services – cheques, receipts etc. The bank seems to have survived at least until 480 BC.

Business in Greece and Rome

In the West, the advent of Greco-Roman society was responsible for sharp increases in the range and scale of business activity. Seaborne trade expanded with a trade in luxuries extending beyond the Mediterranean to the North Atlantic. Within the Mediterranean the grain trade between North Africa and Europe was a major bulk activity. As early as 500 BC, most cities of Greece, with the exception of Sparta, operated cash-based economies. Products as diverse as olives, pottery, jewellery and textiles were traded locally and across much larger distances. Perhaps **the first specialist centre in Europe** was Miletus, which produced wool and woollen products.

At the same time as Greek civilization flowered, the first great Persian empire emerged. Its growth and longevity owed as much to rich iron ore deposits and access to trade routes, as the success of its armies. The trade routes were especially important in providing access to Indian and Chinese luxuries, like spices, silks and porcelain, that could not be matched in the West. The persistence of this trade over hundreds of years is acknowledged by contemporary scholars.

An Ancient Greek bireme, with two banks of rowers. (The better known triremes had three banks of rowers.) Seaborne commerce in the Hellenic world expanded with a trade in luxuries and by 500 BC most Greek city-states operated a cash based economy.
(Peter Newark's Historical Pictures).

Pliny the Elder, for example, blamed trade with India for draining gold from the Roman Empire and provoking perhaps **the first recorded evidence of inflation** seriously affecting economic and social stability. Inflation hit the Roman Empire at different times forcing up prices and wages.

China was at the opposite end of these trade routes. Many of the most valuable trade goods originated there. The period 700 BC to AD 100 was especially fruitful for Chinese business and trade. The imperial dynasties of Zhou, Qin and Han seemed to take a genuine interest in trade and commerce. The Zhou dynasty built **the first major canal programmes**. The Qin established **perhaps the first reliable system of weights and measures**. Inventions as diverse as the cross-bow (circa 200 BC), gunpowder (circa AD 100) and eventually ink and paper (circa AD 200) flowed during this period. The inventiveness of China at this time

contrasts with the lack of scientific or technological innovation during the Roman Empire. Here, the genuine interest in engineering saw some significant developments notably **the first aquaducts** and important developments in bridge and road building. There was, however, a prejudice against the application of science to commerce which was inherited from the Greeks (and might have been passed on to the English middle classes!). Despite that **the first reaping machines** are referred to by the elder Pliny in the first century AD, while large-scale bacon curing was developed in Gaul to supply Roman markets at about the same time. Rome was, at its core, an economy of pillage in which there were few incentives for investment in production. Most of the significant commercial developments occurred outside Italy especially in Gaul. For the true Roman the only respectable business activities were trade and usury.

Business in the Middle Ages

The collapse of the Roman Empire led to a long period of economic and political instability in Europe. It is only with the growth of the North European and Italian

Britain's oldest existing businesses

Company	Date of foundation	Business
Aberdeen Harbour Board	1136	Administration of Aberdeen Harbour
Cambridge University Press	1534	Printers and publishers
Oxford University Press	1586	Printers and publishers
Durtnell Ltd	1591	Builders
Old Bushmills Distillery Co. Ltd	1608	Whiskey distillers
The Post Office	1635	Postal service
Alldays Peacock & Co. Ltd	1650	Industrial fan manufacturers
Hays Ltd	1651	Office support services
Vandome and Hart Ltd	1660	Weighing machine manufacturers
James Gibbons Ltd	1670	Locksmiths & metal foundry

Source: *Dun and Bradstreet*

city-states and the embryonic nation states during the 12th century that the conditions were created for a new surge of economic activity.

Britain's oldest business – the Aberdeen Harbour Board – was established in 1136. The Faversham Oyster Company dates from before 1189 but was really more of a guild, granting fishing rights in the river. The first mention of the Weavers' Company, **the first English guild**, was in 1130. There were, however, enforced guilds, or collegia, during the Roman Empire. Caxton started printing in England in 1476 and **the first book was printed in England** in 1477.

The world's oldest, well-documented company is Stora Kopparbergs Bergslags of Falun (in Sweden). It has been in continuous existence since the 11th century with evidence of transaction from 1288, when a Swedish bishop bartered a part share in the enterprise. The company was granted a formal charter in 1347. Many of these early companies, and the mercantile cities of the North, built their prosperity on

bulk trade in goods like slate, wine, timber and grain. Shifting these products was made easier by the construction of **the first true, deep-sea cargo ship**. The first of these were the solid clinker-built *Kogge* and later *Hooker* – large flat-bottomed ships capable of carrying large cargoes in their hold.

The Hanseatic League was identified as such for the first time in English royal documents in AD 1267. **The first permanent trading posts abroad** – the Kontors – were set up by the Hanseatic League in the 13th century. Some of the first and oldest businesses in Europe date from around this time.

The 11th century saw **the first great maritime code** to regulate shipping and trade in the Mediterranean – the Amalfi Tables . The rival cities of Venice and Genoa have been described as **the first truly capitalist societies** – Venice by Cox (in *The Origins of Capitalism*, 1959) and Genoa by Braudel (in *The Perspective of the World; Civilization and Capitalism in the 15–18th century*, 1979).

The Hanseatic League

The Hanseatic League was a grouping of cities in Northern Germany that came together in the middle of the 13th century as an association (Hansa) to advance their joint commercial interests. The most important cities were Lübeck, Riga, Hamburg, Danzig (Gdansk in Poland) and Bremen, but around 200 towns were members at different times.

The League's strength reflected the weakness of central or national governments and their inability to implement laws, protect trade or help navigation. The League's period of greatest strength coincided with the weakness of the Holy Roman Empire and the younger nation states of Northern Europe. The

Wooden houses in the Hansa port of Bergen, Norway. Bergen flourished in the Middle Ages as one of the most important Scandinavian members of the Hanseatic League. (Ann Ronan Picture Library).

League probably reached its zenith between 1350 and 1500 when it had around 40 members with representatives in countries from England to Russia. In 1370, it defeated its greatest rival, Denmark, and won major concessions from the Danish Empire at the Treaty of Stralsund.

The growing power of the nation states of northern Europe, notably England, France and the Netherlands, forced the League into decline as its rights and privileges declined and competition from London and Amsterdam increased. The last meeting of the League was in 1669 but former members like Lübeck and Hamburg retained special rights and privileges in Germany until the 19th century.

Detail of St Mark's Cathedral in Venice, the greatest of the medieval Italian city-states. By the 13th century Italian businessmen had developed a sophisticated system of credit finance and were acting as international bankers. These facilities made Italy the hub of international trade and Venice, Pisa and Genoa fought one another for control of the lucrative commerce of the Mediterranean. (Image Select).

Europe's oldest businesses

Company	Date of foundation	Business
Stora Kopparbergs Bergslags	c. 1000	Timber and metal products
Bayerische Staatsbrauerei	1040	Brewery
Klosterbrauerei Scheyern	1119	Brewery
Mansfeld Aktiengesellschaft fur Bergbau und Huttenbetrieb	1200	Copper
Lowenapotheke	1241	Pharmacy
Clerget-Buffet et Fils	1270	Wine growers
Raoul Clerget et Fils	1270	Wine growers
Urquell Brewery	1295	Brewery
Burgerspital zum Heiligen Geist	1319	Brewery
Moulin à Papier Richard-de-Bas	1326	Paper makers

The first partnership agreements, or collegaza, appeared in Venice and Genoa around 1072–73 to fund trading voyages with one partner putting up the cash, the other undertaking the voyage and splitting the proceeds.

The oldest surviving bank – the Monte dei Paschi di Siena (Italy) – was established in 1472. Double entry book-keeping was widely used in Venice by the 15th century and the first book on the subject was published by Pacioli in 1491.

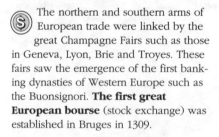 The northern and southern arms of European trade were linked by the great Champagne Fairs such as those in Geneva, Lyon, Brie and Troyes. These fairs saw the emergence of the first banking dynasties of Western Europe such as the Buonsignori. **The first great European bourse** (stock exchange) was established in Bruges in 1309.

Shifts in the pattern and dominance of trade in the 14th and 15th century moved the centre of Northern commerce first to Lisbon then to Antwerp. **Bills of Exchange were first used** in Antwerp around 1500 based on a system employed earlier at the Champagne Fairs.

The growth of trade soon became linked with attempts to restrict some transfers. In the 13th century, the Papacy made the first well documented attempt to ban the export of science and technology when they tried to stop the export of techniques associated with alum production. In the next century the authorities in Bristol banned "any man to take outside this city any kind of cloth known as raicloth".

Business in the East

The centuries of turbulence and low rates of innovation in Europe were not matched elsewhere. Paper had been invented in China some time before AD 110 and **the first paper money** was printed in AD 812. During the Tang (or T'ang; 618–907) and Song (or Sung; 960–1127) dynasties, industrial drills were developed. **The first industrial drills** were used to drill for brine far earlier (c. 500 BC) but during the Tang dynasty reached depths of over 260 m (850 ft). Drills were also used for the first time to obtain natural gas which was used to boil the brine to obtain salt. This encouraged the empire to declare salt a state monopoly. **The first matches** were manufactured in China around AD 577.

Long-distance, seaborne travel for trade is made immeasurably easier by the use of the compass for navigation. **The first dry,**

magnetic compasses date from around AD 1000 although there is evidence that the Olmec people of Mexico had a compass-like device around 1000 BC.

China enjoyed relative stability managed by an effective civil service – the mandarins. External trade prospered in part because of the activities of Indian traders. Sufficient surpluses were created for a diverse social life. **The oldest restaurant in the world** Ma Yu Ching's Bucket Chicken House opened in AD 1153 in Kaifeng, China.

The erosion and eventual destruction of the great trading empire of the Dravidians of central and South India reduced China's links with India and the Arab world. "The ruin of the Empire of Baghdad, the occupation of Central Asia by the Turks, the decadence of the Byzantine Empire and the even greater decadence of the Russian cities put an end to world trade for several centuries. The balance which the twofold hegemony of the Roman Empire and the Chinese Empire had established ... was finally destroyed." (Pirenne, J. *Tides of History* 1963)

Nation states

In Europe, a new economic and political system emerged with the increased power of the nation state. The embryonic states of the pre-Middle Ages had already created **the first Royal Mint** in AD 287. The success of Amsterdam, the capital of the United Provinces, marked the creating of **the first national, trading capital**. The United Provinces probably operated **the first cash crop economy** where goods are produced primarily, or solely, for sale not consumption. Their success prompted one of the first attempts to stimulate national technologies through stimulating innovation or trade embargoes.

In England, **the first system of patents** designed to protect the rights of inventors was created in the 1560s. They were given privileged rights to exploit their inventions for 14 years. The first patents awarded in America came under this scheme: Samuel Winslow was awarded a patent for a new means of manufacturing salt by the Massachusetts General Court in 1641. **The first American patent for a manufacturing process** was awarded in 1646 to Joseph Jenkes for a method of manufacturing scythes.

James I of England tried to keep control of technological advances by banning the sale of English white cloth to the United Provinces in 1614. He wanted to deny their dyeing industry access to high quality English cloth while stimulating local dye makers. In 1622 the Committee of the Privy Council and Foreign Plantations (eventually the Board of Trade) was set up in England. **The first stock exchanges** were created in Hamburg in 1558 and Amsterdam in 1602. Perhaps **the first of the major North European banks** – the Bank of Amsterdam – was formed in 1609.

The first central bank – Sweden's Rijsbank – was established in 1657. The Banks of Venice and Amsterdam performed many of the functions of Central banks but did not, for example, issue banknotes. The success of Amsterdam and the United Provinces was built on excellent and stable trading links with Spain, the Baltic and eventually the Indies. Goods were moved **by the first cost efficient, deep-water trading vessel** – the *fluyt* or *vlieboot*. These sturdy, round-sided ships could carry large cargoes and be manned by a small crew. The Dutch shipyards that built them were among the first to introduce mechanical saws, hoists for masts and inter-changeable parts (1630–1690).

Trade, banks and commerce

By the late 1500s, trade with the Indies was so important that a number of trading companies were given charters by their governments to develop this trade. The

The emergence of banking

Trading banks	Date	Central banks	Date
Monte dei Paschi di Siena (Italy)	1472	Bank of Venice	1585
Banco di Napoli (Italy)	1539	Bank of Amsterdam (Netherlands)	1609
Child's Bank (UK)	1559	Rijsbank (Sweden)	1657
Martin's Bank (UK)	1563	Bank of England	1694
Joh Berenberg, Gossler & Co (Germany)	1590	Bank of Scotland	1695
Bank of Amsterdam (Netherlands)	1609	Banque de France	1701
Banco di Santo Spirito (Italy)	1605	Bank of the United States	1791
Gosling's Bank (UK)	1650		
Sanwa Bank (Japan)	1656		
Smith's Bank (UK)	1658		

dark side of this trade had already been shown when in 1454 the Portuguese established **the first European slaving port** Sao Jorge da Mina in the Azores. **The first of the major trading companies** was the East India Company founded in London in 1599 and granted a charter by Queen Elizabeth I in 1600. Other chartered companies created about this time include The Russia Company (granted its charter in 1619), The New River Company (1619) and the Hudson's Bay Company (1670). In response, the Dutch East India Company – Vereenigde Ooste-Indische Compagnie – was established in 1602 on a much larger scale. It had an initial capital of 6.5 m florins, ten times that of its English rival. Despite that, the use of Dutch capital to finance foreign rivals like the English East India Company provides one of the first examples of public concern about the willingness of bankers to finance foreign trade rivals.

The Swedish iron and steel industry, for example, owes its origins to the use of Dutch money and the transfer of Walloon workers to set up **the first, brick blast furnace** in Bergslag, Sweden. The first blast furnaces in the world date from the 15th century.

In the 1690s, for the first time, the Westminster Parliament agreed to earmark

tax incomes to repay loans. This led to a flood of Dutch money into England to finance government loans. This was followed by significant injections of funds into the East India Company, the South Sea Company and the Bank of England. By 1777, popular economic writers were arguing that the success of Amsterdam as a financial centre was at the expense of the rest of the economy. For perhaps the first time it was argued that the interests of the international bankers in a domestic economy lay in investing monies in rival economies like England. This reduced funds available for investment at home. This argument, since used in both Britain and the USA, was used to explain the very different fortunes of the Dutch banking sector and the rest of the economy in the second half of the 18th century. In the 1740s **the first public (non-religious) poor houses** were established in Amsterdam, Rotterdam and The Hague.

The growth of capital and the expansion of trade led to the emergence and growth of the banking and insurance industries. **The first British bank** was Child's Bank, which was established in 1559.

With banks came the first banking crises. The collapse of the South Sea Company (1711–1720) – the South Sea Bubble – led to **the UK's first banking crisis** and the

Britain's first banks

Company	Date of foundation
Child's Bank	1559
Martin's Bank	1563
Gosling's Bank	1650
Smith's Bank	1658
Hoare's Bank	1672
Lloyds Bank	1677
Coutts Bank	1692
Drummond's Bank	1717
Royal Bank of Scotland	1727
British Linen Bank	1746
Glyn Mills Bank	1753

Britain's oldest insurance companies

Company	Date of foundation
Sun	1710
Union Assurance	1714
Westminster Fire	1717
London Assurance	1720
Royal Exchange	1720
Equitable Life	1762
Phoenix	1782
Norwich Union	1797
Essex & Suffolk	1802
Law Union & Rock	1806
London Life	1806

collapse of a number of London and 'country' banks. This was only a temporary setback to the proliferation of banks in the late 18th century. **The first English interbank clearing houses** were established in 1773. The three great Dutch banking crises of 1763, 1772 and 1780 are closely linked with the decline of the United Provinces as northern Europe financial and trading capital, and the transfer of power to the UK.

The first, fire insurance companies in Britain were created after the Great Fire of London (1666). The first company was started by an individual with the remarkable name – Unless-Christ-Had-Died-For-Thee-Thou-Hadst-Been-Damned-Barebones – subsequently shortened to Dr Nicholas Barbon. The same era saw **England's first national lottery** – The Million Adventure – launched in 1694.

Lloyds was established at Lloyds Coffee House in the Royal Exchange in 1774. The sharp increase in prosperity meant that **the first business directory of London** published in 1677 listed 1786 merchants and traders in the City and Westminster. **London's first newspaper** – the *Daily Courant* – was published in 1702.

Perhaps inevitably, income tax was first introduced in 1799. **The first stock exchange**, named as such, was formally given that title in 1773, although its origins

---

Britain's oldest newspapers

Title	Date of foundation
The Oxford Gazette (later The London Gazette)	1665
Berrow's Worcester Journal	1709
Lincoln, Rutland and Stamford Journal	1710
Lloyds List	1726
News Letter (Belfast)	1738
Hampshire Chronicle	1772
The Times (originally the Daily Universal register)	1785
Observer	1791
Morning Advertiser	1794
The Scotsman	1817

lay in Garraway's coffee house. The communication and trading revolution was reflected in the creation of the Royal Mail in 1784.

Industrial Revolution

These commercial developments fed off the burgeoning industrial sector, the growth of which was increasing through innovations in cotton, iron making and machinery. Perhaps, the crucial first inventions in these sectors were Darby's coke smelting process in 1709, Hargreaves's Spinning Jenny in 1764, Cort's puddling and rolling process in 1783 and James Watt's construction of the **first true steam engine** in 1774. These, together with the transformation of agriculture and the new factories created the **first, great industrial revolution**.

The first true factories appeared c. 1716 in sectors like porter brewing.

Jethro Tull developed the seed drill in 1733. The first description of these changes as an industrial revolution occurred in Arnold Toynbee's *Lectures on the Industrial Revolution* given 1880–81 and published in 1884. The Industrial Revolution was the convergence of four distinct revolutions in science, agriculture, trade and manufacturing.

With the first Industrial Revolution, the pace of change accelerated. Gradually,

Benjamin Franklin (1706-90), the American statesman and scientist. As well as playing a major role in drafting the Declaration of Independence (1776) and the American Constitution (1787) and designing the first lightning conductor, Franklin also founded the first American insurance company, the Philadelphia Contributionship (1752). (Ann Ronan Picture Library).

these innovations and the firsts became increasingly global. Benjamin Franklin founded **the first American insurance company**, the Philadelphia Contributionship in 1752. The first life assurance company in the USA was the Presbyterian Ministers' Fund created in 1759.

 Benjamin Franklin's interest in commerce went much further than setting up insurance companies. He was

America's oldest companies

Title	Business	Date of foundation
J.E. Rhoads & Sons	Conveyor Belts	1702
Covenant Life Insurance	Insurance	1717
Philadelphia Contributionship	Insurance	1752
D Landreth Seed	Seeds	1784
Bank of New York	Banking	1784
Mutual Assurance	Assurance	1784
Bank of Boston	Banking	1784
George R Ruhl & Sons	Bakery Supplies	1789
Burns & Russell	Building Materials	1790

perhaps the first great, national smuggler of science and technology. During his time as Ambassador in Paris he actively encouraged the emigration of skilled workers, especially those with the skills to re-create modern machinery in the US. His involvement in 'Emigrants' Clubs' was specifically designed to encourage people to leave England with the secrets of advanced machinery despite the efforts of the Crown, the Home Office, customs authorities and 'patriotic informers' to prevent the export of these technologies. Franklin offered land, citizenship, monopolies in manufacturing and selling and exemption from military service to migrants.

The early success of **the USA's first industrial network** (the Boston Associates), its **first, true industrial enterprise** (the Boston Company) and the Industrial Revolution in North America owes much to industrial piracy. Francis Lowell, the man behind all these, spent two years in Britain studying the industrial changes that were transforming the country. He smuggled out plans for power looms, dressing machines, spinning equipment and the ways to organize these into a modern, large-scale production unit. The construction of **America's first real factory** in 1813/14 was soon followed by the development of **America's first industrial town**, Waltham/Lowell, Massachusetts. This evolved into the Lowell System at Lowell, by the Merrimack Manufacturing Company in 1822.

For perhaps the first time there was the integration of large capital investments, concentration of all production processes, unified management and specialized production of a single product by relatively unskilled workers. This system in which a paternalistic approach to workers was linked to modern manufacturing became a wonder of the age.

Manufacturing innovations

Half a century earlier, Britain had seen the application of a number of innovations to manufacturing. Textiles, iron making, pot-

tery and mining were among the industries first affected by these changes. Soon transport, food production and processing and a host of industries were reshaped. Textiles had been important in England since the Middle Ages but it was the application of machines to wool, silk and cotton processing that transformed the industry.

The first knitting machine was the Rev. William Lee's stocking frame in 1589. The Wilton Royal Carpet Company dates back to 1655. One of the first users of Samuel Crompton's spinning mule was William Heaton and Sons who were established in 1750. The spinning mule was made by Dobson and Barlow of Bolton and won its name because it combined the features of Arkwright's water frame and Hargreaves' spinning jenny. It produced a thread which could be used as both warp and weft, enabling the manufacture of the first all-cotton fabrics. At the end of the 18th century, Eli Whitney removed one of the major barriers to the growth of the cotton industry in the USA. His cotton gin 'combed' the sticky seeds out of raw cotton. This increased by fiftyfold the amount of cotton that could be processed by one person.

Many wool spinners date their origins from the same era notably Wm Hollins Ltd., established in 1784, C.F. Taylor and Co. of Shipley (West Yorkshire) in 1788, and Jeremiah Ambler of Bradford (West Yorkshire) in 1789. By the middle of the next century, the industrialization of wool production enabled Sir Titus Salt to build one of **England's first 'model towns'** at Saltaire near Bradford (1851). The transformation of the textiles industry was completed in the 19th century when **the first effective power looms** were produced. Edmund Cartwright took out the first patents, but it was not until William Horrocks developed his technology that power looms became successful.

The transformation of iron making was inseparable from all aspects of the Industrial Revolution. At its heart lay Abraham Darby's success in being **the**

The first iron bridge was erected in 1777-79 at Coalbrookdale, Telford (Shropshire, England). After the 1780s, cast-iron structures were used extensively both for engineering purposes and to strengthen conventional architecture. (Ann Ronan Picture Library).

first person to effectively smelt iron with coke in 1709. This made large-scale iron production possible. There were, however, so many technical problems with the process that large-scale production was not possible until the middle of the century. Carron Iron Founders (1759), of Falkirk (Scotland), and the Stockton Heath Forge (1770), of Warrington (Cheshire, England), were among the first that emerged at this time. In the 1780s Henry Cort developed and patented the puddling and rolling process that permitted **the large-scale production of refined iron for the first time.**

Revolutions in transport

The early history of the Stockton Heath Forge is hard to separate from the transport revolution occurring at the same time. The company produced the spades and shovels used for the construction of the Bridgewater Canal by the Earl

of Ellesmere in 1770. **The first true industrial canal in the British Isles** was the Newry Canal in Northern Ireland. **The first industrial canal in England** was the Sankey Brook Navigation Canal (1757) built to move salt and coal between Cheshire and Lancashire, but it was the Duke of Bridgewater's canal of 1761, which moved coal from the Duke's colliery at Worsley, that produced 'canal fever' and transformed inland transport. In Britain the canal era lasted almost a hundred years – until the railways were introduced and expanded after **the first steam railway** from Stockton to Darlington in 1825.

In North America, the canal era was much shorter but its impact was massive. The first major canal was the Erie Canal from Albany to Buffalo which opened in 1825. This linked the Hudson to the Great Lakes and secured New York's dominance on East Coast commerce. The success of the Erie Canal played its part in creating the fortune of **America's first dollar billionaire**, Conrad (Commodore) Vanderbilt. His first fortune was built as a shipowner on the Hudson and Erie, but like the rest of America, he soon moved into railways.

The first US railway was the Baltimore and Ohio completed in 1828. **The first**

steam train ran, unsuccessfully, on the Delaware-Hudson Canal Co. line in 1829. A year later, the steam locomotive *Best Friend of Charleston* ran successfully on the South Carolina Railroad. This marked **the start of the railway age in the USA**. When he died in 1877, Commodore Vanderbilt dominated the railway networks of the North Eastern USA through his Harlem, Hudson and New York Central lines. His fortune of $100M was larger than the US Treasury and would be worth at least $1.5Bn today. It is probable that Europe's first modern, commercial billionaire Nathan Mayer Rothschild was worth a similar sum in the late 1870s.

Nathan Mayer Rothschild

Nathan Mayer Rothschild (1776–1836) was the most remarkable of five talented brothers who between the later 1790s and the early 1830s transformed their father's small money lending and discount house in Frankfurt into the most powerful financial institution in Europe.

The story of how Nathan Mayer Rothschild – a 'red-headed, stocky, bustling, impatient, often ill-tempered man' – led his family to such prominence is full of legends and mysteries. The initial impetus came from two sources. First, there was his decision to migrate from the family home in Frankfurt to England. The second is rooted in the story of the Elector (prince) of Hesse-Kassel's fortune. Some commentators have suggested that Nathan's move to England was part of a wider plan hatched by his father, Mayer Amshel Rothschild (1744–1812), to place a son in each of the major financial centres of Europe. The truth is probably the more mundane desire of an ambitious young entrepreneur to base himself in the fastest growing economy in Europe. Nathan joined many other ambitious central Europeans on the road to the newly, industrializing cities of England.

Initially, Nathan established his business in Manchester in 1798. He soon achieved considerable success by the time honoured, but risky, tactic of taking a highly fragmented business and concentrating its activities. He cut out a number of middlemen and won lower prices by replacing credit with cash and paying promptly. Nathan cut his costs to the bone and used his knowledge of international affairs to exploit opportunities created by the Napoleonic Wars. Within a decade, Nathan was a major force in the Manchester market and ready to move to London; at the same time he moved the focus of the business away from trade in goods to trade in money, especially government bonds and bullion.

The Rothschild legend links this shift with the problems being faced by the Elector of Hesse-Kassel. The prince had angered Napoleon, prompting the Emperor to vow 'to remove the House of Hesse-Kassel from rulership and to strike it out of the list of powers'. The prince's immediate reaction to this threat was to try to remove his vast fortune out of territories controlled by Napoleon. He turned to Nathan's father, Mayer, to hide and protect his wealth, estimated at about £600,000 (or $50,000,000 at present values).

Mayer successfully saved the fortune from French troops by using an audacious ploy. After hiding the Prince's fortune, he left his own wealth, about £15,000, unhidden. The troops found and took this, but did not search any further. In gratitude, the Elector promised that 'my money shall be at your service for 20 years to come and at no more than two per cent interest'. Access to this wealth 'made our fortune' according to Nathan's brother Carl.
Between 1810 and 1815, Nathan Rothschild moved from being one of many London financiers engaged in trades ranging from general merchandise to blockade running to His Majesty's Government's official banker. Access to the Elector's wealth

allowed Nathan to engage in financial dealing at a scale few others in London could match. His superb intelligence system, discretion, hard work and determination to succeed bore dividends on a massive scale. All these factors came in to play when he took responsibility for arranging gold shipments to Wellington's army in Portugal and Spain from 1811.

The growth and scale of the family's international network was an especially important feature of developments from 1810 onwards. Nathan was in London, his brothers James in Paris, Salomon in Vienna, Amschel in Frankfurt and Carl, eventually, in Naples. The entry of British troops into France reinforced Nathan's position and his relationship with the British government. Peace provided new opportunities and threats.

Napoleon's doomed Waterloo campaign added new touches to the Rothschild story. Nathan was the first person in London to hear that the prevailing rumour 'that a battle had been fought and the Duke of Wellington was crushed' was false. He tried to inform the Prime Minister but was turned away by a butler who told him that the Prime Minister had retired for the night and could not be disturbed. The following day, the Prime Minister refused to believe Nathan's account – leaving Nathan the only person in London 'speculating' on Napoleon's defeat. The postwar era saw major increases in the wealth and power of the Rothschilds, who were active in managing the French loans that were used to deal with war reparations and indemnities. An attempt was made to exclude them from this process but a bout of Rothschild inspired speculation against the loan almost ruined those involved while reminding others of the power of the House of Rothschild.

Nathan's ability to influence events was confirmed during the banking crisis of 1825. The Bank of England was close to collapse when the speculative frenzy of that decade came to an abrupt end. During late October and early November 1825 over 70 banks failed and the Bank of England's deposits shrank dramatically. Nathan Rothschild arranged a 'rescue' package of $10M (at 1820s values) to save the Bank.

In his later years, his reputation was so high that he could shift opinions through a simple act. On one occasion, he stopped a run on Masterman's bank by simply entering its offices and placing a deposit while loudly declaiming 'put that to the credit of my account'.

Nathan Mayer Rothschild died during a visit to his native Frankfurt in 1836. *The Times* obituary said that his death was 'one of the most important events for the city, and perhaps for Europe, which has occurred for a very long time'.

The family's fortunes were measured to ensure an equitable share of profits. At current (1995) prices, each brother's share of the capital was:

	1818	1825	1828
Nathan	$78,000,000	$174,687,500	$183,300,000
Amschel	$50,544,000	$123,134,375	$128,009,375
Salomon	$50,544,000	$123,134,375	$128,009,375
Carl	$50,544,000	$123,134,375	$128,009,375
James	$50,544,000	$123,134,375	$128,009,375
Total	$280,176,000	$667,225,000	$695,337,500

The rise of new industries

Many writers identify the start of the industrial age with the creation of the Staffordshire potteries of Josiah Wedgwood (1730–95). His potteries at Brick House Works and then Etruria, at Burslem, were developed between 1764–69. It was one of **the first attempts to link advanced scientific knowledge about production processes, with progressive thinking about the way to organize labour.** The link between science and industry became more pronounced as industrialization progressed. This stimulated the growth of the scientific instruments industry as well as the pressure of better systems of measurement and more qualified engineers. **Britain's first significant commercial producer of scientific instruments** was W. Ottway and Co. established 1640. Wedgwood was among the first to take a systematic approach to sales and marketing his products. Other potteries, notably the Coalport China Company of Stoke on Trent (1750) and Royal Crowne Derby (1750), pre-date Wedgwood but none had a more profound effect on industry and commerce.

All these new industries relied heavily on the extractive industries. Coal, iron and a host of other materials were dug from the ground. One of the main restrictions on mining was the inability of the mine workings to reach deep underground and work with a modicum of safety. Watt's steam engine allowed mine owners to **introduce steam winding into mines for the first time** by the 1790s. This enabled much deeper seams to be reached.

The distribution of industrial activity became increasingly linked with both the source of key raw materials like coal and the inventiveness of citizens. In the UK, Benjamin Huntsman's development of crucible steel in the 1740s was inseparable from the growth of the Sheffield cutlery

James Watt's steam engine, from a cigarette card published in 1915. The sun-and-planet gear converted up-and-down motion of the beam to rotary motion for driving machinery. Watt's steam engine was one of the most significant nventions of the 18th century. (Ann Ronan Picture Library).

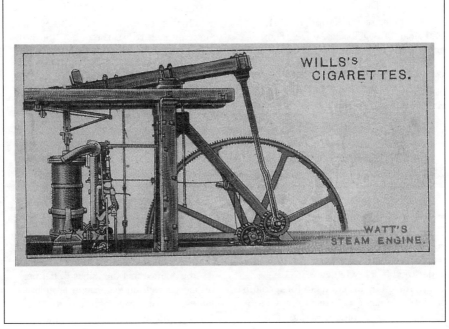

and tool-making industries. The mining industry in Cornwall was one of the first to use Watt's steam engines because they used less coal than rival technologies. This was a major advantage in a region which had relatively small local coal deposits. In Scotland, the North East of England and other areas the link between access to raw materials and industrial growth was more direct. This pattern was repeated across Europe as industrialization gathered pace and became an increasingly worldwide phenomenon.

The second stage of the Industrial Revolution was dominated by new industries like chemicals and engineering. Geigy, founded in 1758, is probably **the oldest chemicals company in the world**. At the start of the 19th century, E.I. du Pont started his chemicals company on the Brandywine River, Delaware. Besides setting up **the USA's first great chemicals company**, he started North America's **first great industrial dynasty**. At the latest estimate, the 1700 descendants of E.I. du Pont have combined assets of over $200Bn.

The link between scientific knowledge and the growth of the chemicals industry was especially evidence in the evolution of the industry in mainland Europe. In 1791, Haussman of Logelbach, Alsace, (France), introduced Berthollet chlorine bleaching for the first time. Thirty years later in 1822, Mulhouse opened one of the first schools of chemical engineering. **The first industrial bank**, Société Générale des Pays-Bas pour favouriser l' Industrie nationale, was founded in Belgium in 1831.

Comprehensive patent laws were introduced in a number of countries. The US Patent and Trade Mark Office was first established by Congress in 1790. It allocated its first patent in the same year to Samuel Hopkins for a process for making soap. Patents have to be enforced. The problems of enforcing patents were well understood by Eli Whitney who was almost ruined by his efforts to force cotton producers to pay for the use of his cotton gin. This adversity produced one of the

most important breakthroughs in manufacturing history. Whitney was given a contract in 1798 to produce guns for the US army. In meeting the order, he developed **the first system of production by using interchangeable parts and employing a structured division of labour** in 1790. He invented mass production a century before Henry Ford.

The growth of leisure and consumerism

The new industrial workforces were far more concentrated than at any time in history. This created larger and new markets for consumer and commercial goods. Some of the world's oldest businesses are linked with leisure and recreation. Few businesses in Britain can trace their histories further back than inns and pubs.

For most of their history, inns and taverns brewed their own beers. Brewing became increasingly centralized during the 19th century with major breweries and distilleries dominating the trade.

The oldest breweries in the British Isles are City of London (1580), Barclay Perkins's Anchor (in Southwark, 1616), and Tomson & Wooton (in Ramsgate, 1634). The oldest British distillery is Haig, founded in Scotland in 1623. **The oldest brewery in the world** is probably the Bavarian State Brewery, Weihenstephan at Freising (near Munich), which traces its origins to about 1040. The Klosterbrauerei, Scheyern, Germany, was established in 1119. The Erven Lucas Bols distillery pre-dates any of those from the British Isles and can trace its origins to 1575.

There is a great deal of debate about which is the oldest producer of bourbon in the USA. Jack Daniels proudly claims on its label, that it is **the oldest registered distillery in the United States**. There is good evidence that the James E. Pepper distillery was founded around 1740 and James B. Bean traces its history to 1794. There is, however, general agreement that

Britain's oldest inns and pubs

Name	Date	Location
Bingley Arms (orig. Priests Inn)	905	Bardsley (W. Yorks.)
Godbegot	1002	Winchester, Hampshire
The Trip to Jerusalem[1]	1070	Nottingham
Skirrid Mountain Inn	1110	Llanvihangel Crucorney, Monmouthshire
George	1420	Norton St. Philip, Somerset
The Fighting Cocks	1070 (origin c.700)	St Albans, Hertfordshire
Ye Olde Ferry Boat Inn	1100 (origin c.900)	Holywell, Cambridgeshire
Angel & Royal	1450 (origin c.1213)	Grantham, Lincolnshire

[1]The Trip to Jerusalem has sometimes been seen as the oldest inn because its history is the best documented of all the contenders.

the first vineyard in North America was established in 1769 at the Franciscan Mission San Gabriel in California. The oldest French vineyard is either Raoul Clerget et Fils, or Clerget Buffet et Fils. Both were established in 1270. The oldest German vineyard is the Burgerspital Zum Heiligen Geist in Wurzburg dating from 1312.

The concentration of people in the industrial cities of Europe and North America stimulated the expansion of the food and beverages industries. Crosse and Blackwell dates its origins to 1706 making it perhaps the oldest broad range food processor. R. Twinning (1706) was one of the first major producers of tea for the mass market. There are older tea companies such as Davidson, Newman and Company (c. 1650) who are reputed to be the first grocers to sell a pound of tea and were certainly old enough to have their tea thrown into the sea at the Boston Tea Party of 1773.

Richard Wall – the founder of Wall's – started his meat business in 1786. The oldest European food companies tend to be linked with the flour, cakes and biscuits industries. They include Jb. Bussink's Koninklijke Deventer Koekfabrieken's bakery in Holland which dates back to 1593 and the Swiss firm of Karl Jakob founded 1753. The oldest US food company is probably the Walter Baker Company, a chocolate maker founded in 1776. It was, perhaps, the first company to offer a money back satisfaction guarantee in 1774.

The concentration of industrial labour and associated struggles over wages, health and safety, and working conditions led to the emergence of trades unions and combinations. The Grand National Consolidated Trade Union of 1834 was the first, large general union. Among its more well-known members were the Tolpuddle martyrs.

The early general unions eventually collapsed because of their weak structure and limited resources. The more tightly defined craft-based unions survived longer. The first of these in the UK was the Amalgamated Society of Engineers (1851). In the USA, employers were quick to use the laws against combinations to restrict the early growth of unions. Early trades union history in the USA followed a similar pattern with the first general union – the National Labor Union – established in 1834 but collapsing within a few years. It was the formation of the craft-based American Federation of Labor in 1886 that established the basis for modern trades unionism in North America.

The Tolpuddle Martyrs

The Tolpuddle Martyrs were six farm labourers who were forcibly transported from England to Australia in 1834 for their part in forming a union of agricultural workers. They organized themselves to resist further cuts in farm wages after the depression in agriculture following the end of the Napoleonic Wars.

Contrary to popular belief, they were not charged with forming a union, which was legal in Britain after the repeal of the anti-union Combination Actions in 1824. Their crime was taking an illegal and secret oath.

Taking secret oaths was an important part of early trades unionism. Unions were said to meet 'on dark nights on the peaks, moors and wastes', where secret oaths, buried records and talk of revolution made up rituals which terrified the landowning classes. The 94th Psalm with its talk of 'vengeance' against the 'wicked' who slay the widow and the stranger, and 'murder the fatherless' while asking 'who will rise up against the evildoers?' was an especially popular part of the ritual. All were enjoined to keep the secrets of the union with the call 'taisez vous' (keep quiet).

The fears of the local landowners were increased by the 'swing' riots of 1830, which occurred across the southern English counties of East and West Sussex, Wiltshire, Hampshire and Dorset and were protests against poor wages and unemployment.

When the authorities regained control, 250 people were condemned to death, 500 were transported and 600 imprisoned.

Memories of these events and a determination to 'nip any problems in the bud' persuaded the local magistrates to act quickly and ruthlessly against the six agricultural workers who had formed the Tolpuddle Society (affiliated to the Grand National Consolidated Trade Union) to protest against their low wages. They were being paid eight shillings (40p) a week when labourers in the rest of the district earned ten shillings (50p).

On the advice of Lord Melbourne, a powerful government minister, the local magistrates decided to try the workers under the 1797 Mutiny Act, an Act of Parliament originally passed in response to a strike by sailors in the Royal Navy.

At the trial, the judge summed up the case by pointing out that the aim of trades unions was 'to shake the foundations of society and ruin their masters'.

The six men were found guilty and sentenced to be 'transported to such places beyond the seas as His Majesty's Council in their discretion shall see fit for a term of seven years'.

The trial, conviction and sentence provoked widespread protests. It, however, was two years before pardons were obtained, eventually forced out of the government by evidence that members of the Orange Order including the Duke of Cumberland, the King's brother, took a similar oath.

After their return, only one of the martyrs stayed in Britain. The other five eventually emigrated to Canada.

In 1844, the Rochdale Pioneers (of Greater Manchester, England) **started the world's first retail cooperative.**

The retail revolution

The end of the 19th century saw the transition from the heavy industry based society of the first Industrial Revolution to the light, consumer industry based society of the 20th century. Large retailers grew to prominence.

John James Sainsbury open his first shop in 1869. Jesse Boot opened his first shop in 1873 and launched his first major advertising campaign in 1877. Michael Marks opened his first stall in the Kirkgate market

An advertisement for Sears Roebuck, the largest retailer of general merchandise in the world. The company's headquarters in Chicago (USA) are depicted in the early part of this century; the company presently operates from Sear Tower (Chicago), which, when it opened in 1973, was the world's tallest building.
(Advertising Archive).

in Leeds in 1884. Charles Harrod moved his department store to 101, 103 and 105 Brompton Road in 1884. The oldest fish and chip shop Malins opened in London in 1865.

America's first department store, Macy's, was opened in 1877. By the end of the century (1895) Sears Roebuck and Co.'s mail order products were opening up the American hinterland to new products and novel ideas. At the same time, F. W. Woolworth was turning his five and ten cent stores into a world retail empire.

The communications revolution

A new transport and communication revolution was emerging. Samuel Morse had designed **the first intercity telegraph** in 1837. He sent the first message 'What had God wrought' in 1844. Before the end of the century the separate efforts of Thomas Alva Edison, a former telegrapher, and Alexander Graham Bell

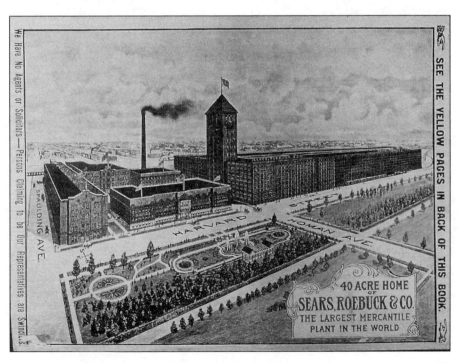

had produced the invention that was to overtake the telegraph – the telephone. **The first telephone message**, sent by Alexander Graham Bell, was the rather more mundane – 'Mr Watson, come here, I want you'. A few year later in 1896, Marconi's wireless telegraphy completed the transformation. In Germany during 1883, Gottleib Daimler was building **the first effective light petrol engine**. Daimler's **first practical petrol drive car** was built in 1886. The modern age was born.

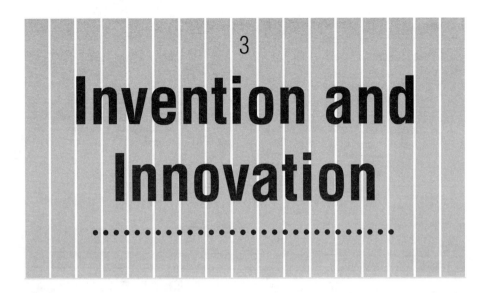

3

Invention and Innovation

 Few processes are more important to business than invention and innovation. A host of inventors saw their ideas and technologies converted into major corporations. Bell, Benz, Le Bic, Davy, Dunlop, Edison, Gillette, Goodyear, Kellog, Otis, Pilkington, Pitman, Siemens, Singer and Westinghouse are just some of the inventors and innovators whose names are still synonymous with firms and industries inseparable from their invention.

Other inventors were just as influential but are not immortalized in the same way. Jean-Antoine-Brutus Menier (1795–1853) invented the chocolate bar. By 1825 production at his factories was 854,000 kilos per year; by 1869 it was 3,846,648 kilos per year, by 1879 it was 15 million kilos. He was the largest chocolate maker in the world but how many purchasers of Hershey bars in the USA or Cadbury's dairy milk in Britain recognize his achievement?

 Edwin Land's **invention of the instant camera** and Cyrus McCormick's **development of the reaper** eventually prompted them to build major corporations like Polaroid and International Harvester but the personal link is less clear. Many inventors have seen their inventions used by others to create wealth, companies and industries. Sometimes this resulted from the revolutionary and pervasive nature of the invention. Henry Bessemer's **invention of the Bessemer converter** transformed iron and steel production. It provided types of metal and metals production that were essential to industrialization across the world in the second half of the 19th century.

Missed opportunities

Sometimes, the decision not to exploit the invention or discovery personally reflected the particular interests and preoccupations of the discoverers and inventors. Alexander Fleming's **discovery of penicillin** was reported in a scientific paper in the 1920s but his researches led him elsewhere and the development was ignored for a decade. All too often, discoverers and inventors fail to gain advantage from their developments. Satori Kato is widely credited with being **the first to devise**

Britain's oldest chocolate bars

Name	Date
Fry's Chocolate Cream	1866
Cadbury's Dairy Milk	1905
Cadbury's Bourneville	1908
Fry's Turkish Delight	1914
Cadbury's Milk Tray	1915

powdered, instant coffee but others exploited his idea. The practice of drinking coffee had been invented in Arabia where it is first reported by ar-Razi (sometimes known as Rhazes) – an Arab doctor – in the 10th century. The first coffee house was opened in Paris in 1643 and was followed by coffee houses in Oxford (1650) and London (1652).

Kato's fate was, however, happier than that of John Kay who **invented the flying shuttle**. His invention won him the undying hatred of the handloom weavers whose livelihood he destroyed and he died hated and in poverty.

Failure to profit from their original invention spurs some inventors to even greater achievements. The modest reward Edison gained from his improvements to the ticker-tape machine prompted him not only to establish **the world's first research laboratory** but to make sure that he won a significant return from the fruits of his inventiveness. Edison was the greatest inventor of all time. This is true both in terms of the number of significant inventions – over 1000 attributed to Edison and his immediate colleagues – and the scale of the corporations he created. Edison produced a powerful sense of system and discipline into the process of invention. However, he never ignored the scope for accidents leading to major new developments. His flair for publicity ensured that his primacy was never in doubt – even when he was not strictly the first to make the breakthrough. His contemporary, Alexander Graham Bell, was the beneficiary of perhaps the most remarkable act of serendipity. He was attempting to invent an effective hearing aid when he came up with the telephone.

Links between innovation and invention

The close link between invention and innovation or commercial exploitation is relatively recent. It is important to understand the difference between the key terms and concepts of technical change, invention, innovation and product or service development.

• **Technical change** is the environment of adaptation, development and modification in technology surrounding the firm, its customers and the market.

• **Invention** is the process of creativity and discovery, usually involving a specific addition to the sum of human knowledge, but although new, not necessarily useful, desirable or commercially successful.

• **Innovation** consists of the technical, industrial and commercial steps which lead to the marketing of new manufactured products or commercial services and the use of new technical processes, products or services.

• **Product development** is the introduction of adaptations, changes or modifications into existing products, brands or services designed to extend their viable life, adapt to new markets or introduce new uses.

Early Chinese inventions and innovations

Date (circa or earliest reference)	Invention
550 BC	Kites
500 BC	Magnifying lens
300 BC	Industrial drill
210 BC	Navigation canals
200 BC	Organic pesticides
180 BC	Magic lantern
50 BC	Paper
50 BC	Hot air balloons
AD 300	Fireworks and gunpowder
AD 580	Toilet paper
1127	Dry compass

Early inventions

Some of the most important early inventions – the wheel, gunpowder, paper, the waterwheel, etc. – are lost in time, although a Chinese eunuch is attributed with the invention of paper in about AD 50. Even where the authorship is known, such as Archimedes' screw converter for irrigation, the link between invention and commercial exploitation – if it existed – is lost in time.

In the East, invention blossomed under the Shang, Han, Tang (or T'ang), Song (or S'ung) and M'ing dynasties of China.

The Hellenic and Persian civilizations saw invention affect life in areas as diverse as communication, weapons and mining. Julius Caesar is sometimes given credit for inventing the flyposter to support his political ambitions in Rome. His publication of a regular, hand-written sheet for distribution in Rome around 59 BC might mean he was the first newspaper baron.

In India, South America, and Northern and Central Africa there are many examples of change in agriculture, architecture, warfare and medicine prompted by invention. In the West the link between scientific, cultural and industrial change became clear in the 15th and 16th centuries. The scientific revolution that emerged in the late 1400s is hard to separate from the industrial and commercial revolution of the late 1500s and early 1600s. For perhaps the first time, invention was initiated for a clearly commercial end.

No-one epitomized the transition that occurred at the end of the 14th century more clearly than Leonardo da Vinci. His range of interests prompted him to prepare sketches for a host of 'inventions' that were impossible with the technologies of his era. These ranged from the driving chain to the helicopter. His curiosity led him to research human anatomy in an attempt to understand the way the body worked and his correspondence shows he was, also, capable of showing the kind of pragmatic approach to science employed by modern inventors.

Da Vinci's letter to Ludovico Sforza of Milan, seeking employment, promises that he will "contrive catapults, mangolets, trebuchets and other machines of marvellous efficiency and not in common use". His contemporary Johan Gutenberg's **invention of movable type** is one of the clearest links between invention, innovation and business development.

Evolution and revolution

 The scale of recorded invention increased during the 16th century. This was especially evident in England, the Netherlands and France. Iron production increased by six hundred per cent between 1540 and 1620 in England. The French were **the first to use cannon on a ship** at the battle of Rapallo in 1494. **The newspaper was invented** by Abraham Verhoeven in Belgium, in 1605. His publication – *Nieuwe Tijdingen* – was expensive but showed all the key characteristics of the modern newspaper – even the gossip.

The link between inventors and their inventions are very different from that seen today. The notion of intellectual property was imperfectly developed, with the laurels resting 'less with those who said things first than with those who said things best'. (Nef, J.U. *War and Human progress* Cambridge, Harvard University Press, 1950).

The earliest known English patent was granted by Henry VI in 1449 to Flemish-born John of Utynam for making the coloured glass required for the windows of Eton College. However, it is slightly misleading to use the term patent in this context as any rights were awarded by the Crown often for reasons which had little to do with intellectual property rights. This notion gains its first currency at this time with the formation of the first, scientific, learned societies. The convergence of science and invention

The earliest learned societies

Society	Country	Foundation
Accademia dei Lincei	Italy	1609
Royal Society	England	1660
Academie Royale des Sciences	France	1666

is vividly illustrated at this time by the careers of individuals like Robert Hooke whose inventions included the air pump (used by Robert Boyle for his famous experiments on gases), the balance spring for watches, the universal joint and, per-

haps, the learned scientific journal, along with early speculation on the rotating, milling lathe.

The 16th and 17th centuries saw the systematic accumulation of inventive activity

Hooke and Newton

Two people vividly illustrate the tension between science and invention. Robert Hooke (1635-1703) was a brilliant inventor who constantly sought to transfer his ideas into applications. Before he was thirty he had worked for Robert Boyle (1627-91) on the design of air pumps. Later he invented the balance spring of the modern watch, the universal joint and the iris diaphragm. He also produced the first book of drawings of microscopic animals. In 1662, he was appointed curator of experiments to the Royal Society. His life and reputation were,

however, blighted by a bitter row with Isaac Newton. Their conflict was initially sparked by Hooke's criticisms of Newton's early work on optics. It was sustained by their wholly different philosophies. Hooke wanted to try out a host of ideas, convert them to inventions and introduce them as quickly as possible. Newton sought order in his experiments. Painful exactitude underpinned by powerful mathematics was his lodestar. This conflict has recurred repeatedly over the last three hundred years.

Invention and application in the 16th and 17th centuries

Item	Date
Pencil, dredger, naval mine, rolling mill, theodolite, vice and spanner, wallpaper, dressings for wounds.	1500–1550
False limbs, newspapers, knitting frame, pendulum, microscope, thermometer, foot rule	1551–1600
Telescope, slide rule, micrometer, calculating machine, barometer, submarine	1601–1650
Balance spring, cigarette, pressure cooker, air pump, universal joint, steam engine	1651–1700

Francis Bacon

Francis Bacon (1561–1626) was an English statesman and philosopher who has been called the father of modern science. He was a determined empiricist who criticised Aristotle and rejected deductive logic as the route to scientific knowledge. Bacon argued for a wholly empirical basis for understanding. It could be argued that he died for his belief. Bacon was conducting an experiment of the effects of extreme cold on the preservation of flesh – in his case, stuffing a fowl with ice – when he caught the cold that killed him.

Bacon held a number of important political offices including Solicitor General (1609), Attorney General (1613), Lord Keeper of the Great Seal (1617), and Lord Chancellor (1618), but in 1621 he was found guilty of accepting bribes and was removed from his offices.

into a body of scientific knowledge and commercial exploitation, for perhaps the first time.

The same era saw the emergence of the equally important divergence between pure and applied science. In the Royal Society, the bitterness that grew between Isaac Newton and Robert Hooke went beyond Newton's fears of plagiarism to his deeper concern about Hooke's inter-est in a host of novel ideas for application – perhaps at the expense of sustained, systematic, basic research. Both could claim to be the heirs of Bacon. He welcomed the application of scientific knowledge "to the production of wonderful operations", but argued against the purely "luciferous" (money grabbing) use of scientific knowledge (Francis Bacon *Philosophical Works*, 1620).

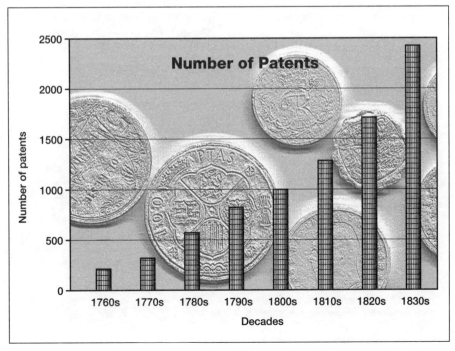

Number of Patents

The age of the inventor

 The end of the 16th century in England saw sharp increases in coal mining, iron production and other forms of manufacture many of which were stimulated by inventions and innovations. These included covered crucibles to separate materials in glass-making, the printing press, the blast furnace, and the stocking knitting frame. Besides these developments the sharp increase in the use of coal (instead of wood) in glass-making, steel-making and brick-making, boosted industrial output.

 In the century of that followed, this progress stopped and indeed regressed in many places. The pressure from invention declined, along with opportunities and markets, as exploration, colonization and war absorbed the invention and enterprise of people. This is illustrated by the number of patents registered in England. During the boom of the 1690s, the numbers of patents peaked at 102 only to decline. From the 1770s numbers started to surge, exceeding 300 by the end of the decade. They rose to over a thousand during the first decade of the next century, and almost 3000 during the 1830s.

The 19th century saw inventions and their commercial application affect every aspect of human life. Initially, agriculture, materials technologies, mining, and mechanical production processes were most affected. Many of these sectors linked 18th century inventions, like the flying shuttle and the spinning jenny, to new technologies and emerging markets. Later, transport, public health, construction and warfare were transformed. By the end of the century, communications, electronics, chemicals, domestic life, health and leisure were shaped by the success with which inventions were converted into successful businesses. The ability of inventors to protect their rights through patents was an important element in the creation of a link between invention and commercial exploitation. A hundred years after the inception of the US Patent Office in 1790, an international system of patent protection was created under a convention of 1883.

 The first industrial sector affected was spinning. Inventors like James Hargreaves, in 1764 and Samuel Crompton, in 1779, built spinning machines and organized them into production systems which were recognizable as factories. Both men illustrated another aspect of the link between invention and business. (This is the difficulty that many innovators face in establishing successful businesses.) Their compatriot, Richard Arkwright, lacked their inventiveness – he probably stole his patents – but he had

---

Richard Arkwright

Richard Arkwright (1732–92) was born in Preston, Lancashire (England). Although Arkwright was a self-educated man, he invented many machines for mass-producing yarn. His greatest achievements lay in the development of production systems and processes for cotton production and he has been described as the father of the modern industrial factory system.

Arkwright improved on the spinning jenny with a machine with a mechanical tread-spinner able to draw carded cotton into threads of any thickness. This quality improvement overcame the main barrier to the widespread adoption of machine-produced yarns. He built a number of his own mills and created one of the first true industrial empires. The first producer to use Watt's steam engine to power textile machinery, his later years were surrounded by controversy as his collaborator successfully challenged his patents. Despite that, Arkwright left a large fortune at his death.

entrepreneurial skill to turn his invention into a commercial success.

Inventions like Cort's invention of puddling had a similar impact on the iron industry. The iron industry also saw one of the first successful steps in the process of freeing production from its dependence on natural sources of energy. In 1776, John Wilkinson used Watt's steam engine to power his factory.

Ⓢ Steam engines were known since the start of the 18th century. Thomas Newcomen installed the first in his factory in 1712. These **early steam engines** were both inefficient and dangerous. They had to be cooled off each time they were used, which took time and wasted energy. It was not until James Watt asked the classic inventor's question – why do we do it this way? – that the breakthrough took place in steam technology. His breakthrough lay in condensing steam in a separate container, so that the steam chamber could be kept hot all the time. This 'invention' broke the link between production and animal muscle or water or wind power. Watt's partnership with Matthew Boulton linked the inventor with the industrialist. Boulton's use of a form of leasing to promote the use of engines was a further innovation. Although the savings were often very large, it was hard to persuade the owners of the metal mines to pay the agreed price.

The application of steam power to cotton production led to dramatic increases in productivity that created wealth for some, while destroying traditional production processes. Watt and Boulton were typical of the inventors/entrepreneurs who were coming to dominate British and world industry. They continually sought improvements to their systems and linked their investigations to a wider understanding. Josiah Wedgwood's determination to improve temperature control in his kilns led to **the invention of the pyrometer**. This gave him the tools to make the fundamental scientific discovery that at high temperature all materials glow in the same way, i.e. that colour measures temperature.

From the end of the 18th century to late in the 19th century, the spirit of invention spread across the world. Sometimes inventions solved specific problems such as the New Yorker John Greenwood's invention of the dental drill in 1790. Elsewhere, they tackled major commercial problems. Eli Whitney's cotton gin (1792) transformed the business prospects of the Southern US cotton plantations. This simple machine increased productivity fifty-fold. Whitney was perhaps the first of the great New England inventors. His creativity allowed him to move beyond the cotton gin into pioneering mass production through a host of inventions, especially in machine tool manufacture.

Inventions in Europe

On the European mainland, a similar surge of creative energy was seen. J. M. Jacquard's **invention of the punch card system** of automatic pattern weaving transformed cloth production. In France, this was followed, later in the 19th century by Huart Chapel's reverbatory furnace, Thimonnier's invention of the sewing machine, Berthollet's chlorine bleacher and Girard's flax spinner.

Ⓢ For much of the 18th century, the most advanced economies in the world outside Britain were found in the Benelux countries. Sometimes their industries were built on successful technology transfer. Brugelman built a version of Arkwright's water-frame as early as 1783 – an early example of the biter-bit. Nearby, Bockmuhl invented one of the first machines for making bootlaces. The textile industry was the centre of attention for many of these inventors, notably Heilman who **developed the power loom** in early 1826. He followed this up with a series of inventions culminating in an effective wool-combing machine in 1846.

The great surge in German industrial development and invention can be dated from the middle of the 19th century. Some of the most successful German companies, including Siemens and Mercedes Benz, date their foundations back to this era. As the century progressed, these commercial inventions ranged from **the first motor cars** (Carl Benz in 1884) through the electricity generator (Friedrich von Hefner-Alterneck in 1872) to aspirin (Felix Hoffman in 1897). By this time, the link between invention and commercial development was well established, and occurring in a host of countries. **The safety match** was invented by Anton von Schrotter in Austria (1845), **the electric motor** by the Belgian Zenoble Gramme (1873) and **wireless communication** by Guglielmo Marconi in Italy (1896).

Farming, transport and communications

The population explosion of the 19th century provided labour for the new factories, and markets for the new products. This explosion occurred, in part, because of the breakthroughs in hygiene and medicine which cut infant mortality rates.

The opening up of large areas of North America, Australasia and Southern Africa was closely linked initially with the search for new lands, and later with growth in agricultural production to feed the industrial workforces. No decade was more important for this first 'green revolution' than the period 1825–1835. Without these inventions, the industrial workforce for the second half of the 19th century could not have been fed.

 The new industries and their associated businesses were concentrated in the rapidly growing cities of Northern Europe and North America. Moving their products, and shipping food and raw materials into them, required a comparable revolution in transport. Steam provided the motor force, while iron and then steel provided the means to contain, transform, and determine the movement of people and goods. **The first steam ship** was built and sailed by Patrick Miller in Scotland in 1799.

Within ten years the idea was taken and used by an American, Robert Fulton, to establish **the world's first steam packet line** between New York and Albany. Within fifty years, the whole face of seaborne transport was transformed when Brunel's *Great Britain* linked **three great inventions: steam propulsion, the screw propeller and the iron hull**. Land-based transport was transformed with comparable speed. It took only 40 years for the 50 kilometres of railway between Liverpool and Manchester to stretch to over 100,000 kilometres across the world.

Sharp increases in the number of people travelling prompted other related inventions. Thomas Cook **invented the package tour and travel agents** in 1841. The traveller's cheque was invented in 1891 by American Express. **The credit card was first introduced** by Ralph Schneider in 1950.

The movement of people and goods, the expansion of trade, and the increased inter-dependency of businesses, markets and technologies placed enormous pressure on information and

Inventions and the green revolution			
Inventions	**Inventors**	**Country**	**Date**
Corn reaper	Patrick Bell	Scotland	1826
Food canning	Peter Durand	England	1830
Threshing machine	Andrew Meikle	Scotland	1830
Crop rotation	Jethro Tull	England	1831
Refrigeration	Jacob Perkins	USA	1834

A Thomas Cook poster of 1868. Thomas Cook (1808-92) invented the package tour and may be described as the first travel agent. (Peter Newark's Historical Pictures).

communication. Thomas Edison started his career by introducing improvements into primitive ticker-tape machines. The electric telegraph ushered in a series of inventions which transformed communication from a low speed, personal and local process to an instant, impersonal and global network. The English inventors W.F. Cooke and C. Wheatstone invented (1836), patented (1837) then installed (1838) **the first commercial electric telegraph** (for the Great Western Railway). Within a decade, Samuel Morse had invented his code, installed a commercial telegraph, and introduced relays to expand its range.

Three inventors dominate the half century

Michael Faraday

Michael Faraday (1791–1867), one of the most important scientists in history. His inventions – the electric motor (1821), the dynamo (1831), and the transformer (1831) – were the platforms on which Edison built.

Faraday won his recognition, however, in the research community while Edison's monuments are as much in the business community.

Faraday had little formal education. He was, however, apprenticed to a bookseller and book binder and used this as an opportunity to read widely. Faraday became particularly interested in the many new ideas that were then emerging in physics and chemistry.

In 1811, he attended a series of lectures and sent him the notes he had made of his lectures. These persuaded Davy to make Faraday his assistant at the Royal Society in London.

Faraday's early work was with Davy on chemistry and he successfully liquefied chlorine and other gases, and was the first to isolate benzene. This work was crucial to the development of organic chemistry.

It is Faraday's work on electricity and electrolysis that is most famous. He built the first electric motor as part of his experiments on the relationship between electricity and magnetism.

In 1831, Faraday discovered that if a magnet is passed through a closed loop of wire, a current will flow through the wire while the magnet is moving: this process of electromagnetic induction is crucial to the understanding of electromagnetism and is a vital stage in the development of applied science, and to the development of the dynamo, or electrical generator.

James Clark became convinced of the notion of lines of force by Faraday's demonstrations of the effects of electromagnetism. Maxwell went on to put Faraday's ideas into mathematical form: this, in turn, led to the development of modern field theory.

Faraday's later discovery of the rotation of the plane of polarized light in a strong magnetic field – the Faraday Effect – has been used as a basis for discoveries about molecular structures and galactic magnetic fields. Faraday introduced the term eletrolysis to describe the process by which molecules can be split by using an electric current. Faraday's Laws, the quantitative laws of physics are named after him. Faraday was a popular lecturer and, in his later years, was committed to increasing interest, especially among children, in science. His six children's books The Chemical History of a Candle are classics of popular scientific literature. A very modest man, refused both a knighthood and the Presidency of the Royal Society. His achievements are well summed up by his patron Sir Humphry Davy, another great scientist. When Davy was asked "What was your greatest discovery", he immediately replied 'Michael Faraday'.

of revolution in communications that followed: Alexander Graham Bell, Thomas Alva Edison and Guiseppe Marconi. Their careers represent wider shifts in the link between invention and business development. Each linked their inventions with major corporations which survived long after their deaths.

The corporation comes of age

The end of the 19th century saw a major shift in the form of industrial organization.

The highly personal businesses of earlier days were replaced by corporations managed by professional managers. This, in turn, produced a determined effort to professionalize invention and its conversion to successful business. The career of Thomas Edison symbolized this transition. He is probably the greatest inventor in recorded history.

Edison bridged the research laboratory, the financial system and the corporation. This was especially evident in 1882 when, with the backing of J. P. Morgan, the Edison Electric Illuminating Company won the contract to supply customers in New York

Thomas Alva Edison

No-one more clearly represents the link between invention and business success than Thomas Alva Edison (1847-1931). He was responsible for more significant inventions than any other person in recorded history. His key inventions were underpinned by over 1000 patents and a willingness to organize invention. He was born at Milan, Ohio (USA), but his family soon moved to Port Huron, Michigan. Although he had little formal education, he built his first laboratory in his parent's basement at the age of 10. His introduction to practical invention occurred when he was asked to produce a practical and reliable stock printer. From then, inventions flowed. At the heart of his success was his willingness to organize research systematically.

He once commented that his greatest invention was "the research laboratory". He was also willing to accept failure – he actually stated that he had no failure but learned about thousands of ways that did not work. He was determined to concentrate his effort on practical problems and vowed to "never invent anything that nobody wants". He recognized the value of 'failure'.

City. This success led eventually to the formation of the Edison General Electric Company – now known as General Electric. His career sharply contrasts with the life of Michael Faraday. Faraday's inventions – the electric motor (1821), the dynamo (1831), and the transformer (1831) – were the platforms on which Edison built. He won his recognition, however, in the research community while Edison's monuments are as much in the business community.

 Edison was not alone. Perhaps his greatest rival was George Westinghouse, the inventor of the air brake and the first alternating current (1886). Westinghouse built the firm named after him into a major and successful rival to Edison's companies. The corporations became the host to inventions which transformed production processes, products, services and science itself. The automobile industry epitomized this process.

Henry Ford's **large-scale introduction of mass production** took Eli Whitney's invention of production through components (1798), added the band conveyor developed to shift bulk foods in Liverpool (1868) to produce **mass assembly line production (1908)**. This production system soon dominated mass production of goods as diverse as small consumer products to ships.

The inventions of Thomas Alva Edison (include)

Invention	Year
The research laboratory	1876
The phonograph	1877
The incandescent light bulb.	1879
The moving picture camera.	1891
The dictating machine.	1911
Over 1000 other patents	

Thomas Alva Edison (1847-1931) listening to a recording on his phonograph. Edison, who had over 1000 patents to his credit, set up the world's first industrial research laboratory at Newark, New Jersey. (Ann Ronan Picture Library).

The new industrial concerns required a constant flow of inventions to win competitive advantage over their rivals. Ford's rival, General Motors, sponsored a series of inventions to challenge Ford's dominance during the first 25 years of this century. These included the air-cooled engine, the copper-cooled car, synchromesh gears, instalment selling, the used car trade, annual model changes and branding, until the combination of the best of these with the 'closed body' led to success.

The expansion of the car industry prompted novel developments elsewhere. **Car hire was invented** in 1918 by a second-hand car dealer in Chicago. His business was bought out in 1923 by John D. Hertz, who renamed the company the Hertz Self Drive System.

 Even Scotch Tape or Sellotape has its origins in the car industry – it was invented in 1925 by Dick Drew when he was working for 3M. Drew was trying to develop a method of 'masking' around the paintwork of cars so that colours did not mix. Glued paper, which had been used before, often stripped away the paint it was supposed to mask. Scotch tape now has a host of uses in the home, commerce and industry. This pressure for invention to win competitive advantage allied to the cost of research shifted attention away from the individual inventor to the corporation or research laboratory for

most of this century.

European industry saw the same processes at work. In Britain, entrepreneurs like Alfred Lever and George Cadbury built their business through a studious mixture of invention, production improvement and marketing. It was, however, in Germany that many of the best examples of integrating invention and business occurred over the last century. Three industries epitomize this process: chemicals, engineering and pharmaceuticals.

The early chemicals industry grew out of the production of dyes. The first breakthrough was achieved by an Englishman, William Perkin, who, at the age of 18, patented **the first commercial dye** (1856). Within a short period of time, the production of synthetic dyes proliferated, especially in Germany, where chemistry held a powerful position in science education. Between 1870 and 1900, employment in the German chemicals industry grew from 30,000 to 260,000. At the same time, Germany's share of world trade in chemicals grew from less than 15% to over 90%. Nobel Prizes for Chemistry were won by German scientists five times between 1901 and 1910 by Hermann Fischer, 1902; Adolf von Baeyer, 1905; Eduard Buchner, 1907; Wilhelm Ostwald, 1909 and Otto Wallach, 1910. It was not until World War I, when supplies of German products were cut off, that the

The face of invention

Number of US patents granted

	1981	1991
Corporations	27,189	35,029
Independent inventors	10,241	13,193
Universities	434	1,306
US Government	1,115	1,180
Other	244	475
Total US origin	39,223	51,183
Total foreign origin	26,548	45,331
Total patents	65,771	95,514

chemical industries in North America and Britain became significant forces in world production.

Wartime transformation

The two World Wars of this century are associated with a remarkable range of inventions which were quickly converted into products and services. Some were directly associated with warfare itself. These included the tank (1915), gas masks (1915), sonar (1916), radar (1935), the jet engine (1939), napalm (1942), the aqualung (1943), the ballistic missile (1944). Other inventions were either sponsored by the military, financed because of military developments, or developed and extended because of military use; notably DDT (1874), synthetic materials (1902),

oxyacetylene welding (1903), gyro-compass (1912), stainless steel (1912), rockets (1926), antibiotics (1928), Titanium (1937), computers (1943), transistors (1946).

The pressure of war created markets for inventions as diverse as the zipper (1893) and the atomic bomb (1945). Although **the zipper was developed** by Whitcomb Judson in 1893 and 'perfected' by Gideon Sundback in 1913, there was no market for the product until the USA joined the First World War. The initial orders came for troops' uniforms in 1916.

Only wartime pressures could persuade the US government to allocate the vast resources needed by the Manhattan Project which led to the production of the atomic bomb. Even the humble cat's eye was only accepted by the British authorities after it

Serendipity

Accidents play an important part in the history of business inventions. Sometimes, the inventor started with one idea in mind and ended up with another: Bell was looking for a better hearing aid and came up with the telephone.

Occasionally nature takes a hand. Sir Alexander Fleming (1881-1955) was responsible for one of the greatest modern pieces of scientific serendipity when he 'accidentally' discovered penicillin (1928). In the course of his research, a staphylococcus culture was accidentally exposed to the atmosphere and became contaminated by a mould which, he noted, dissolved the surrounding bacteria. Fleming correctly inferred that the mould was producing a substance which was toxic to the staphylococcus bacteria. He named the antibacterial substance penicillin after the mould (Penicillium notatum) that produced it.

Fleming published his results the following year but gained little support for his

research from his colleagues. He lacked the technical skills to refine or purify penicillin for medical use, but in the late 1930s two other British researchers, Howard Florey and Ernst Chain, developed the techniques to refine and purify penicillin. (Fleming shared the 1945 Nobel Prize for Physiology or Medicine with Chain and Florey.)

The drug was first used to treat wounded soldiers during World War II. Once sufficient quantities were available penicillin became one of the most important drugs in modern medical history. Fleming made no attempt to establish or protect the patents or licence for penicillin. His reluctance to exploit his discovery commercially probably led to its widespread use very early, saving many lives.

Firms today try to spot this type of opportunity quickly. Scotchguard fabric protector began when a 3M technician spilt a polymer sample onto her shoes and could not clean it off.

was shown during the war that no light was reflected upwards.

The new Industrial Revolution

The interwar years and the post World War II era saw the fit between invention on the one hand and business formation and development on the other hand become stronger and better organized. Major corporations were restructured to increase the resources available for research, and their ability to exploit inventions. In the UK, ICI was formed in 1926 from the merger of four companies: British Dyestuffs, Brunner-Mond, United Alkali and Nobel Industries. The Anglo-Dutch giant Unilever was formed in 1929 to exploit the inventions of their component firms in industries ranging from soaps to food processing. Despite this, small firms remain vital contributors to invention and innovation. Products as diverse as the aerosol can and the zipper have their origins in the entrepreneurial activities of small businesses.

At the other extreme, inventions defended by patents provided a platform for the expansion of Pilkington Glass starting with continuous polishing and grinding (1930). In North America, the search for access to important inventions, patents or technologies, and the wish to achieve greater scale in research, prompted General Motors to acquire Bendix (1929), Westinghouse to set up Station KDKA (1920) and independent producers of film came together to form Metro Goldwyn Mayer, Paramount and First National.

Invention is so important to national economic performance that the US Department of Commerce, the US Patent and Trademark Office, and the US National Council of Patent Law Associations created a National Inventors Hall of Fame in 1973. Not surprisingly Thomas Alva Edison was its first member.

The importance of scale for invention was vividly illustrated by the financial difficul-

ties of Warner Brothers in 1927. This was the year that the firm **invented 'talking pictures'** with the production of The Jazz Singer. The cost of this film almost sent the company to the wall, but the movie's success transformed the industry and secured the company's future. Leisure, transport, materials and communications saw dramatic changes fed by invention and the determination of firms to capitalize on the markets created. Cinema and radio exploited established inventions, but television was based on several novel developments.

Although **the first television** was built by John Logie Baird (1926), the widespread development of television was based on the alternative technologies invented by the Russian-American Vladimir Kosma Zworykin, (1938), whilst in the USA, and introduced by RCA. Baird's original television system was basically mechanical, using a mechanical scanner in the transmitter to create the signal and a scanner in the receiver to convert the signal to a 30 line image. This was overtaken by Zworkin's electronic television system, which used the kinescope cathode ray tube to produce a 60-line, higher definition image. Baird improved on his own system to produce a 240-line system, but by this time the technology based on the electronic system was well established. The cost of protecting an invention is well illustrated by RCA's support for this development. RCA was the first company to spend more than $10m on research and patent protection for a single project.

Modern inventions

The business inventions associated with transport during the interwar and postwar era ranged from means to expand the application and capability of novel forms of transport to ways to control and limit their use. Anti-knocking gasoline (1912) and catalytic cracking of petroleum (1915) made cars, then aircraft, more efficient while the hydraulic clutch (1924) and power steering (1924) made cars more accessible. Cars had such an impact on communities they were forced to turn to

An experimental television demonstration by John Logie Baird in 1930. Although the first television was built by Baird, his 'flying spot system' was abandoned in favour of Vladimir Zworykin's electronic scanning system in 1937. (Image Select).

Carlton Magee's invention – the parking meter (1932) – to control their distribution. The first parking meters were used in Magee's home town of Oklahoma City, USA, in July 1935.

New industries like automotive production needed novel materials to get the best from their capabilities. The materials industry was shaped and reshaped during this century by a host of inventions including float glass (1902), silicones (1910), Plexiglas (1912), nylon (1927), Polyethylin (1930), Stelvatite (1954), safety belts (1963), air bags (1974) plus a host of related inventions which affected the production process. These ranged from the injection moulding of plastics (1952) to Just In Time (1958) management.

A revolution was started in the food industry when Clarence Birdseye 'invented' the frozen food process and launched his **first range of frozen foods** in March 1930. The ubiquitous fish finger was launched in the USA by Gortons in 1953, and in Britain by Birdseye in 1955. Ice cream predates frozen food. **The ice-cream cone** was invented by Italo Marcioni in 1904 and caught on at the St Louis World Fair in 1904. (Using snow or ice to cool or preserve food has a much longer history. The Emperor Nero's tutor, Seneca, railed against the habit of putting snow in drink c. AD 60. **The oldest ice house** dates back to 1700 BC in the Mari kingdom of Northern Iraq. There is evidence of ice houses in China in the 7th century BC. The ice lolly (originally the Popsicle) was probably invented by Frank Epperson in 1923.

At least as important as the revolution in food processing were inventions and innovations in food retailing. Pierre Parissot **invented the department store** format in Paris. His store, La Belle Jardinière, opened in 1824. The first US department store – Harper's Building – opened in New York during 1854. Four years later the Crystal Palace Bazaar, the UK's first department store, opened in 1858.

Clarence Saunders **invented the self-service store** in 1916 with his Piggly Wiggly store in Memphis, Tennessee. Britain's first self-service store was opened by the London Co-operative society in 1942. **The cash register was invented** by James J. Ritty in November 1879 for his saloon. **The supermarket trolley** was invented in 1937 by the owner of the Humpty Dumpty store in Oklahoma City.

The information and communication revolutions

The rate and pace of development in the communications and information sector encourage many observers to describe today's economic conditions as a new industrial revolution. Surveys in the USA of the most innovative companies put firms like Microsoft and other information and communications companies at the top of the league.

 The parallel with the first Industrial Revolution is strengthened when the surge in the world population of the last thirty years and the innovations in agriculture are considered. The invention and widespread use of introduction of hybrid corn (1964), new strains of rice

The most innovative companies

Rank	Company
1	Microsoft
2	General Electric
3	3M
4	AT&T
5	Motorola
6	Apple Computer
7	Intel
8	Merck
9	Wal-Mart Stores
10	Chrysler

Source: *Fortune, 1994*

This US survey was quoted in *Fortune* but took little account of global shifts in research, development and innovative activity.

Patent registrations in the USA are drawn from across the world, with Japanese companies featuring as powerful contributors. Hitachi became the first organization to file over a thousand patents in the USA, in a single year, in the late 1980s.

The US maintains the largest research and development activity but outside the USA, in particular, Japanese research is increasingly fruitful at generating patents.

US patent Top 10 – changing fortunes between 1979 & 1989

1979 Corporation	No. of patents	1989 Corporation	No. of patents
General Electric	611	Hitachi Ltd.	1053
Bayer AG.	360	Toshiba Corp.	961
Westinghouse	347	Canon K. K.	949
IBM.	327	Fuji Photo Film Co.	884
Hitachi.	308	General Electric Co.	818
Siemens	305	Mitsubishi Denki K.K.	767
US Philips	304	US. Philips Corp.	745
US Navy	297	Siemens A.G.	656
RCA	286	IBM Corp.	623
Ciba Geigy.	250	Bayer A. G.	589

European and US patent applications with percent change (1984-89)

	Patents (US)	Per cent increase	Patents (Europe)	Per cent increase
US	58,819	31	14,991	23
Japan	23,168	36	12,272	71
Germany	7599	3	10,467	4
France	3280	23	4537	21
Switzerland	1290	4	2090	14
UK	2629	2	2902	-16
Italy	1438	34	2036	26

(1968, 1972) and new insecticides (1953, 1961) produced dramatic increases in crop yields. This has helped to sustain the much larger populations seen in the developing world. The revolution in communications is driven by a series of inventions which created a host of new business in travel, entertainment and person to person communication.

No invention is more closely linked with the transport and travel revolutions of this century than **the aeroplane**. From the day in 1903 when the Wright Brothers flew for 251 m (825 ft), to the space shuttle programme, inventions have stimulated business growth directly and indirectly. Excluding war, many of the most important inventions are linked with expansion of postal services, parcel and now wider arrays of goods travel. **The invention of the gas turbine engine** (1939) reduced costs while increasing reliability. This invention coincided with **the development of alloys** (1939), which reduced weight and further expanded the capacity to move goods and people at competitive prices. The postwar expansion of international and transcontinental air transport was made possible by these inventions. **The jet engine** – for which the first patents were taken out in 1913, but which only became a practical reality in 1939 – further transformed the situation. Higher speeds, lower costs and greater payloads were the key to further expan-

sion. The jumbo jet (1966) brought these elements together.

The electronic computer is perhaps the greatest symbol of the current industrial revolution. Charles Babbage foresaw the potential of coding systems or punch cards. His Difference Engine (1823) and Analytical Engine (1836) were, in a real sense, **the prototypes for modern computers**. It was, however, the electro-mechanical tabulating machine(s) devised by Herman Hollerith of the United States Bureau of the Census, in the 1880s, that demonstrated both the potential of calculating machines to tackle large-scale computational tasks, and the efficiency of devices driven by electricity. Hollerith was one of the founders of the firm that is most closely associated with the expansion of electronic computers – IBM. The pace of development in computing accelerated in the post-World War II period. In part, this was because the key problems were solved just before or during the war. Konrad Zuse invented **the binary code** for problem solving (1942), the Mark1 computer was built at Harvard (1943) and the Colossus at Bletchley Park (Buckinghamshire, England) in 1943.

These early developments came together, first in the electronic computer ENIAC (Electronics Number Indicator And Calculator, 1946), then in **the first programmable computer**

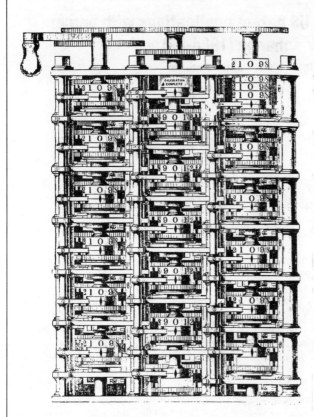

*The first computer':
Charles Babbage's 'dif-
ference machine'
(designed in 1822), an
advanced form of calcula-
tor for application for navigation problems. He was
helped by Ada, Countess
Lovelace (Byron's daugh-
ter), who pursued the idea
that the analytical engine
could be made programma-
ble. (The programming lan-
guage ADA was named
after her.)
(Ann Ronan Picture
Library).*

(ATLAS, 1948). It was, however, **the invention of the transistor and the switching device** at the Bell Laboratory (1949) that transformed these vast, cumbersome and relatively unreliable machines into marketable commercial products. The mass production of computers started with the IBM 700 series in 1954. The history of computers and information technology for the next 40 years was driven by a mixture of invention-based technological push and market pull. The inventions often drove costs down while increasing speed and reliability. The market pull constantly widened the array of uses.

(S) **The invention of the microchip or integrated circuit** by Robert Noyce (1959) symbolized these technological innovations. It reduced costs, cut down the size of machines and increased reliability. The invention of **the first true, user friendly personal home computer** (1977) by Steve Wozniak and Steve Jobs represented a vital breakthrough in making computing accessible to all – creating new markets and innovative uses. It built on the earlier Altair 8800 (1974) and Tandy's computer (1977).

(S) Since then the rate and pace of invention has increased with **software developments like spreadsheets** (Visicalc, 1979) and word processors (Wordstar, 1980) vying with hardware innovations (the Intel 80286, 80386, 80486 chips), the transputer (1985), Graphical User Interfaces, GUIs (1985) and **laser printers** (1986) to open up new markets.

The convergence of these computational

Seymour Cray

The father of supercomputing shares many characteristics with other great inventors who were also business people. Like Edison, he had a laboratory in his home by the age of 10. One of his first projects was an automatic telegraph machine that could translate a punched card into Morse code. World War II interrupted his studies but he used his military training to good effect. He was lucky to come under the influence of William C. Norris, the founder of Control Data Corp. They shared a vision to create the biggest and the best computers in the world.

However, Seymour Cray was not willing to work for someone else indefinitely and a determination to build his own vision of the future prompted him to start up on his own. Before he left CDC he built the first computer capable of executing 3 million programme instructions per second – the CDC 6600 in 1963. He built a host of novel features into his invention, ranging from the first use of reduced instruction set computing (RISC) to the use of the coolant Freon to cool down the computer. His next and last machine for CDC was five times faster – the CDC 7600. He left soon after to set up Cray Research and go on to 'invent' the supercomputer.

The Cray-1, built in 1976, far outperformed any other available machines. For example, it was 10 times faster than the CDC 7600 but was a quarter of its size. He made this breakthrough by inventing the first successful vector processor. This executed not one but 32 arithmetic operations simultaneously.

His next machine, developed jointly with Steve S. Chen, introduced dual processing and was three times as fast as the Cray-1. The Cray-3, built in 1989, pushed the technology even further – new super, high quality chips crammed together at unheard of levels. The machine was designed to go so fast that no machine existed that could test it. It had pushed the technology further than anyone else – until a new invention came along.

technologies with other inventions has transformed a host of business environments. The introduction of robots into factories (1986) played a large part in improving quality while cutting costs. Telecommunication systems are linked with computers to provide information to business. **Fibre optic cables** (1970) increase the capacity of information systems. **Videotext** (1977) and **viewdata** (1980) systems make information widely available, while **portable telephones** (1988), **faxes** (1987) and **internet-type computer systems** (1991) show how quickly inventions can supplant existing technologies, reach maturity and be overtaken by further inventions.

 The final shape of this third industrial revolution is not clear, but it has demonstrated the capacity of invention to revolutionize the business environment. The use of computers is extending from the workplace to the home from practical pursuits to leisure.

The greatest inventions

It is hard to draw any firm conclusion about the most important or valuable invention.

The wheel, the plough, the stirrup, perhaps vaccination, or one of the innovations in agriculture have a claim. It is not possible to put any contemporary value of these.

The most valuable 'modern' (over the last hundred years) invention is probably the electric light and power generator with a

The greatest business inventions (turnover)

Invention	Attributed turnover ($Bn. 1990)
The electric light and power generator	270
The computer	270
The automobile	265
The telephone	227
The aeroplane	185
Synthetic drugs	148
Television and radio	126
Plastic and rubber processing	122
Metals processing	110

Leading Holders of Patents

Edwin Herbert Land (1909–1991) is second only to Edison in the number of patents registered at the US Patents Office. He is, probably, best known for his invention of the Polaroid Land Camera which takes, and instantly develops, photographic images. This emerged from his wider researches into light 'polarisation' which he started at Harvard University. He applied his research to reduced glare sunglasses, camera filters and antiglare automobile headlights. It is said that he offered the technology to Kodak and, when it was rejected, set up his own production facilities and introduced it to the US market in 1948. Around 40 years later, he won one of the largest patent infringement cases in history when Kodak were required to pay $600M for infringing his patents with their 'instant' cameras.

Jerry Lemelson (b. 1924) holds over 500 patents for items as diverse as robots to satellite-based navigation warning systems. Lemelson started his work as an industrial inventor in the 1950s with projects to develop innovative toy designs. Since then, his work has expanded across the commercial environment, and he has become a powerful defender of 'inventors' rights' especially against corporate infringements of copyright.

Lemelson's inventions include:

- Devices to record and read digital and analogue information

- Computer controlled injection moulding machines

- Automatic warehousing

- Faxes

- 'Stand alone' computer stations

- Video filing systems

- Metal-on-silicon microchips and circuit structures

- Electronic still photography

- Disease detection systems

- Computer controlled surgical tourniquets

- Dart boards using Velcro balls

The most inventive people (commercially)

Person	Patents
Thomas Alva Edison	1069
Edwin Land	823
Jerry Lemelson	532
Alexander Graham Bell	321

Research and development

Invention and innovation is full of risks. It is estimated that nine out of ten new products or services launched onto markets fail or are withdrawn after losing large sums of money. It is, sometimes, not necessary to be the inventor or first into the market to gain the most benefits. Some firms thrive by being 'poisoned apple' marketers i.e. they let someone else bite the apple first.

current value of about $270Bn. It is probably no coincidence that its development has its roots in the inventive genius of Thomas Alva Edison. He, also, holds the record for the most US patents held by a single individual.

Corporations and larger organizations dominate patenting and patent activity. In the last decade, corporations, universities and governments account for three times as many inventions as private individuals,

The world leaders in R&D spending, 1994

R&D Rank	Company	Country	Sales ($M)	R&D ($M)
1	General Motors	United States	135,696	6030
2	Daimler-Benz	Germany	60,228	5474
3	Ford Motor	United States	108,448	5021
4	Siemens	Germany	51,946	4759
5	International Business Machines	United States	62,716	4431
6	Hitachi	Japan	60,515	4025
7	AT&T	United States	67,159	3428
8	Matsushita Electric Industrial	Japan	56,659	3227
9	Fujitsu	Japan	27,799	3107
10	Alcatel Alsthom	France	30,614	2863
11	Toshiba	Japan	37,159	2503
12	RWE	Germany	33,984	2431
13	Nippon Telegraph and Telephone	Japan	52,227	2372
14	NEW	Japan	28,225	2208
15	Fiat	Italy	48,469	2132
16	Philips Electronics	Netherlands	33,571	2087
17	Bayer	Germany	27,334	1988
18	Hoechst	Germany	30,136	1865
19	Sony	Japan	32,063	1864
20	Hewlett-Packard	United States	20,317	1761

Source: *Business Week*

and the gap is widening. The contribution of organizations to innovative activity partly reflects the scale and strategic importance of research and development expenditure, especially in manufacturing.

Britain's largest spenders on R&D are ICI, Glaxo, Smithkline Beecham, Unilever and Shell.

 Inventiveness and innovation is not confined to the scientific, the wholly new or the vastly expensive. Ernst Thomke invented the 'Swatch' watch by converting the traditional functional role of the watch into a fashion accessory in 1979. Post-it notes were invented by Spencer Sylver in 1970, but only when Arthur Fry found he needed to mark pages in his music book without damaging the paper was the opportunity recognized. The Maclaren Baby Buggy was invented in a stable (in 1965) by retired engineer Owen Maclaren because of the problems faced by his daughter in getting around with her child.

Not all inventions – even those which eventually have a major impact – are followed up quickly. DDT took 70 years to move from the laboratory to the market place; the ballpoint pen took almost 60 years to reach the market, and penicillin over a decade.

Major modern inventions taking more than ten years to get to market

Product and process	Invention	Innovation	Years between invention and innovation
DDT	1874	1942	68
Ballpoint pen	1888	1946	58
Float glass	1902	1957	55
Synthetic detergent	1886	1930	44
Fluorescent lamp	1901	1938	37
Silicones	1910	1946	36
Automatic drive	1904	1939	35
Zipper	1891	1923	32
Helicopter	1904	1936	32
Tungsten carbide	1900	1926	26
Continuous steelcasting	1927	1952	25
Anti-knock petrol	1912	1935	23
Cotton picker	1920	1942	22
Hydraulic clutch	1925	1946	21
Catalytic cracking of petrol	1915	1935	20
Diesel locomotive	1895	1913	18
Radio	1900	1918	18
Phototypesetting	1936	1954	18
Cinerama	1937	1953	16
Penicillin	1928	1943	15
Rocket	1929	1944	15

Plexiglass	1912	1926	14
Kodachrone	1921	1935	14
Terylene	1941	1955	14
Television	1923	1936	13
Jet engine	1928	1941	13
Xerography	1937	1950	13
Hovercraft	1955	1968	13
Nylon	1927	1938	11

The rewards of innovation

The returns from success can be vast. Sometimes they transform the lives of people and corporations. Few firms have been changed as quickly as the Haloid Company of Rochester, USA. It introduced the Xerox copier in 1959. In its first year, its revenues were $33M. In 1961, they had grown to $66M; in 1963, $176M and by 1966 $500M. By 1974, just 15 years after its introduction, Xerox (by now the company's name) had revenues of $3600M. The costs of failure can be equally large. IBM's failure to keep up with changes in the information industries led to job losses of over 35,000 in the two years to 1994.

500 years of innovation

The chronology of innovation that closes this chapter highlights just some of the inventions and discoveries over the last 500 years that have transformed the business world.

16th century

Year	Invention
1560	False limbs
1569	Wallpaper
1588	Pendulum
1589	Knitting machine
1590	Compound microscope
1591	Thermometer

17th century

Year	Invention
1608	Telescope
1621	Slide rule
1625	Blood transfusion
1636	Micrometer
1642	Adding machine (basic)
1643	Barometer
1656	Pendulum clock
1658	Balance spring
1666	Calculus
1676	Universal joint
1679	Pressure cooker
	Binary arithmetic

18th century

Year	Invention
1701	Seed drill
1709	Piano
1712	Steam engine
1716	Diving bell
1731	Sextant

Year	Invention
1733	Flying shuttle
	Achromatic lens
1740	Crucible steel process
1749	Marine chronometer
1756	Hydraulic cement
1760	Bifocal spectacles
1764	Spinning jenny
1775	Water closet
1779	Spinning frame
	Spinning mule
1780	Steel pen
1781	Stethoscope
1783	Steel rolling mill
1785	Power loom
1786	Thresher
1789	Soda from salt
1791	Metric system
1792	Semaphore
	Ball bearings
	Illuminating gas
1793	Cotton gin
1795	Hydraulic press
1796	Lithography
	Vaccination
1797	Cast-iron plough
	Parachute
1798	White paper making
1799	Bleaching powder
	Anaesthetics

19th century

Year	Invention
1800	Jacquard loom
1804	Canning
1805	Electroplating
1810	Printing press (modern)
1812	Hydraulic jack
1814	Spectroscope
1815	Miner's safety lamp
1820	Elastic
1821	Thermocouple
1823	Mackintosh (raincoat)
1824	Portland cement
1827	Matches
1829	Typewriter
1830	Platform scales

Year	Invention
	Sewing machine
	Railways
	Ice-making machine
1831	Dynamo
	Reaper
1832	Tram
1834	Electrolysis
1835	Calotype photography
1837	Telegraph
	Steel plough
	Screw propeller
1838	Morse code
1839	Vulcanized rubber
	Daguerreotype photography
	Steam hammer
	Bicycle
1840	Blueprint
1842	Postage stamp
1843	Facsimile
1846	Rotary printing press
1849	Reinforced concrete
1850	Paraffin
1851	Refrigerating machine
1852	Gyroscope
1853	Condensed milk
	Hypodermic syringe
1855	Bunsen burner
1856	Bessemer steel
	Steel converter
1858	Harvester
	Open-hearth steel process
1860	Cylinder lock
	Voltaic cell
	Internal combustion engine
	Can opener
	Linoleum
1861	Electric furnace
1863	Pasteurization
1864	Drive chain
1865	Web-fed rotary press
1866	Dynamite
1868	Dry cell
	Plastics
1873	Barbed wire
1874	Rayon
	Arc lamp
1875	Research laboratory
1876	Telephone
1877	Phonograph
1878	Microphone

The Bessemer process in operation at Sheffield (South Yorkshire, England), from Great Industries of Great Britain; c. 1880. Henry Bessemer's invention transformed iron and steel production. (Ann Ronan Picture Library.)

1879	Cash register
	Incandescent lamp
	Cathode-ray tube
1880	Blow lamp
1883	Linotype
	Manganese steel
1884	Fountain pen
	Motor car
	Steam turbine
1885	Comptometer
	Flexible film roll
	Transformer
	Motor cycle

	Gas mantle
1886	Aluminium
1887	Combine harvester
1888	Adding machine
	Kodak camera
	Pneumatic tyre
	Ball-point pen
1889	Aspirin
	Brassiere
	One-armed bandit
1890	Milk test
1891	Carborundum
	Zipper
1892	Vacuum flask

Benz's motor tricycle of 1885, showing a general view (top) and a view of the vehicle's machinery from the back (below), from Motor Vehicles and Motors, published in 1900. The invention of the first motor car by Carl Benz in 1884 was part of a great surge of German industrial development from the middle of the 19th century. (Ann Ronan Picture Library.)

1893	Photoelectric cell
	Carburettor
	Diesel engine
1895	X-ray
	Thermite
1896	Rubber heel
1897	Breakfast cereal

20th century

Year	**Invention**
1900	Airship
	Kodak Brownie camera
	Paper clip
	Radio (commercialized 1912)
1901	Vacuum cleaner
1902	Disc brakes
1903	Power controlled aircraft
	Safety razor
	Electrocardiograph
1904	Diode
	Automatic drive in vehicles
	Bakelite
	Ultraviolet lamp
	Caterpillar track
	Bottle-making machinery
	Gearless tractor elevator
1905	Directional radio antenna
1907	Gyrocompass
1908	Cellophane

	Tungsten filament
	Oxyacetylene welding
	Sulphonamides
	Conveyor belt
1909	Commercial colour film
1910	Neon light
	Geared turbines
1911	Practical air conditioning
	Heavy oil marine engine
	Lewis machine gun
	Electric self-starter for cars
1912	Antiknock petrol
	Stainless steel
1913	Assembly line production
	Synthetic detergent
1914	Anticoagulants
1915	Catalytic cracking in petrol
	Pyrex
	All-metal aircraft
1916	Military tank
	Automobile windscreen
	wipers

The Wright Brothers' first flight. No invention is more closely linked with the transport and travel revolution of the 20th century than the aeroplane. From the day in December 1903 that Wilbur and Orville Wright made their first flight at Kill Devil Hills, North Carolina, USA, he modern era had begun. (Image Select.)

Ford Motor Company's first moving assembly line located in Highland Park (Michigan) c.1913. Here the automobile body is being lowered onto the chassis outside the factory building. (Image Select.)

1918	Diamond-edge cutting drill
1919	Wide band radio Synthetic fertilizers
1920	Continuous hot strip steel Insulin Submachine gun
1921	Kodachrome
1922	Sound motion picture Echo sounding
1923	Bulldozer
1924	Loudspeaker
1925	Television Photoelectric cell Quick-frozen food
1926	Liquid fuel rocket
1927	Continuous steel casting Nylon Continuous casting of non-ferrous metals
1928	Magnetic recording tape

	Geiger counter Quartz clock First working robot Elastoplast Penicillin
1929	Mechanical computer 16mm film
1930	Bathysphere
1931	Stereophonic sound Cyclotron
1932	Parking meter Electron microscope
1933	Polyethylene Frequency modulation (FM)
1934	Drum scanner facsimile process Catseye
1935	Radar
1936	Cotton picking machine
1937	Titanium Nylons Jet engine
1938	VW Beetle
1939	Terylene Helicopter Insecticides

1940	Freeze drying of foods		Teflon
1941	Aerosol spray	1956	Videophone
1942	Nuclear reactor		Video tape recorder
	Xerography	1957	Interferon
1944	Automated digital computer	1958	Laser
1945	Atomic bomb	1959	Integrated circuit
1946	Electronic digital computer	1960	Heart pacemaker
	Liquid crystal display	1961	Silicone chip (patent)
1947	Holography	1963	Friction welding
	Streptomycin		Carbon fibre
	Microwave oven	1964	Word processor
1948	Velcro	1965	Soft contact lens
	Long-playing record	1966	Fuel injection car engine
	Transistor		High yield ('miracle') rice
	Aqualung	1967	Dolby noise reduction
1949	Disposable nappies	1968	CAT scanner
	Cortisone	1970	Floppy disk
1950	Colour TV	1971	Microprocessor
	Antihistamines		Nuclear magnetic resonance
1952	Pocket-size transistor radio		imaging
	Float glass	1972	Electronic pocket calculator
1953	Radial ply tyres	1974	Personal computer
1954	Silicone transistor	1975	Disposable razor
	Polio vaccine	1976	Super computer
1955	Optical fibre	1979	Parallel computing
	Artificial industrial diamonds	1979	Compact disc
	Hovercraft		
	Contraceptive pill		
	Carbon dating		

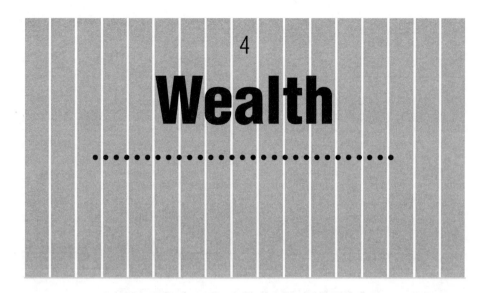

4
Wealth

Wealth has a constant fascination for observers. Phrases like "as rich as Croesus" have been used to describe the wealth of business people from Sir Josiah Child in the 17th century to Ross Perot today. Sir Josiah established England's first bank (Child's). He was the largest shareholder in the East India Company, with shares worth about £50,000. These and his other holdings were worth about £500,000 at the time or at least £500M today. (It is estimated that a typical labourer's wage at the end of the 17th century was 1 shilling a week or 5p.)

Ross Perot made his wealth in selling computer services and speculating. He sold his original company Electronic Data Systems to General Motors in 1984 for $1Bn. He won a further $700M from General Motors when he left the board and reduced his shareholdings. Perot was **the first person in history to make and lose a $billion in less that two years**. The value of his shares in EDS went from $150m to $1476m between their issue in September 1968 and March 1970, over the next three months the price dropped from $164 to $33 giving him a paper loss of $1179m. His cash loss was $74 per second over that period.

Wealth in ancient times

The phrase "as rich as Croesus" comes from the fabled wealth of the king of Lydia in Asia Minor who reigned from 560 BC to 546 BC, but the saying gains a double edge when the final fate of Croesus is understood. His wealth encouraged Cyrus the Great of Persia to invade and conquer Lydia. Croesus was utterly defeated. Cyrus ordered Croesus to be burnt alive and only relented at the last minute. Croesus did better than one of Rome's richest men – Crassus who was a member of the first Triumvirate of Roman rulers (Julius Caesar, Gnaeus Pompey the Great and Marcus Crassus). They ruled Rome from 59 BC to the death of Crassus in 53 BC. Crassus's wealth allowed Caesar and Pompey to build their political and military power-base. He was, it is said, jealous of their military reputation and led an army against the Parthians, but was totally defeated and taken prisoner. He was killed by a Parthian general who poured molten gold down his throat.

Wealth in the modern world

Today's wealthiest people often try to keep the extent of their wealth a secret. It seems that **the richest individual in the world** is the Sultan of Brunei, HM Haji Hassanal Bolkiah Mu'izzaddin Waddaulah. The tiny country of Brunei has vast reserves of oil and gas. Besides these assets, the Sultan has real estate, hotels and other investments. Despite the extent of his business portfolio, he cannot really be described as building or maintaining a business fortune.

The richest business people are probably the Walton family, who are the heirs of Sam Walton, the founder of the Wal-Mart stores – the largest retailer in the world with a turnover of $67.3Bn. **The wealthiest, individual business person** is probably Bill Gates of Microsoft with an estimated fortune of $10Bn.

 It is hard to compare their wealth with the fortunes established by business people in the past. None has a fortune which compares with **the first cash billionaire – John D. Rockefeller**, who was the first person acknowledged as having a personal fortune in excess of $1Bn. In 1918 it was estimated by C.B Forbes, the founder of *Forbes* Magazine, that John D. Rockefeller's fortune was already $1.25Bn. This would probably be worth around $17-20Bn at today's values, although, if he had maintained his holdings in the oil companies he founded and controlled, he would have been worth far more.

The wealthiest business people today

Rank	Person*	Wealth $ bn (est. 1995)
1	William H. Gates III (USA)	9.5
2	Warren Edward Buffett (USA)	9.2
3	Minoru Mori and Akira Mori (Japan)	6.5 (13)
4	John Werner Kluge (USA)	5.9
5	Robert Owen Perelman (USA)	4.5
6	Richard Martin deVos	4.5
7	Jay Van Andel (USA)	4.5
8	Helen, S. Robson, John T., James C. and Alice L., Walton (USA)	4.3 (21.7)
9	Samuel I. and Donald E. Newhouse (USA)	4.0 (8)
10	Forrest Mars Snr and Jnr, John Mars and Jacqueline Mars Vogel (USA)	3.5 (14)

* Where the members of a family are identified, the gross wealth of family members is equally divided unless there is information suggesting a different division is appropriate. The figure in brackets is the family wealth.

A hundred years on – some comparisons

Individual	Wealth $M (year)	At today's values ($M)
J.D. Rockefeller	1250 (1918)	17,000
Henry Ford	1100 (1923)	14,000
Andrew Carnegie	500 (1905)	6000
J.P. Morgan	400 (1901)	4500
Marshall Field	400 (1938)	3240

William Vanderbilt	200 (1883)	2000
Andrew Melon	325 (1925)	2000
Mayer Rothschild	170 (1875)	1700
Cornelius Vanderbilt	100 (1869)	1000
The Duke of Westminster	50 (1883)	500

Andrew Carnegie (1835-1919), a cartoon showing him holding four of the many libraries which he endowed. A Scottish industrialist, who became an American citizen, Carnegie proclaimed a 'Gospel of Wealth', according to which one half of an individual's duty was to accumulate wealth and the other half was to redistribute the surplus for the general good.
(Peter Newark's American Pictures.)

There are more billionaires in the USA than anywhere else in the world.

Wealth in Britain

Wealth in Britain has traditionally been associated with land and property. In 1994, for the first time *The Sunday Times* listing of the richest people in Britain put two business people ahead of the Queen. These were Gad and Hans Rausing. They

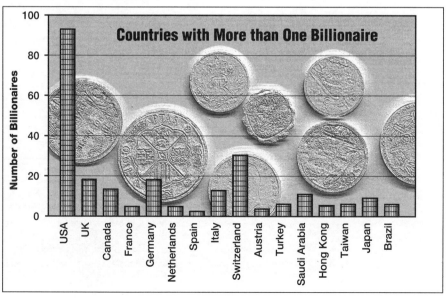

The Wealthiest Business People in Britain Today

Rank	Person*	Source of wealth	Wealth £M (est. Jan1,1995)
1	Gad and Hans Rausing	Food packaging	4000
2	David Sainsbury and Family	Food retailing	2520
3	Garfield Weston and Family	Food production	1700
4	The Duke of Westminster	Landowner	1500
5	John & Peter Moores	Stores & football pools	900
6	Gopi & Sri Hinduja	Finance & trading	850
7	Sir J. Goldsmith	Finance & politics	790
8	Sir John & Sir Adrian Swire	Shipping & aviation	770
9	Richard Branson	Airline & retailing	725
=10	Joe & Sir Anthony Bamford	Construction equipment	650
=10	Viscount Rothermere	Newspaper publishing	650

Source: *Sunday Times*

* Where the members of a family are identified, the gross wealth of family members is equally divided unless there is information suggesting a different division is appropriate.

had overtaken the Duke of Westminster a year earlier as the growth of their fortune matched the decline in the property values which underpinned the Duke's wealth. The Queen remains Britain's richest individual but, just like the Sultan of Brunei, her wealth does not rely on business activities. The Rausings are the richest family in Britain, somewhat ahead of the Sainsbury and Moore families.

Among the super rich in the UK, four kinds of business activities are especially well represented – finance, the media, retailing and food.

 It is harder to get a proper picture of the wealthiest business women. This is not just because of the widespread reluctance to give women credit for their business achievements. It is often hard to

Gad and Hans Rausing

Gad Rausing (b. 1922) and Hans Rausing (1926) are the sons of Ruben Hausing (1901–1983), the inventor of the tetrahedron-shaped cardboard carton for holding liquids. Ruben Hausing's invention in 1952 revolutionized the packaging and transportation of liquids: its growth in popularity coincided with the success of supermarkets and their demand for packaging for liquids that minimized weight and space.

The family company, TetraPak, rapidly expanded and diversified during the late 1950s and 1960s, but faced major problems in the late 1960s when it was forced to contract its operations sharply. Since then, the company's growth has been focused more closely on its areas of core strength. TetraPak employs 16,000 people worldwide with sales of over 68 billion cartons annually worth £5Bn.

establish the extent to which they are active in business and to separate their funds from other family members. This is clearly seen in the case of Lady Grantchester – the eldest child of Sir John Moores, the pools billionaire. Lady Grantchester is a main board member of Littlewoods and had equal prominence with her two brothers in the will of her father, who is known to have been impressed by her business acumen. However, her brothers are regularly listed among the richest people in Britain, but she is seldom mentioned.

The wealthiest businesswomen in Britain today

Rank	Name	Source of wealth	US $M
1	Lady Grantchester	Retailing	500
2	Freddie Murphy	Property	435
3	Ann Gloag	Buses	270
4	Clarice Pears & family	Property	195
5	Anita Roddick	Retailing	156
6	Phyllis Somers	Investments	133
7	Margaret Barbour	Clothing	125
8	Lady Anne Cavendish-Bentinck	Landowner	117
9	Mary Foulston	Computers and racing circuits	94
10	Lady Porter	Property & retailing	89

Source: In all cases, the most recent estimate from *Fortune, Forbes* and the *Sunday Times* has been used.

The Body Shop headquarters at Littlehampton, West Sussex (England). *Anita Roddick, the founder of the Body Shop, is one of the wealthiest businesswomen in Britain. Not only is her company internationally successful, it has also encouraged numerous environmental, health and other campaigns.*
(The Body Shop)

The wealthiest businesswomen in the USA today

Rank	Name	Source of wealth	US $M
1	Helen and Alice Walton and families	Retailing	21,500
2	Jacqueline Mars Vogel	Confectionary	12,000
3	Barbara Cox Anthony; Anne Cox Chambers and families	Newspapers & broadcasting	6,000
4	Martha R. Ingram and family	Distribution	1,700
5	Joan Beverley Kroc	Retailing	1,600
6	Mary Alice Dorrance Malone	Food industry	1,200
7	Margaret Cargill and family	Grain trading	1,200
8	Magaret Hunt Hill and family	Oil industry	1,100
9	Kathryn McCurry Albertson and family	Retailing	1,100
10	Abigail Johnson	Fidelity Investments	1,000

Source: In all cases, the most recent estimate from *Fortune, Forbes* and the *Sunday Times* has been used.

The richest business families in the world (excludes monarchs etc.)

Rank	Family	Wealth $Bn*
1	Waltons (USA)	22
2	Mars (USA)	14
3	Mori (Japan)	13
4	Du Pont (USA)*	10
4	Newhouse (USA)	10
6	Rausing (UK)	7
7	Thomson (Canada)	6
8	Cox (USA)	6
10	Mellon (USA)	5
10	Rockefeller (USA)	5
10	Ito (Japan)	5

*(rounded to nearest whole number)
Source: In all cases, the most recent estimate from *Fortune, Forbes* and *The Sunday Times* have been used.

International wealth

The gap between the very wealthiest in Britain and the USA is stark.

The richest business family in the world are the Waltons who seem to have overtaken the Du Ponts over the last few years.

Some sources put the wealth of the richest US families even higher. These estimates go beyond the immediate family and include control of the assets of family trusts and foundations. On this basis, it claimed that the Du Ponts are worth $150Bn, the Fords $70–100Bn and the Rockefellers $50–70Bn.

Cornelius Vanderbilt shared the belief of the leader writer of *The New York Daily News*, that it was easier to create wealth than hold on to it. Over the last century, a significant number of US business families have managed to do both. In the *Forbes* listing of the richest families in the USA, 25 of the 30 families identified as having

The Vanderbilts

Cornelius 'Commodore' Vanderbilt told his son William shortly before he died in 1877 that "any fool can make a fortune. It takes a man of brains to hold on to it after it is made". Initially, it seemed that his descendants had heeded his lesson well. William Vanderbilt doubled his father's fortune in the eight years after his father's death. William died in 1885 - the richest man, by far, in the world with a fortune of at least 200M dollars, or at least $4Bn at current values. Within thirty years, his eldest grandson Neily was a near bankrupt. It seemed to confirm a prediction made at the time of Cornelius 'Commodore' Vanderbilt's death in the *New York Daily Tribune*, which commented that "the ruling idea of the Commodore's latter years was to amass a high fortune which should stand as a monument to the name Vanderbilt, and make the head of the house a permanent power in American society. He chose one son out of his many children, and trained him alone to possess the inheritance of this vast wealth, as a king's firstborn is educated for a crown; and this favoured son he doubtless expected to transmit the deposit, unimpaired and perhaps increased, to the head of the next generation. American law and American customs discountenance such preferences, and have never favoured the confining of wealth to a single narrow channel. There is

no country in the world where fortunes are made so quickly, none where so large a proportion of the men of business have succeeded in amassing a comfortable independence; yet there is none where ancestral wealth is so rare, and none in which ancestral wealth has done so little for its possessors.

Every few years a new Croesus dazzles us with his sudden abundance; he has plundered the stock exchange, he has negotiated a railway subsidy, he has speculated in land, he has found a silver mine, he has floated a construction company, he has gambled in rotten steamships, he has held an army contract, or he has, perchance, built up prosperity by shrewd adventures in legitimate commerce. What becomes of all these stupendous fortunes? Most of them vanish as quickly as they came."

The decline of the Vanderbilts over the next fifty years reinforced this. Some families of this era, however, kept enough of their wealth together to remain powers in society. The Du Ponts, Rockefellers, Mellons, and the newspaper-owning Pulitzers founded their wealth in the same era or earlier and retain family fortunes more easily measured in billions than millions.

wealth of over $1Bn were built on fortunes created at or before the turn of the century. The sources of these fortunes have shown surprising stability over the century. Analysis of the sources of wealth of the

richest families that have survived the century shows that the media, food and drink, manufacturing, retailing and oil and chemicals are the most important.

The richest men in Britain at the turn of the century

Rank	Name	Approx. wealth 1900 value $M	Approx. wealth 1990 value $M
1	Lord Leverhulme	200	1200
2	Sir John Ellerman	175	1050
3	Duke of Westminster	170	1020

4	Edward Guinness, Earl of Iveagh	170	1020
5	Charles Morrison	125	750
6	James Williamson	125	750
7	Sir Julius Wehrner	125	750
8	Alfred Holt	125	750
9	Henry O. Wills	60	360
9	Alfred Beir	60	360
9	Sir Joseph Beecham	60	360
9	Lord Northcliffe	60	360
9	Nathan Rothschild	60	360
9	Herman Stern	60	360
15	Marcus Samuel	50	300

Keeping hold of wealth

There is relatively limited information of the fortunes of Britain's richest business people at the start of the century. The data that exists suggests that William Hesketh Lever (1851–1925) was the richest man in Britain

The richest families excluding the landed aristocracy were the Rothschilds ($170M, 1900; $1,250M at 1990 values), Wills ($125M, 1900; $1000M, 1990) and Coats ($100M, 1900; $850M, 1990).

 The scale of these fortunes falls far short of the riches accumulated by North America's business billionaires at the turn of the century. They, also, contrast with the wealth of their predecessors at the end of the 19th century. Between 1809–1819 William Crawshay, the ironmaster, **was the single non-landed millionaire** in Britain. **The first, true, industrial millionaires** Sir Richard Arkwright (1755-1843) and Sir Robert Peel (1750-1830) created their fortunes in the first quarter of the century. In 1858, there was probably only one industrial or business £ sterling millionaire but by 1900 there were at least

The Richest Business Families in Europe

Family	Nationality	Source of wealth	Worth (1994, $Bn)
Rausing	Sweden/UK	Food packaging	6.5
Wallenberg	Sweden	Manufacturing	6
Thyssen	Germany	Manufacturing	5
Quandt	Germany	Motor industry; securities	4.5
Heineken	Netherlands	Brewing	4.5
Sabanci	Turkey	Banking; insurance; textiles; rubber; hotels	4
Flick	Germany	Investments	4
Henkel	Germany	Chemical industry	4
Hoffman	Switzerland	Pharmaceuticals	4
Agnelli	Italy	Motor industry; art	3.75

50 in the UK. There were no female millionaires or half-millionaires in the middle of the last century; there were at least six millionaires by the end of the century.

Before *The Sunday Times* started publishing lists of the richest people in Britain, there was no reasonably reliable information on the richest people in Britain. Twenty five years ago (in 1969) the *Daily Express* claimed that Garfield Weston was already the richest business person in Britain. Fifty years ago, it seems that this position was held by one of the trio: James Rothschild, the Duke of Westminster and Sir John Ellerman.

Some of the greatest business fortunes have shown a remarkable resilience. The Harmsworths (Lords Northcliffe and Rothermere), Pearsons, Guinness family (Lord Iveagh), the Swires, Vesteys and Rothschilds were among **the richest business families at the start of the century** and remain firmly entrenched among the super rich in *The Sunday Times* listing in 1995. Some of the richest business families in Europe show the same ability to survive economic and political turbulence.

Just as in North America, wealth created can be lost. At the start of the century, the Stern family challenged the Rothschilds for leadership in the finance community. A century later, the name is little known. The events of the mid 1990s might consign the Baring family to a similar fate. Several British families have successfully built on their inheritance: the Swires and the Vesteys have significantly increased their wealth over the century.

There has been relatively little change in the types of industry on which great fortunes are built. Food and drink, retailing, the media, oil and chemicals, finance and banking were the dominant sources of wealth for the Guinness, Rothschild and Northcliffe families in Britain and the Rockefeller, Du Pont and Busch families in North America. The Sainsbury, Weston and Goldsmith families in the UK as well as the Walton, Murdoch and Buffett families in North America have the same roots. However, some major sources have declined or disappeared: these include shipping (the foundation of Ellerman's wealth and railways) – the source of the Vanderbilt fortune. Others, like computers and telecommunications, have grown in importance.

Top earners

Business wealth is not restricted to the owners and founders of business. The earnings of managers, executives and other employees can match, or exceed, the rewards available to owners and shareholders. **The first business executive to report earnings of over $1M per annum** was Charles Schwab –

HIS FAVORITE REMEDY.

John D. Rockefeller (1839-1937),
a cartoon of 1903. The founder of Standard Oil and of one of America's greatest business dynasties, John D. Rockefeller amassed a vast fortune. He, and his son John Jnr., gave away $930 million dollars in a programme of planned philanthropy.
(Peter Newark's American Pictures).

the President of US Steel from 1901 to 1903. His earnings increased even more when he moved to join Bethlehem Steel when it was reported that his total remuneration approached $2M per annum. Inflation means that his remuneration compares favourably with the current top US earners. These include Sanford I. Weill of Travellers Inc. who earned $45.7M in 1993–94. This remuneration package was primarily made up of options on stocks in Travellers Inc. **The highest basic salary** in the same year was paid to Dwayne O. Andreas of Archer Daniels Midland who

earned $2.6M. There is a big gap between Sanford Weill and the number two earner – George Fisher who earned $25.4M. However, both earn far less than Michael Eisner earned in 1993. During that year, Eisner's total income from Disney Corp. exceeded $200M which included stock options and bonuses that he chose to exercise in that year. Even this falls far short of **the largest remuneration package ever** which earned Michael Milliken of Drexel, Burnham Lamber Inc $550M in salary and bonuses in 1987.

Name of Chief Executive Officer	Company	Salary ($000)	Bonus ($000)	Other ($000)	Value of long-term incentives and stock grants	Total ($000)
Sanford I. Weill	Travelers Inc.	1019	3030	245	41,367	45,660
George M. C. Fisher	Eastman Kodak	331	154	5,000	19,908	25,392
Gerald M. Levin	Time Warner	1050	4000	244	15,870	21,164
James R. Mellor	General Dynamics	670	1350	12,879	5380	20,279
James E. Cayne	Bear Stearns	200	8137	0	7578	15,915
Louis V. Gerstner	International Business Machines	1500	1125	5085	7542	15,252
John S. Reed	Citicorp	1150	3000	69	8906	13,125
Reuben Mark	Colgate- Palmolive	901	1264	94	10,658	12,916
Harvey Golub	American Express	777	1850	335	8878	11,840
Alston D. Correll	Georgia-Pacific	817	550	667	9625	11,659
Richard B. Fisher	Morgan Stanley Group	475	4438	24	5628	10,565
Richard K. Eamer	National Medical Enterprises	974	0	8040	1547	10,561
Daniel P. Tully	Merrill Lynch	500	6200	161	3605	10,466
Robert B. Palmer	Digital Equipment	738	0	9	9473	10,220
Charles S. Sanford Jnr	Bankers Trust New York Corp.	750	8116	301	1013	10,180
John F. Welch Jnr	General Electric	1750	2200	441	5414	9,805
Donald B. Marron	Paine Webber Group	600	6300	534	2213	9,647
Charles F. Knight	Emerson Electric	800	1100	45	7593	9,538
Kenneth L. Lay	Enron	960	1040	1512	5912	9,424
William J. Alley	American Brands	1054	862	5263	1708	8,887

Source: *Fortune.*

However, Michael Milliken had little chance to enjoy his earnings. He was arrested and convicted of trading offences by the US Securities Exchange Commission.

 The pay of Britain's top managers seldom matches these vast sums.

The first salaried millionaire in the UK was Henry Greenwood Tetly, Chairman of Courtauld Limited. His basic salary at the turn of the century was about $20,000 pa or roughly $1.2M pa today. He was very much the exception as a salaried employee with no family link with the ownership family and not owning some significant part of the assets of the company in which he worked. In the early 1990s, Peter Wood of Direct Line Insurance – a subsidiary of the Royal Bank of Scotland – consistently topped UK rankings of the highest paid executive with an income of about $10M a year.

 The first year in which more than one UK business executive earned

more that $10M was 1993. In the 'top ten', only Jim Fifield comes from a predominantly UK manufacturing environment. Among those who lead very large, UK corporations Roland 'Tiny' Rowland of Lonrho, Clifford Schofield of Tetrosyl and Bob Bauman of Smithkline Beecham have been consistently among the highest earners during the 1990s.

The most highly paid Chief Executive Officers of large British Plcs

Individual	Income $000
David Sullivan	3075.38
Bob Bauman	2922.92
Clifford Schofield	2490.18
Tiny Rowland	2488.64
Sir Paul Girolami	2220.7

Top business wage earners in the UK (1993)

Individual	Annual Income ($000)
Peter Wood (finance)	28,448.42
Graham Kirkham (retailing)	13,528.9
Jim Fifield (manufacturing)	11,012.5
Michael Morton (services)	6980.82
Matthew Harding (services)	6977.74
Derek Crowson (finance)	6808.3
Octav Botnar (finance)	5865.9
Steve Rubin (trade and manufacture)	5212.9
John Madejski (publishing)	4567.5
William Brown (finance)	4387.4

The highest paid business people in Europe (1993)

Individual	Income $000
Leonardo Vecchio (Italy)	11,200
Silvio Berlusconi (Italy)	8,900
Gianni Agnelli (Italy)	5,800

Mark Wossner (Germany)	2,200
Gert Schulte-Hellen (Germany)	2,200
Jan Timmer (Netherlands)	1,800
Eberhard von Kuenheim (Germany)	1,500
Edzard Reuter (Germany)	1,400
Lo van Wachem (Netherlands)	1,300
Antoine Riboud	930

The wages earned by UK business people are generally at the upper range of those earned in Europe.

The earnings of business people are dwarfed by the sums earned by entertainers like Phil Collins. He earned $18M and $16M in 1992 and 1993 respectively.

Consultants and advisors can also earn large sums. **The highest paid investment consultant** is Harry G. Schultz who earned an estimated $7.2M a year in the early 1990s. This was made up of a standard consultancy fee of $2400 per hour weekdays and $3400 at weekends. He charges $40 per minute for shorter consultations. **The highest paid management consultant** is Tom Peters who is claimed to earn $6.4M per annum from consultancy, lectures and book royalties. Sir John Harvey-Jones is said to earn over $1M per year from the same mix of activities.

The largest earners tend to be those benefiting from performance bonuses, commissions or share options. Performance bonuses generally explain the high earnings of city traders or financiers. Sales staff can benefit from commissions on large contracts. Share options allow executives to buy their shares at heavily discounted rates, and sell them after a time at a large profit. The share options of Michael Eisner of Disney Corp. are worth $202M. In 1992, three UK directors earned over $1M from exercising share options – Greg Hutchins of Tomkins, Brian Pearse of Midland Bank and Lord Swaythling of Rothmans International.

Dividends and pensions further boost earnings. David Sainsbury earned more from dividends than from earnings during the late 1980s and early 1990s. His earnings of $100M over the decade are probably the largest consistent dividend earnings in UK business history, with $50M in the two years 1992–93, his shares in J. Sainsbury were worth about $3Bn in 1994.

Pensions contributions can have a similar impact on real earnings. The $10M pensions contribution by the Royal Bank of Scotland was probably **the largest annual pensions contribution** for a non-asset holding individual in British corporate history.

Not all managers leave on retirement or voluntarily. Many of these departures are marked with 'golden handshakes'. **The most generous golden handshake** was the $53.8M given to F. Ross Johnson on his exit from RJR Nabisco in 1989.

The highest 'golden handshake' in British corporate history was the $4.7M awarded to John Cahill after his short tenure at British Aerospace.

The wealth created by the sale of a business or asset can dwarf the amounts won in other ways. The largest cash settlement to an individual, in real terms, was the $546M ($1.092Bn at 1995 values) paid to buy out Howard Hughes's holdings in TWA. In Britain the $1Bn paid by THORN-EMI to Richard Branson is the largest comparable payment, followed by the $700M paid to Jack Walker by British Steel.

The sources of wealth are relatively concentrated with land holding, real estate, music and investments being the main sources from which British millionaires have built their fortunes.

The other extreme

 It is much harder to identify **the worst paid people**. The greatest concentrations of low pay in Britain are among housekeepers, hairdressers, office juniors, care assistants, kitchen porters, chamberstaff, catering and shop assistants. The disparities between the resources available to the wealthiest and the needs of the poorest prompt some rich people to give large sums to the needy. Andrew Carnegie once commented "there is but one right mode of using great fortunes - namely, that the possessors from time to time during their own lives should so administer these as to promote the permanent good of the communities from which they were gathered". Another, more jaundiced commentator said that Carnegie would have endowed the Parthenon – if it had been re-named after him.

Foundations

Many of the richest early US business people endowed massive foundations. The largest of these is probably the Ford

The largest early US foundations

Established pre-1940	$M (1995)
Ford	5150
Kellogg	1865
Rockefeller	1700
Kresge	1300
Lilley	1300
Mott	1000
Duke	1000
Carnegie	1000

Foundation with total assets which now exceed five billion dollars.

The largest post-1940 US foundations

Post-1940	$M (1995)
MacArthur	2331
Johnson	1942
Pew	1865
Mellon	1709

 The total assets of the largest foundations founded before 1940 are roughly $15Bn. The post-1940 era has not seen the creation of a similar number of giant US foundations, or trusts, by individuals or families. The largest – the J. Paul Getty Foundation – had a total asset value of $3.850Bn in 1994. This foundation differs from those listed above as it makes no endowments or grants outside and exists only to fund the J. Paul Getty Museum. The largest post-1940 foundation is the John D. and Catherine T. MacArthur Foundation.

The tax structure of the USA makes the creation of these large unitary foundations effective and tax efficient. In mainland Europe the largest foundation is the Alfried Krupp von Bohlen und Halbach Foundation with total assets of $550M. In Asia, the Toyota Foundation is probably the largest.

The largest Japanese foundations

Foundation	$M 1995
Toyota Foundation	150
Mitsubishi Foundation	100
Honda Foundation	50

 The history of charitable giving in the UK by business and business people goes back beyond the Middle

Ages. Many of the guilds and liveried companies established and retained a significant charitable element in their work. Sir Thomas Gresham (1519–1579) – famous for Gresham's Law – was one of the earliest great charitable givers. After his only son died in 1564, Sir Thomas devoted his fortune to good works including the creation of a bourse or stock exchange to rival that in Antwerp. He endowed eight almshouses and Gresham's College, London.

Industrialization was closely linked with sharp increases in the gap between the rich and poor. Some of the beneficiaries used their wealth for charitable giving. In the late 17th century, Thomas Firmin gave away his whole estate of £20,000 (roughly £2.5M at current prices) to various charities. In the first half of the 18th century Edward Colston spent almost £280,000 (about £28M, today) on 'good works' in his native city of Bristol. Around the same time John Thornton disposed of £180,000 (approx. £18M at today's values) on charitable pursuits. Just after the turn of the 20th century, Lady Rylands left the bulk of her fortune of £3.602M to various charities, mainly in the North West of England.

Britain's 19th- and 20th-century entrepreneurs and business people were active in a host of charitable activities. They have created a large number of charitable foundations and trusts.

The top grant making trusts by size of income

Ranking in 1992	Name	Income £000
1	Wellcome Trust	124,700
2	Tudor Trust	21,695
3	Royal Society	20,571
4	British Academy	17,647
5	Henry Smith (Estates Charities)	15,669
6	Wolfson Foundation	13,144
7	Gatsby Charitable Foundation	13,084
8	Leverhulme Trust	12,699
9	Garfield Weston Foundation	11,190
10	Baring Foundation	9704
11	Joseph Rowntree Foundation	8575
12	Esmee Fairbairn Trust Fund	7705
14	Nuffield Foundation	6181
15	Rank Foundation	6098

Source: *Charities Aid Foundation*

Companies giving more than £1m to the voluntary sector (1993)

Name	Total corporate support £000
British Telecom plc	14,646
British Petroleum plc	11,000

National Westminster Bank plc	10,202
Barclays plc	7520
Abbey National plc	6020
Marks & Spencer plc	5800
Shell UK Ltd	5523
ICI plc	5500
Unilever plc	5000
Lloyds Bank plc	4972
Source: Charities Aid Foundation	

George Cadbury

George Cadbury (1839–1922) was a true symbol of the best of his age. This Quaker businessman built his chocolate manufacturing company into one of the most successful enterprises of his age. He took over the chocolate company with his brother Richard from their father in 1861. He was, however, dissatisfied with the working and living conditions in which the company operated. In 1895 he acquired 120 acres of land adjoining his factory and established the model village of Bournville (Birmingham). He used some of the ideas originally developed by Sir Titus Salt for his model village of Saltaire but decided that the community would not be restricted to his own employees. A democratically elected council was set up to run the village's affairs. Cadbury did, however, establish some basic rules. Elementary and adult education were provided but public houses were banned. The Bournville Village Trust was set up in 1901, by which time there were 370 houses on the estate. Cadbury's business instincts prompted him to insist that the trust earn a five per cent profit to reinvest.

A melangeur, a crushing machine with eight heavy granite rolls, in operation at Cadbury's works at Bournville (Birmingham) in 1880. In 1879 the Cadburys (George and Richard) moved their business from Birmingham city centre to what was then a rural site, which they called Bournville. There they developed working conditions, a social security scheme and (from 1894) company housing, all far ahead of their time. (Ann Ronan Picture Library).

During this century in the UK, the focus has shifted towards donations by companies to charities and voluntary activities.

Corporate giving is sometimes closely linked with direct commercial benefit. This is especially true when trade is linked to giving. Several countries, including the UK, operate 'aid and trade' provision: this means that poorer countries receiving aid are required to spend aid money with firms from the donor country. Balfour Beatty, the construction company, is Britain's largest beneficiary of this type of trade deal.

Charity and sponsorship

Some companies make a major contribution to improving the built environment and contributing to charities.

Largest charitable donors by company 1986/87–1993/94 (UK)

Company	Amount ($M)
NatWest	151
Barclays	133
BP	119
M&S	83
BT	72
ICI/Zeneca	53
British Gas	48
Glaxo	36
BAT	35
Shell	30

Many charities have learned lessons in trading and business development from commerce and apply them to their retail and other enterprises. Oxfam's shops generate significant profits which make a major contribution to their operation. Oxfam is **the largest and most profitable charity shop operator** with

profits of over $60M produced in the first five years of the 1990s. The Imperial Cancer Research Fund and the Spastics Society's shops are the next most profitable with surpluses of $40M and $25M respectively over the same period.

Commercial sponsorship often is designed to create awareness among specific sectors of the community and reinforce key aspects of the firm or bank image. This scope and potential benefit of this was vividly illustrated when C.R. Smith, the Scottish double glazing company sponsored both Rangers and Celtic in the Scottish Premier League. This audacious act won the firm far greater levels of awareness than the sum of the two clubs supporters.

The largest individual sponsorship in the UK is the Volvo sponsorship of the PGA European tour, which is worth almost $20M.

These figure are dwarfed by the $100M that Coca Cola are reported to be investing in their sponsorship of the Atlanta Olympics. This will be **the largest ever corporate sponsorship.** (The most commercially successful Olympics to date was the Barcelona Olympics of 1992.)

Sponsorship has emerged as an important area of marketing activity.

Worldwide sponsorship activity by value (1992)

USA	$3200M
Japan	$1550M
Germany	$705M
UK	$580M
Italy	$550M
France	$520M
Spain	$485M
Netherlands	$260M
Sweden	$145M
Canada	$120M

The bulk of business sponsorship is split between the arts and sport.

Motor sport is the most heavily sponsored sport in the world with a gross sponsorship income of $150M in the UK and an estimated world income of $1Bn. It is followed by golf and tennis with total sponsorship of between $300M and $250M per annum. Estimates of sponsorship income for US sports are much harder to derive because of the different pattern of sports sponsorship in the USA.

The Scottish double-glazing firm C.R. Smith simultaneously sponsored both Rangers (represented by Dave McPherson, back left) and *Celtic (represented by Danny McGrain, back right) in the Scottish Premier League, a sports sponsorship that considerably raised public awareness of the company in Scotland (C.R. Smith).*

Estimating the scale of arts sponsorship poses great difficulties. At the heart of these problems lies the dis-

Sports sponsorship in the USA and UK 1993

USA		UK	
Sport	**Amount $M**	**Sport**	**Amount $M**
Golf	160	Motor sports	150
Tennis	100	Soccer	80
Baseball	85	Horse racing	50
Athletics	75	Cricket	40
Motor sports	75	Golf	40

tinction between endowment and sponsorship. The Getty Museum, in California, USA, for example, received **the largest arts endowment in history** from the estate of John Paul Getty. This totalled over $1Bn giving the gallery an annual budget of £150M. For the sake of this analysis this type of endowment is excluded from the analysis of arts sponsorship below.

The New York Metropolitan Museum of Art is **the most successful arts institution in the world** at raising sponsorship income with an annual sponsorship income of $50M. Globally, classical music is largest area of arts sponsorship with total sponsorship revenues of $750M. It is followed by the visual arts (including museums) and theatre with, respectively, $650M and $500.

Arts sponsorship in the USA and UK (1993)

USA Medium	Amount $M	UK Medium	Amount $M
Classical music	200	Classical music	30
Visual arts	170	Theatre	25
Opera	90	Visual arts	14
Dance	82	Festivals	13
Theatre	75	Dance	10

The Workers

The organization of labour to economic, industrial and social ends is a defining feature of business activity. The scale of this organization can sometimes be vast. **The largest workforce in the world** is that employed by Indian Railways, which at its peak in the 1960s and 1970s employed almost 3 million people. It remains **the world's largest employer** with 1,546,310 employees in 1993. **The largest employer in Britain and Europe** is the (British) National Health Service with 1,103,000 employees in 1994 (including NHS Trusts but excluding general practitioners). **The largest US employer** is the US Postal Service with 780,000 at the end of 1994.

Among private sector enterprises, General Motors is the largest employer with 700,000 employees followed by Wal-Mart stores with 528,000 and Pepsi-Co. with 423,000 staff. At its peak of 753,000 workers in 1988, General Motors was **the largest, business employer in history**. A significant part of this workforce was drawn from non-automotive sectors. The workforce committed to vehicle production peaked during World War Two and in the early 1960s at just over 600,000 people. General Motors also took part in **the largest employee training programme** in history for a business concern when it recruited and trained 750,000 new workers during World War Two.

Among British companies, Unilever leads the way with 302,000 employees. The next largest in the UK is the Post Office with 193,163 staff and British Telecom with 165,700 workers. In the Britain and the USA, the largest employers are often drawn from the service sector while in mainland Europe and Asia, the largest employers are drawn from manufacturing.

Europe's largest employers

Siemens is **Europe's largest employer**. Founded in 1847 by Ernst Werner von Siemens, the company soon built up an international reputation for excellence in telegraphic equipment. The company expanded slowly at first so that the entire electrical industry in Germany only employed 1690 people in 1882, but the

The biggest recruitment programme in history by one company (General Motors)

Year	Numbers recruited and trained
1942	244,000
1943	332,000
1944	156,000

Britain's largest employers: 1907–1995.

c.1907 Company	Number of Employees	1935 Company	Number of Employees	1995 Company	Number of Employees
Fine Cotton Spinners' & Doublers' Association	30,000	Unilever	60,000	Unilever	294,000
Royal Dockyards	25,580	Guest, Keen & Nettlefold	50,000	Post Office	193,163
Whitworth & Co.	25,000	Imperial Chemical Industries	49,706	BAT	190,308
Vickers, Sons & Maxim	22,500	Vickers	44,162	British Telecom	165,700
Calico Printers' Association	20,495	London, Midland and Scottish Railway	41,301	BTR	129,814
Great Western Railway Co.	17,770	Cooperative Wholesale Society	36,831	J. Sainsbury	124,841
John Brown & Co.	16,205	London, North Eastern Railway	36,789	British Rail	121,052
Royal Ordnance Factories	15,651	Naval Dockyards	31,680	BET	105,123
Metropolitan Amalgamated Railway Carriage & Wagon Co.	13,868	Imperial Tobacco	30,000	HSBC Holdings	104,027
London & North Western Railway Co.	13,500	Fine Cotton Spinners' & Doublers' Association	30,000	Lonrho	99,309

Source: *Business History; Financial Times*

expansion of the telephone, and the construction of the cables for cross-country transmission of high voltage electrical power, stimulated the growth of Siemens and the rest of the electrical and telecommunications sector in Germany. In 1895, Siemens was the largest employer in an industry that employed 26,000 workers; within 15 years this had grown to 142,000 people. Siemens' interests now extend across the range of electrical and electronics industries. Its wealth and fiscal prudence have given it the nickname of the 'bank with a handful of industrial subsidiaries'.

Europe's largest business employers

Company	Employees
Siemens (Germany)	391,000
Daimler-Benz (Germany)	371,107
DBT (Germany)	321,000
Unilever (UK/Netherlands)	294,000
Fiat (Italy)	260,951
Volkswagen (Germany)	253,108

Philips (Netherlands)	252,214
Deutsche Bundesbank (Germany)	217,725
Nestlé (Switzerland)	209,733
ABB Asea Brown Boveri (Sweden/Italy)	206.490

Japan's largest employers

Company	Employees (1994)
NT&T.	232,198
Fujitsu	163,990
NEC	147,910
Toyota	109,279
Bridgestone Corporation	87,332
East Japan Railways	79,679
Hitachi	79,339
Toshiba	74,558
Nippondenso	56,622
Nissan	53,071
Nippon Express Co.	51,538

Daimler-Benz in contrast to Siemens spent most of its history dedicated to the principle of sticking to its last, i.e. concentrating on its traditional businesses and building on its established expertise. Its founders had, after all, invented the automobile. Concentration on vehicle production was perhaps inevitable. However, it is unclear whether Carl Benz or Gottleib Daimler was the first off the mark. They were working within 50 km (30 miles) of each other and both produced a motorized vehicle in 1886. They never met and the firms merged in 1926, a year after the death of Karl Benz and 24 years after Gottleib Daimler died. The name Mercedes comes from the daughter of a part-time salesman – Emile Jellinek – who worked for Daimler at the turn of the century. He was a keen racing driver and agreed to order 36 of Daimler's cars if they were named after his daughter. The famous three-pointed star was introduced in 1911 to symbolise the three places Mercedes engines were used – land, sea and air.

During the 1980s, Daimler-Benz expanded rapidly into new sectors by acquiring MTU, Dornier, and AEG besides building joint ventures with Pratt & Whitney, Aerospaciale, and Mitsubishi, as well as moving into Eastern Europe.

Asia's largest employers

Japan's largest employer is the telecommunication's giant Nippon Telegraph and Telephone (NT&T). NT&T is also **the largest company in the world by market capitalization** and **the world's largest telecommunication company** with total telecommunications revenues almost twice that of AT&T.

Toyota is Japan's largest car maker and produces one in three of the cars sold in Japan. Its origins, however, lie in the textile industry and the invention, by Sakichi Toyoda, of the first Japanese power loom. The wealth created by success in the textile industry enabled Kiichiro Toyoda, the founder's son, to start his car company in the 1930s. The family link was maintained when Kiichiro's son, Shoichiro Toyoda, was sent to spearhead the firm's operations in the US market. The launch of the Lexus in 1989 transformed the image of Toyota and established a genuine challenger to the traditional dominance of US and European car producers in the prestige end of the car industry.

The image of vast labour forces is quickly dispelled by a close analysis of the workforces of other Asian nations. **The largest industrial employer outside Japan is the Steel Authority of India,** but its workforce is dwarfed by that of Indian Railways.

The overwhelming dominance of the public sector in China means that large commercial concerns are relatively few. The Chinese People's Army may be regarded as **the largest employer in the world** with 4,700,000 members while the Bank of China has only 175,524 employees. (The US military has 2.2 million members – roughly the same as the top five US corporations combined.) China also saw **the**

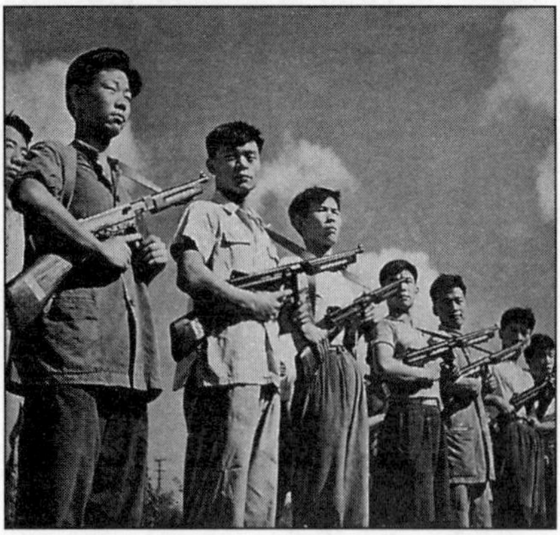

Members of the Chinese People's Militia in Shanghai in 1959.
The Chinese People's Army, with 4,700,000 members, is the world's largest employer.
(Peter Newark's Historical Pictures).

largest workforce engaged in a single project when 300,000 people worked for 10 years to build the Great Wall of China starting around 220 BC.

China has the largest population of economically active people with over 513 million people between 15 and 64 years old. China also has the largest number of workers involved in unproductive work. Over one hundred million Chinese workers are involved in unproductive work which adds little to national wealth or gross national product, i.e. the sum of all productive activities in the country.

Other large employers

Small-scale enterprises dominate the Muslim world and Africa. **The largest firm in the Muslim world** is Koc Holdings in Turkey with 41,397 employees. **The largest commercial ventures in Africa** are concentrated in South Africa. Barlow Rand employs 145,743 people, while the telecommunication utility Transnet has 140,000 workers and South African Breweries employs 109,800. In Latin America, large-scale enterprise is dominated by banking, telecommunications and natural resource development. The Banco do Brasil is **the largest employer in Central or South America**.

It is much harder to arrive at accurate figures of **the industry that employs the most workers.** Today, it is probably the electronics industry with a total worldwide labour force of 3,869,000 people. The automobile industry is the second largest employer with 3,328,000 people. The former is more likely to be an underestimate as the costs of start-up are much lower in electronics than automobile production.

Vehicle producers have been among the world's largest employers since Henry

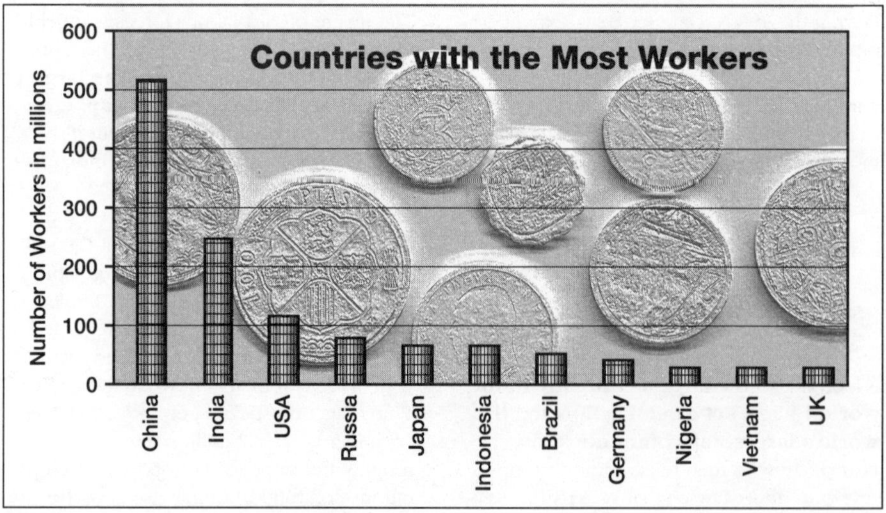
Countries with the Most Workers
Number of Workers in millions
600
500
400
300
200
100
0
China
India
USA
Russia
Japan
Indonesia
Brazil
Germany
Nigeria
Vietnam
UK

Latin America's largest employers

Company	Area of activity	Employees (1994)
Banco do Brasil	Commercial banking	125,894
Pemex (Mexico)	Petroleum refining	106,951
Telebras (Brazil)	Telecommunications	93,574
Telefonos de Mexico (Mexico)	Telecommunications	71,453
Petrobras (Brazil)	Petroleum refining	56,852

Source: *Fortune*

Ford showed the scope for economies of scale in car production when he built his factory at Highland Park, Michigan, USA.

At the time, this was **the largest factory in the world** covering 23 ha (57 acres) and employing 14,336 workers on one site.

Today's largest factory – a single manufacturing unit in a physically enclosed space – is even larger. It is the Boeing Plant at Everett, Washington.

The Boeing 747 and 767 manufacturing facility is the largest enclosed facility in the world at 27 million square metres (291 million square feet) yet the factory workforce of 6000 is much smaller than Ford's labour force at Highland Park at its peak in 1912.

The Boeing Plant at Everett, Washington State (USA), the world's largest factory:
an enclosed facility of 27 million square metres (291 million square feet).
(Image Select).

The cotton industry in 1919

Country	Employed in Cotton Mills (1919)
USA	690,000
UK	650,000
Russia	370,000
India	277,000
Italy	220,000

At the start of this century, the largest commercial employers were cotton production, railways and mining. In 1919, 2,900,839 people were employed in cotton mills across the world with the USA and Britain the largest employers.

Railways employed almost 5,000,000 people and mining over 2,500,000 in the first twenty years of this century.

Service industry employers

Industrial processes like vehicle production and electronics generally employ people on a full-time, semi-permanent basis. The retail sector and many other service industries offer much more variable terms and conditions of employment. Their total labour forces, taking full-time, part-time and temporary staff into account, can be far larger. The 11 largest supermarket and departmental store groups in the USA alone employ almost 2.25 million people. This is a far greater concentration than in any area of manufacturing especially as employment in large enterprises, including those above and other large retailers, makes up less than half of all retail employment.

The story of Wal-Mart vividly illustrates the ability of a first generation business in retailing to grow rapidly and create large numbers of jobs in a relatively short time.

Wal-Mart is largely the creation of Sam Walton, who started his retail career with J.

C. Penny in Des Moines, Iowa in 1940. Five years later, he quit to take up a franchise for the Ben Franklin 5 and 10 Group. Although he struggled at first, even losing the lease of his first outlet, by 1959, he was the largest franchisee in the chain and wanted to change the group's direction. His aim was to build a major, high volume discount store. His ideas were rejected by the owners of the Ben Franklin Group. He sold up his franchise and started the first Wal-Mart discount store in Rogers, Arkansas. Twenty five years later he was the richest man in the USA with a fortune estimated at over $15Bn in 1985. Today, there are 2000 Wal-Mart and Sam's Club stores in the USA and Mexico. On his death in 1992, control of the company passed to his wife and children. Their estimated fortune according to *Forbes* in 1995 is $21.7Bn.

Retail employment in the USA

Company	Employees
Wal-Mart	520,000
KMart	344,000
Sears Roebuck	308,500
J. C. Penny	192,097
Kroger	190,000
American Stores	127,000
May Dept Stores	113,000
Woolworth	111,000
Safeway	111,000
Melville	111,000
Wyn-Dixie	105,000
TOTAL	**2,232,597**

In the UK, retailing, distribution and related industries are the largest sector of business employment, accounting for eight per cent of male employment and 17 per cent of female employment. The five largest retailers alone account for almost 400,000 jobs.

Retailer	Number of employees
J Sainsbury	124,841
Tesco	93,339
Boots	80,099
Marks & Spencer	62,120
Great Universal Stores	30,154
TOTAL	**390,553**

pany sustained a high reputation for quality based on its own speciality lines. Expansion continued during the interwar years. However, the period after 1950 saw the fastest growth. Sainsbury introduced its first supermarket during 1950; five years later, it opened the largest superstore in Europe. During the 1980s and early 1990s, its operations have spread across the UK, and it continues to offer a combination of premium, own label brands and a strong commitment to quality and value.

Ⓢ J. Sainsbury regularly appears in lists of Britain's best employers. The firm was founded as a dairy at the end of the 1860s by John James Sainsbury. Within twenty years, he operated fourteen branches and two depots in the South East of England. Growth in the years before the start of World War One was rapid. In 1914, the group operated 115 outlets across London and the Home Counties. The com-

Ⓢ Sweden, the USA and the UK have **the highest rates of female participation in the labour market**. Sweden has over 80 per cent of women economically active in the labour force, while the USA and UK each have over 65 per cent. In Hungary, however, **women's share of employment is the highest in the world** at almost 50 per cent of the workforce.

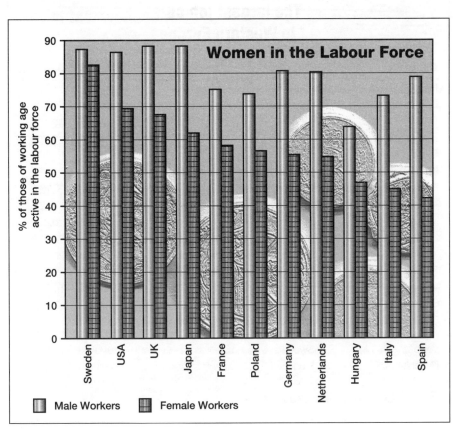

Women in the Labour Force

Male Workers   Female Workers

Longest careers

The growth of female participation in the workforce over the last 30 years can disguise the major role that women have always played in business. **The longest recorded industrial career in one job** in Britain was that of Miss Polly Gadsby who started work for Archibald Turner and Co. of Leicester at the age of eight. Eighty six years later, in 1932, she was still at her bench wrapping elastic. **The longest working life recorded in the UK** was that of Susan O'Hagan (1802–1909), who was in domestic service with the Hall family for 97 years from 1812–1909. She joined when she was ten and was still undertaking 'light duties' almost a hundred years later. In this century, Catherine Bramwell-Booth's 84 year service with the Salvation Army between 1903 and 1987 is a record.

The longest recorded working career in the world was that of Mr Izumi. He started work at a sugar mill in Tokunoshima, Japan in 1872 and retired 98 years later aged 105. **The oldest recorded British working employee** was Richard John Knight (1881–1984) who was company secretary to seven companies when he died aged 103 years.

Job losses

Economic turbulence makes this kind of long working life rare. There is growing evidence that fundamental changes in the nature of work will reduce the chances of long-term employment with single employers increasingly rare. Even large and successful companies are reducing their labour force and changing the nature

The largest job cuts in Western Europe

Company	Country	Sector	Period	Job cuts
Philips	Netherlands	electronics	1990–93	75,000
Bundesbahn	Germany	railway	1992–93	50,700
Ferrovie D. Stato	Italy	railway	1993–95	43,100
British Telecom	UK	telecommunications	1992–93	39,800
British Coal	UK	energy	1992	31,000
ICI	UK	chemicals	1991–93	21,000
Daimler-Benz	Germany	autos, technology	1992–93	33,000
Volkswagen	Germany	autos	1993–94	30,000
Telekom	Germany	telecommunications	1993–96	20,000
Fiat	Italy	autos	1993	20,000
Michelin	France	tyres, rubber	1991–94	20,000
Electrolux	Sweden	appliances	1990–91	15,000
SKF	Sweden	ballbearings	1990–93	14,000
Siemens	Germany	electrical engineering	1993	13,000
ABB	Sweden	energy	1993	12,000
Volvo	Sweden	autos	1990–93	11,000
Renault	France	autos	1991–93	10,600

Source:*Wall Street Journal 28 June 1993.*

of the job opportunities offered. Philips shed more jobs than any European company during the 1990s and its experience shows that even growth industries, like electronics and telecommunications, are cutting the size of their workforce to cope with competition and new technologies.

A similar pattern is seen in Britain with British Telecom, British Aerospace, BAT, ICI and Unilever cutting their workforce by almost 90,000 over the four years from 1990 to 1994.

Cutting back on jobs in Britain during the 1990s

Company	Jobs Lost
British Telecom	39,800
British Aerospace	14,700
BAT	13,027
ICI	11,100
Unilever	11,000
TOTAL	**89,627**

 IBM's reduction in its workforce of 129,000 between 1989 and 1994 is **the largest ever, single labour force cutback by a continuing business enterprise**. General Electric, General Motors and Philips (Netherlands) made the next largest cuts of around 70,000 jobs each. In the public sector and publicly owned utilities, much larger cuts are known. Indian Railways, for example, reduced its labour force by over 350,000 between 1988 and 1993.

Unemployment rates vary considerably between countries. Spain has the highest unemployment rate in the Western industrial world followed by Ireland and Finland.

The levels of unemployment contrast sharply with the average number of years spent in the employ of a specific organization or firm. Japan offers **the greatest**

Unemployment in industrial advanced countries

Country	Unemployment % (1993)
Spain	21.75
Ireland	19.00
Finland	18.00
France	11.5
Britain	11.5
Italy	10.75
Denmark	10.75
Belgium	10.00
Germany	9.25
USA	7.00
Japan	2.50

security of employment measured as years spent with an individual employer. The average length of time with a specific employer in Japan is just under eleven years. Germany and France have the next highest with over ten years as the average tenure. At the other extreme, workers in the USA have the shortest time with specific employer at less than seven years. Australian employers have a slightly higher average. The average time with a specific employer in the Netherlands is seven years.

Danger and stress at work

Unemployment is not the only reason for absence from work. Absenteeism costs billions of dollars every year. In countries like the Netherlands and Britain, absenteeism rates exceed five per cent of all working days.

 High absenteeism rates are closely associated with illness, stress and danger in the workplace. The most common causes of absence from work given by employees are colds or influenza, stomach upsets and back problems. Employers agree about the most common

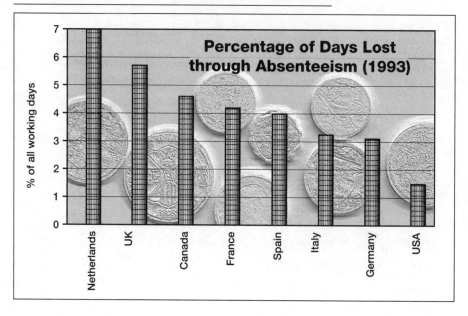

Percentage of Days Lost through Absenteeism (1993)

cause of illness – colds or influenza. They believe, however, that stress or emotional upsets are the second most important cause of absence.

Work-related deaths in manufacturing (annual average per 100,000 workers 1987–91)

Country	Number
Pakistan	59
South Korea	17
Malaysia	11
India	8*
Singapore	7
Thailand	6*
Bangladesh	4*
Burma	4*
Hong Kong	4
Japan	4*

*1982–86

The most stressful occupations

Ranking	Occupation
1	Coal miner
2	Construction worker
3	Police officer
4	Pilot
5	Prison officer
6	Advertising executive
7	Journalist
8	Actor
9	Dentist
10	Doctor
11	Broadcaster
12	Musician
13	Nurse
14	Firemen
15	Teacher
16	Social worker
17	Ambulance service worker

Source: *Professor C. Cooper, School of Management, U.M.I.S.T.*

The most dangerous jobs

USA (injury per 100 workers per year)		UK (injury per 100 workers per year)	
Meatpacking plants	33	Coal mining	65
Mobile home manufacturing	30	Construction	30
Vending machine manufacturing	28	Man-made fibres	27
Manufacture of wooden roof supports	27	Railways	25
Raw cane sugar processing	26	Metal manufacturing	23
Prefabricated wooden building	26	Food, drink and tobacco	23
Reclaiming scrap rubber	26	Extracting oil & natural gas	23
Special sawmill products	25	Agriculture, forestry & fishing	17
Boat building & repair	24	Motor manufacture	14
Manufacture of china plumbing fixtures	24	Air transport	7

Danger and personal risk occurs in many jobs. In North America, meatpacking is the most dangerous occupation. In the UK, mining remains the most dangerous job.

The most common causes of injury are: handling, lifting or carrying; slipping, tripping or falling and being struck by a moving object.

There are wide international variations in the dangers faced by workers. Among those countries studied by the International Labour Organisation (ILO), Pakistan has the highest rate of work-related deaths followed by South Korea and Malaysia.

Trades unions

The difficulties, risks and threats to workers are major reasons for the creation and growth of trades unions.

The largest trades union in the world is the (Russian) Professionalnly Soyuz Rabotnikov Agro-Promyshlennogo Kompleksa (Agricultural Industrial Complex Workers Union), which had 15.2 million members in 1993.

The largest union in the UK is Unison with 1.5 million members in 1995. The largest ever union in the UK was the Transport and General Workers Union,

Europe's largest unions

Union	Membership (000s)
Confederazione Generale Italiana de Lavoro – GGLI (Italy)	5200
Metalworker's Union – IGM (Germany)	3600
Confederazione Italiana Sindicati – CISL (Italy)	3500
Public Service and Transport Union – (OTV) (Germany)	2100
Unison (UK)	1400

which, at its peak, had a membership of 2.3 million.

The largest US union is the Teamsters with 1.9 million members.

The largest union in Europe is the (Italian) Confederazione Generale Italiana de Lavoro (GGLI) with 5.2 million members.

(S) The smallest union ever was the (British) Jewelcase and Jewellery Display Makers union which had two members when it was dissolved in 1986. The smallest union currently in the UK is the Sheffield Wool Shear Workers Union with 14 members.

It is impossible to provide an exact date for the origin of trades unionism. There were combinations of journeymen in Britain from the 16th century. Their role was to negotiate with guild masters and other employers. These combinations were drawn largely from skilled trades, with the woollen trades and weavers in particular, very prominent.

A labour dispute concerning the monotony of diet and working conditions was recorded in 1153 BC in Thebes, Egypt. **The earliest recorded strike** was one by an orchestra leader named Aristos from Greece, in Rome c. 309 BC. The dispute concerned meal breaks.

The burgeoning strength of unions during the Napoleonic Wars led employers to lobby for, and eventually get passed, a series of Combination Acts in Britain (1799,1800) and the Law of Le Chapelier (1791) in France to outlaw trades union activities. This forced 'union' activity underground and encouraged the creation of friendly societies to protect members' interests in a legal way. Despite this unions and societies persisted.

The oldest union banner in existence of the United Tin Plate Workers' Society dates from this time – 1821.

(S) It took 25 years for the Combination Acts to be repealed in 1824. This led to the creation of a number of relatively small, short-lived unions. The first union to achieve a membership of over 50,000 workers was the National Union of Cotton Spinners. The first to break through the 100,000 member barrier was the National Association for the Protection of Labour. However, these unions were very short-lived. The first major strike after the repeal of the Combination Acts was called in April 1831 by the miners of Durham and Northumberland, but this strike failed and eventually collapsed in September in the same year.

The failures of these craft or local unions prompted reformers like Robert Owen to argue for much larger, more diverse, unions. In 1833, Owen announced the creation of the Grand National Consolidated Union, which was the first British union to achieve a total member of a million members. The union collapsed a year later. The next thirty years saw union activity concentrated on the creation of trade or craft

---

The first well-documented example that we have of an organized and at least semi-permanent combination to raise wages is that of the Journeymen Feltmakers. In 1696 we hear of a delegation of twelve journeymen in this trade negotiating with their masters in an effort to prevent a cut in wages, and two years later they were induced to give 'an ingenuous account and full discovery of their combinations and collections of money against the Company', which later provided a basis for the prosecution of several of them. Early in the 18th century, combinations are more frequently mentioned, and sometimes appear to have been very elaborate.

Henry Pelling, *A History of British Trade Unionism*, Penguin (1987).

Robert Owen (1771–1858)

Owen, the conscience of the Industrial Revolution, was a brilliant, prodigious businessman who fought for just working conditions and the abolition of the atrocities of child labour. Born in Powys, son of a saddler, he was well educated by the village lawyer, clergyman and Methodist women, his reading convincing him by the age of eleven that: "There is something fundamentally wrong in all religions", a rationalist philosophy still shocking in a conformist age. He developed his socialist doctrines while managing, at the age of 20, Drinkwaters Mill in Manchester. His mastery of the business and rationalization of production earned him a partnership in four years. There he was troubled by the fact that business "cared more for dead machinery than the living".

When Owen bought out Dale's mills in New Lanark (South Lanarkshire) in 1795, he set up a town where workers were well paid, lived in decent housing and sent their children, as soon as they could walk, to Owen's community school, the 'Institution for the formation of character'.

Owen devoted himself in the 19th century to a new view of society. He proposed a reduction in the number of hours worked by children, and nobody would second it.

A contemporary of Bentham and John Stuart Mill, and, it seems, responsible for Napoleon's conversion on Elba, Owen became an indefatigable fighter for a "new view of society". Most of his cotton fortune was spent on a failed Utopian community in America, 'Harmony', but his lasting achievements were the 1819 Factory Act, which he considered far too lenient to manufacturers, and the formation of the Cooperative Society.

David Cohn

unions. The first major national union in mining was created in Wakefield (West Yorkshire) in 1841 and, by its Convention in Manchester in 1844, claimed a membership of over 60,000 miners. Other important early unions in England were the Amalgamated Society of Engineers (1851) and the Amalgamated Society of Carpenters and Joiners (1851).

After the collapse of the Grand Consolidated Union in 1834, there were several attempts to draw together the different elements in the union movement in Britain into a national organization.

In 1845, the National Association of United Trades for the Protection of Labour was created but died away within a few years. **The world's oldest, national association of trades unions** is the UK's Trades Union Congress (TUC) created in 1868. Its oldest member – the Educational Institute of Scotland – was already 21 years old when the TUC was formed. By 1890, the total membership of affiliated members of the TUC reached its peak during the 19th century of 1,927,000 workers.

Trades union activity in North America dates largely from the second half of the 19th century. **The first major, general US union** was the Knights of Labor, which was formed as a secret society around 1869. Their activities became largely open by 1880, and they had over a million members by 1886. The collapse of the Knights in the late 1880s left a gap for a national organization of trades unions in North America. This was filled by **the oldest surviving association of US trades unions**, mainly craft – the American Federation of Labor (1886). It was, however, not until 1914 that trades union membership in the US exceeded two million. The peak of union membership in North America during the first half of the 20th century was 16 million in 1933.

Annie Bessant

Annie Bessant, née Wood, (1847–1933) was one of the leading radicals, free-thinkers, socialists and, eventually, theosophists of the late 19th and early 20th centuries. Born in London of Irish parents, she married the Rev. Frank Bessant in 1867 and separated from him in 1873.

An early proponent of free thought, birth control and woman's rights, Annie Bessant joined Charles Bradlaugh in the National Secular Society around 1873. She joined the socialist Fabian Society soon after and became actively involved in socialist agitation in the London Docks. (The Fabians rejected Marxism and sought change through education, research and publicity.)

Annie Bessant was a famous sight and sound in London's East End with her 'red tam-o-shanter, loose blouse, flaming red tie, flowing skirt and remarkable eloquence'. George Bernard Shaw regarded her as the

The matchgirls' procession.
Some of the Bryant and May workers involved
in the successful strike led by Annie Bessant.
(Mary Evans Picture Library).

greatest woman orator of her time. She became involved in the 1888 matchgirls strike when she discovered that the girls lost most of their earnings through a vicious system of fines and that many suffered from dreadful industrial injuries and the effects of pollution. One ailment, known as 'phossy jaw' rotted their teeth through contact with phosphorus.

Bessant's anger was further inflamed when she discovered the vast profits earned by the company. She wrote a powerful article in The Link, a leftwards leaning newspaper, which she titled *White Slavery in London*. She attacked the company and its directors for their ruthless exploitation of their workers. She wrote: "Born in slums, driven to work as children, under-sized because under-fed, oppressed because helpless, flung aside as soon as worked out, who cares if they die or go on the streets provided only that Bryant and May shareholders get 23% . . ."

Bessant worked hard to create awareness of the matchgirls' plight and, soon after, 200 of the girls went on strike. The matchgirls

had no union organization or source of funds and they turned to Bessant for help. She advised them to return to work and petition their employers for better conditions. They followed this advice but the company rejected their petition and sacked their leaders. The workers turned again to their 'dear lady' and all 1400 London-based Bryant and May workers went on strike. Bessant recognized that without funds the matchgirls stood no hope of success. She organized a public appeal for help through two newspapers – The Star and The Pall Mall Gazette. Substantial funds were raised and the London Trades Council acted as mediator with the employers. The company soon conceded the matchgirls' demands and even suggested they form a union.

Soon afterwards, Annie Bessant became involved in the Theosophical Society, founded in New York by Helena Blavatsky and Henry Olcott. Bessant became dedicated to the work of the Theosophical Society for the rest of her life, moving to India in the early 1890s.

She became leader of the Society in Europe and Asia on the death of Blavatsky in 1901. She also became active in Indian politics arguing for Home Rule. Annie Bessant became President of the Indian National Congress in 1917, a position she held until 1923. Among her other achievements in India, Bessant established the Hindu Central College in Varanasi.

Trades unionism in France dates back as far as in Britain, but unions faced a much harsher political regime and it was not until 1864 that unions were recognized. They had no legal rights until 1884. **The first French national organization of trades unions** – the Fédération des Bourses du Travail was founded in 1894. At the start of World War One, union membership in France was just over one million.

The first trades unions in Germany were created later, i.e. in the 1840s, but they faced major legal barriers and did not reach two million members until 1914.

The years immediately after World War One saw the greatest ever increases in union membership in democratic societies. Numbers more than doubled in the UK, USA, Germany and France to 8,024,000, 5,607,000, 11,900,000 and 2,500,000 respectively.

The years between World Wars One and Two saw the greatest challenges to the attempts by trades unions to develop their role while protecting the interests of their members. The year of Britain's General Strike (1926) saw **the most days lost through industrial**

action in a single year. The General Strike of 4–12 May, 1926, **the most serious single labour dispute in the UK**, was called by the Trades Union Congress in support of the Miner's Federation. During the nine days of the strike 1,580,000 people were involved and 14,220,000 working days were lost. In 1926 as a whole a total of 2,750,000 people were involved in 323 different labour disputes in Britain and the working days lost during the year amounted to 162,300,000, the highest figure ever recorded in the UK.

The 162 million days lost is twice that of the next highest year. The number of

The highest number of days lost through industrial action in the UK

Year	Days lost through industrial action
1926	162,230,000
1921	85,870,000
1912	40,890,000
1919	34,970,000
1893	30,440,000

Ernest Bevin

From the 1930s to the 1990s, the largest trades union in Britain was the Transport and General Workers Union. Ernest Bevin led the Union for many of its formative years. He went on to play a vital part in Britain's war effort and held the post of Foreign Secretary during the 1945 –51 Labour government.

Bevin's remarkable life started in the tiny village of Winsford, Exmoor (Somerset), and ended shortly after his appointment as Lord Privy Seal in 1951. His family was very poor; he never knew his father and his mother died when he was eight. Until the age of 30, Bevin's working life was a mixture of unemployment and poorly paid jobs as delivery boy, tram conductor, carter and waiter. In 1911, he was appointed local organizer for the docker's union in Bristol.

During World War One, he played an important role in eliminating congestion in the docks. By the end of the war, he had drawn up a programme to build a strong national union for transport workers. He became assistant general secretary of the dockers' union in 1920. The same year, he was nominated to represent all the dock unions in an enquiry into the case for a minimum wage for all dock workers. His outstanding performance during this hearing won him the title the 'Dockers King's Council' and gained the dockers a minimum wage of 16 shillings (80p) a day for a 44 hour week. A year later, Bevin persuaded a number of waterside and transport unions to come together to form the Transport and General Workers Union (The T&G). The T&G continued to develop during the 1920s and 1930s, so that by 1937 it was the largest union in the free world with 650,000 members. Bevin played a prominent part in the General Strike especially as a powerful and energetic speaker at rallies across the UK. The collapse of the National Strike left him to spend the next decade defending then building the T&G. He stood unsuccessfully for Parliament in 1931 but in 1937 was elected Chairman of the Trades Union Congress. He shared with Walter Citrine much of the credit for holding the union movement together after the defeat of the National Strike, the collapse of Ramsey MacDonald's second government in 1931 and the subsequent split in the Labour Party.

He became an MP in 1940 and served most of the Second World War as Minister of Labour. During the war, he was second only in power and influence to Churchill. He oversaw a mobilization of labour that exceeded that managed in Nazi Germany. He achieved this despite rejecting the use of compulsory powers and endorsing a policy of 'voluntarism' based on persuasion. Bevin achieved a net increase in the labour population despite mobilizing five million men for the armed forces and the loss of half a million people through death in action, at sea and through air raids. He was the architect of the all-party commitment to full employment after the war.

The end of the war saw another shift in the fortunes of this pauper's son, when the Labour Prime Minister, Clement Attlee appointed him Foreign Secretary in 1945. In this post, he played a key part in the Potsdam Agreement, and he was active in building European wide links which gradually incorporated the defeated powers. He helped to create the Organisation for European Economic Cooperation (now the OECD) and the North Atlantic Treaty Organisation and was a principle negotiator during the development of the Marshall Plan, but he was less successful with the Colombo Plan to build up economic collaboration in South and South East Asia. His efforts to achieve a solution to the British withdrawal from Palestine largely failed.

working days lost to strikes in Britain in 1991 was the lowest since records began in the 1890s, with 761,000 in 369 separate stoppages. The highest number of stoppages in a wartime year was 2194 in 1944. In the post-World War Two era, the peak of industrial action was in 1979 when 29,474,000 days were lost through strikes.

In the interwar years, industrial action in North America peaked in 1939 when 1,170,900 workers were involved in industrial action. But also in the 1930s, the trades unions in Germany were absorbed within the state when the Nazi party came to power.

 In the post-World War Two era, trades union membership continued to grow. In the UK membership peaked in 1979 when the total number of people affiliated to trades unions was 13,498,000. Of these, 12,128,000 were members of TUC affiliated unions. The total number of unions in 1979 was 454 (109 in unions affiliated to the TUC). The number of unions in Britain was at its highest in 1920 when there were 1360 unions, and the number of unions affiliated to the TUC was greatest in 1918 when there were 266 members. The smallest number of trades unions affiliated to the TUC prior to the 1990s was 302 in 1928.

The largest number of stoppages in Britain occurred in 1970 when 3906 strikes occurred with 10,980,000 working days. The nature of industrial disputes had changed in the postwar era with more stoppages than in the prewar era but generally of shorter duration.

The world's longest recorded strike ended on 4 January, 1961, after 33 years. It concerned the employment of barber's assistants in Copenhagen, Denmark.

 The longest recorded major strike was that at the plumbing fixtures factory of the Kohler Co. in Sheboygan, Wisconsin, USA, between April 1954 and October 1962. This strike is alleged to have cost the United Automobile Workers' Union about $12 million to sustain.

 The period since 1980 has seen the sharpest collapse in trades union membership in Britain since the 1920s. Total membership dropped by four million during the 1980s. The largest reduction in one year took place between 1920 and 1921 when union membership dropped by 1,700,000. In 1995 there are fewer unions affiliated to the TUC – 260 – than at any time in the TUC's history.

In North America, the American Federation of Labor (AFL) concentrated its efforts on craft unions and made little effort to build, support or incorporate unskilled or semiskilled labour. This kept union membership relatively low until the 1930s and Roosevelt's New Deal. The late 1930s saw the growth of large unions in the mass production industries like automobile production. The United Autoworkers Union was the first modern American union to exceed 500,000 members (1937). The autoworkers' unions came together to form the Congress of Industrial Organizations (CIO). Rivalry between the AFL and the CIO made little difference to the growth of unionism in the United States before, during and just after the Second World War, and the greatest threat to the growth of American unions occurred with the Taft Hartley Act, which attempted to ban the closed shop, in which non-union labour could not be hired. President Truman vetoed this bill but Congress forced the bill through. The AFL and the CIO merged in 1955 to create **the largest federation of trades unions in the free, industrial world.** The membership of affiliated unions of the AFL-CIO reached 22 million in 1980 before starting to drop back.

The USA is the home of t**he union with the longest name** – the International Association of Marble, Slate and Stone Polishers, Rubbers and Sawyers, Tile and Marble Setters' Helpers and Marble, Mosaic and Terrazzo Workers' Helpers (IAMSSPRSTMSHMMTWH) of Washington DC.

Despite the size of the AFL-CIO, union membership rates in North America are

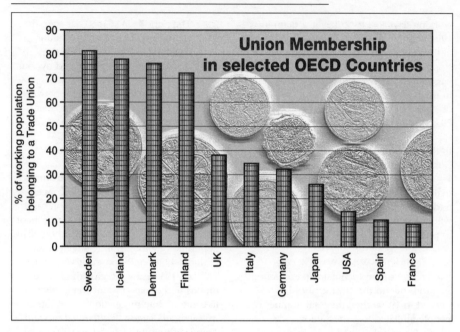

Union Membership in selected OECD Countries

low compared with most industrial developed countries. The highest density of unionization is in Sweden where over 80 per cent of all workers are members of a trades union.

In the UK, **the highest rates of union membership** are found in central and local government with, respectively, 80 and 85 per cent union membership. In the commercial sector, the metals and mineral processing industries, energy and posts and telecommunications have the highest rates of membership with, respectively, 77, 77 and 64 per cent participation.

Female membership of trades unions has generally been lower than among men, but this seems to be changing. Women's participation in trades unions has increased over the last few years and 1994 saw the highest ratio of female membership with 44.3 per cent of all union members, in the UK.

Cooperatives

Trades union activity is not the only means by which workers protect their position

and try to ensure their well being. Cooperative societies, which have existed since the early part of the 19th century, take four basic forms – producers, retail, bankers and farming or fishing cooperatives. Britain's Cooperative Congress of 1832 was the first major attempt to bring together the goods produced cooperatively and sell them. Few significant producer cooperatives managed to survive very long in Britain (apart from those linked to retail cooperatives). During the 19th century, in France, however, the number of cooperatives grew more rapidly and by 1906 there were 338 producer cooperatives.

The largest British producer cooperatives were formed in the 1970s: Norton Villiers Motorbikes at Meriden; The Scottish Daily News and Kirkby Engineering Limited, Merseyside. The 1250 workers at Meriden (Warwickshire) were **the largest workforce ever in a British workers cooperative.**

Retail cooperatives originated before the Napoleonic Wars. The modern cooperative movement has its origins in the work of the Rochdale Pioneers to establish a shop in Toad Lane, Rochdale (near Manchester) in December 1844. The high point of the British retail cooperative movement was in the 1920s when 1300 societies held 30 per cent of the retail market.

The cooperative movement in Britain extended its activities to include wholesaling (The Cooperative Wholesale Society, 1863), insurance (The Cooperative Insurance Society, 1867) and banking (The Cooperative Bank, 1872).

Ⓢ The first retail cooperative in France opened in 1835. **The earliest recorded US cooperative** was a dairy farming question, which can be traced back to 1810 in Goshen, Connecticut. The dairy famers cooperative established a tradition of small farmers 'cooperating' to get better and more stable

prices, and seeking economies of scale in purchasing supplies. Dairy cooperatives proved so popular that by the start of the US Civil War there were over 400 cooperatives in the dairy industry of the eastern USA. By 1890, there were over 1000 active farmers' cooperatives in the USA, and in 1902, they formed the Farmers Educational and Co-operative Union of America, also called the Farmers Union.

Banking played a much larger role in the cooperative movement in Germany than in Britain. Cooperative banks were established in most German cities during the 19th century and in rural areas cooperative land banks were created. The greatest number of German cooperative banks was in 1890 when there were 1729 rural land banks and 395 urban banks.

The largest contemporary cooperative movements are probably in Scandinavia, where 3000 societies have over a million members, and Italy, where 9000 societies have two million members.

The Rochdale Principles (of the Rochdale Pioneers)

Each member shall have one vote, regardless of how many shares he holds.

Anyone may join regardless of his race or religion.

Goods and services are sold at market prices. After business expenses are paid, profits are returned to members in proportion to their purchases, not their shareholdings.

Dividends are strictly limited.

Interest on capital invested is strictly limited.

All sales shall be based on cash.

All members shall be educated on the principles and values of cooperation.

Employee-owned companies

Cooperatives should be carefully distinguished from employee-owned organizations. In these, the workers might own all, or much of, the stock, but this gives them no right to 'cooperate' in running the enterprise. **The largest employee-owned company** in the UK is The John Lewis Partnership with over 40,000 partners. Peoples Provincial Buses (UK), with 270 employees, fits more clearly into the conventional model of ownership by employees, being 100 per cent owned by workers and the employees share-ownership plan. In the USA, employee owned companies cover a wide range of business activities.

The John Lewis Partnership in Britain and Publix Supermarkets in the USA have many things in common besides being retailers. Both were founded by retail entrepreneurs with a strong desire to make work enjoyable. John Spencer Lewis believed that the main purpose of a busi-

The USA's largest employee-owned companies

Company	Type of business	Number of employees
Publix	Supermarkets	65,000
Health Trust	Hospital management	30,000
Avis	Car rental	15,000
EPIC	Hospitals	10,000
Science Applications	R&D	10,000
Parsons	Engineering	10,000
Charter Medical	Hospitals	9000
Amsted Industries	Manufacturing	8300
Weirton Steel	Steel	8100
Avondale	Shipbuilding	7500

ness was "the happiness of its members".
George Jenkins, the founder of Publix,
wanted to open stores "where working is a
pleasure". Both were active innovators.
Jenkins introduced the first electronic eye
doors and the earliest electronic scanners.
John Lewis and Publix have generous
profit share schemes. At Publix, 20 per
cent of a store's profits are distributed to
employees every quarter. At John Lewis,
the profit sharing partnership bonus was
£30M, or just over 30 per cent of profits, in
1993.

John Lewis store in Oxford Street, London.
The John Lewis Partnership is, technically, the
largest employee-owned company in the United
Kingdom, with over 40,000 partners.
(Ann Ronan Picture Library/John Lewis).

6
Markets, competition and conflict

The existence of markets, competition and some conflict is intrinsic to business. The development of a market encourages producers to create a surplus to trade. The existence of more than one producer or intermediary produces competition. Competition stimulates innovation and change but may result in conflict. Just like armies, companies "do not want conflict – but they do want the market share and the profits that go with it" (James, B.G., *Business Wargames*, Penguin, 1984). Investing resources in success in the marketplace can produce a competitive edge which can ensure success in business conflicts. Advertising, promotion, merchandising, selling and research are integral part of this effort to produce this edge.

The oldest forms of advertising are the signs which producers or merchants use to inform potential buyers of the availability of their wares. These signs and accompanying symbols can be found in all ancient civilisations. **The oldest known advertising signs** are probably the advertisements for booksellers reported in Horace's *Ars Poetica*. The oldest of these signs existing come from Pompeii and date from around AD 79.

The signs used by English inns in the 17th century show that they could be just as obscure as contemporary advertising. The promise inherent in the Hog in Armour or the Three Squirrels was probably as cryptic as the offer made by Benson & Hedges today. (Benson & Hedges' advertisements in the UK have no obvious connection to the product or its use.) In all likelihood, a memorable name was as important in the past as it is today.

Today's equivalent to these inn names are the brand identities, symbols or trade marks that are such important features of the contemporary marketplace. The Coca-Cola brand name and its various symbols is **the world's strongest image** according to various world, US and UK surveys. The world survey put it ahead of Sony and Mercedes Benz while the US study saw it outperform Marlboro. In the UK, its nearest rivals are Marks and Spencer, and Kellogg.

A powerful brand name or identity makes it harder for rivals to present their offerings as substitutes. This might mean that the owner can win a price advantage, control key sources of distribution, retain the loyalty of consumers, or keep marketing costs down.

Even in societies where advertising expenditures are small, or the promotions industry is relatively new, brand awareness can

The world's most powerful brand names

World	USA	UK	EU
Coca-Cola	Coca-Cola	Coca-Cola	Coca-Cola
Sony	Marlboro	Marks and Spencer	BMW
Mercedes Benz	Pepsi-Cola	Kellogg	Adidas
Kodak	McDonald's	Gillette	Mercedes-Benz
Disney	Miller	=Guinness	Philips
Nestlé	Budweiser	=Mars	Kodak
Toyota	Ford	Heinz	Sony
McDonald's	Wendy's	Sainsbury	Volkswagen
IBM	Chevrolet	Nescafe	Gillette
Pepsi-Cola	Burger King	Cadbury's	Pepsi-Cola

be high. A survey of Eastern European consumers found high levels of awareness of 'western' brands like Sony, Coca-Cola and Adidas, but some differences in esteem.

A recent study of the value of brand names by *Financial World* made Marlboro and Coca-Cola **the two most valuable brand names in the world**. The Marlboro brand name was valued at just under $40Bn and the Coca-Cola name at

over $30Bn. Intriguingly, this study was performed just before Marlboro was forced to cut its prices in the USA in the face of cut-price competition and Coca-Cola faced a threat from own label brands in the USA and Britain.

The success of Coke is more remarkable given the relatively small sums spent on advertising by Coca-Cola and Pepsi Cola. Procter and Gamble, the detergents company, spends over twice as much a year

Brand esteem in Eastern and Western Europe

Rank	Eastern Europe Brand name	Western Europe Brand name
1	Coca-Cola/Coke	Coca-Cola/Coke
2	Sony	Levi's
3	Mercedes-Benz	Kodak
4	BMW	Philips
5	Adidas	Nestlé
6	Philips	Gillette
7	Kodak	Adidas
8	Ferrari	Nescafe
9	Honda	BMW
10	Volvo	Volkswagen

Source: *Campaign*

The world's strongest advertising image: the Coca-Cola bottle and symbol.
A study of brand names by Financial World valued the Coca-cola name at over $30Bn (second only to Marlboro at just under $40Bn). (The Coca-Cola Company).

advertising its brands of detergent than Pepsi spends on its brands.

Unilever, and its rival Procter and Gamble, are **the largest UK advertisers**. Unilever's portfolio of products ranges from detergents, through soaps and cosmetics to foods. Unilever was the first company to spend more that £200M in a single year – 1993 – when it spent £211M on advertising. Procter and Gamble was the second largest advertiser with £140M but over a smaller array of products.

Coca-Cola

Coke is the most heavily consumed beverage in the world after water. The Coca-Cola company estimates that if all the Coca-Cola ever consumed by the human race by 1994 was poured over Niagara Falls, the falls would flow at their normal rate for 38 hours and 2 minutes. In the early 1990s, Coke was served 600 million times every day of the year. A year's consumption would fill one of the towers of New York's World Trade Centre almost a hundred times.

The early years of Coke gave little sign of the global marketing phenomenon that was to emerge. John Stith Pemberton, an Atlanta-based producer of patent medicines, invented Coca-Cola in 1886 from a mixture of sugar, water, various flavourings and an additional secret ingredient. Pemberton died two years later and eventually the recipe ended in the hands of Asa Candler, another Atlanta pharmacist, who had great faith in its ability to cure headaches and dyspepsia. He spotted the chance to promote Coke as the standard drink in the vast number of soda fountains that were opening across the USA.

Candler recognized the value of advertising and promotion. He invested in Coca-Cola signs, posters and merchandising so that by 1895 it was sold in every state in the USA. Four years later, Candler was approached by Benjamin Franklin Thomas and Joseph Brown Whitehead who wanted the concession to bottle Coca-Cola. Candler sold them the rights to bottle Coke in the USA for one dollar. This ranks as one of the best or worst deals ever made in business history. It was Thomas who developed the Coke bottle in 1915. He employed another classic marketing ploy – the competition – to "find a bottle that anyone would recognize even in the dark, a bottle unique in the whole world".

In 1919, the Candler family sold their company to Ernest Woodruff for the, then, vast sum of $25M. This was one of the biggest business transactions in US history at the time and the largest concluded in the southern USA. It was Woodruff's son, Robert, whose marketing genius turned a successful product into a national symbol. He was helped by the advent of prohibition, which made Coke a widely accepted product, and by the success of its distribution system. The split between the production of the Coke syrup and the bottling of the drink allowed production capacity to expand across the USA at a relatively low cost.

The breakthrough into global markets occurred during the Second World War. Woodruff achieved perhaps the most amazing coup in the history of distribution when he decided that wherever American GIs went, Coke would follow – at a cost of no more than five cents a bottle. Woodruff convinced the US Department of Defense that Coke was a vital morale booster. Simultaneously, he persuaded the government to contribute significantly to their investments in bottling plants around the world. By the end of the war, the number of

overseas markets served by Coke had increased from under forty to almost eighty. Coke had become a universal symbol of American prosperity, power and life styles. The term 'Coca-Cola diplomacy' became associated with the growth of US influence across the world.

The competition between Coca-Cola and Pepsi Cola has added another chapter to the Coke story. The so-called Cola Wars saw the first sustained threat to the dominance of Coke. Pepsi has steadily made up ground especially in North America. Coke's early success was based on its dominance of soda fountains and other non-retail consumption. Pepsi built up a powerful retail franchise. The shift in demand to retail sales eventually led to Pepsi achieving brand leadership in the USA in 1985.

Largest UK advertising expenditures in the 1990s

Rank	Company	Expenditure £M (1990–1994)
1	Unilever	972
2	Procter & Gamble	671
3	Nestlé	382
4	HM Government	370
5	Mars	347

Source: *Marketing Week*

The largest advertisers in the USA (1990–1993)

Rank	Company	Spend £M (1990-1993)
1	Procter & Gamble Co.	8998.1
2	Philip Morris	8149.7
3	General Motors Corp.	5852.6
4	Sears Roebuck & Co.	5217.9
5	PepsiCo	3720.4

Sources: *World Advertising Expenditures (Starch INRA Hooper Inc.); Advertising Age*

Europe's biggest television advertisers in 1993

Country	Advertiser	Spend (£M)
UK	Unilever	174.4
Italy	Ferrero	163.9
Germany	Procter & Gamble	144.5
France	Nestlé	113.6

The Netherlands	Procter & Gamble	52.3
Spain	Procter & Gamble	35.4
Norway	Procter & Gamble	14.5
Denmark	Procter & Gamble	12.1
Switzerland	Procter & Gamble	10.6
Austria	Henkel	9.8

Source: *Campaign.*

Europe's biggest press advertisers in 1993.

Country	Advertiser	Spend (£M)
Germany	C & A Brenninkmeyer	98.4
The Netherlands	Procter & Gamble	57.1
Switzerland	Migros	50.3
Italy	Fiat Auto	41.3
France	Renault Automobiles	33.1
UK	Dixons Stores	33.0
Spain	Fasa Renault	19.8
Denmark	Dansk Supermarked	11.6
Austria	Media Markt	9.0
Norway	OBS	4.8

Source: *Campaign.*

The curious case of the Procter and Gamble symbol

The Procter and Gamble 'Moon and Stars' symbol was at the centre of controversy during the 1980s. Various writers suggested that it was a satanic image while others asserted that it indicated that the firm was owned by the 'Moonies', followers of Sun Myung Moon and the Unification Church.

These claims were vigorously rejected by the company. It pointed out that the symbol was adopted as the company's trade mark in 1882, the same year that Ivory soap was launched by Harvey Procter, the son of one of the company's two founders – William Procter and James Gamble.

The largest US advertiser is Procter & Gamble which was also the first company in the world to spend over a billion dollars in a single year in 1988. Since then, two other companies have matched this figure: Phillip Morris and General Motors.

Procter and Gamble is **the biggest advertiser in Europe** with a total advertising spend of $465M in the European Community in 1994.

Trade marks

 Very few trade marks survive as long as the Procter and Gamble's symbol. Britain's oldest trade mark is the Bass

Triangle which was registered in 1876.

More trade marks applications are registered in the USA than anywhere else in the world – 187,000 in 1994 compared with 36,000 registered in the UK.

Some of the most powerful symbols and trade marks owe more to a whim or quirk of fate than any sophisticated advertising or research process. The origins of the Shell 'shell' lie in the small shells company owned by Simon Marcus, the company's founder in the UK. The shell has changed shape over the last hundred years but remains instantly recognisable.

The Kodak – K – was even more clearly the result of the whim of the firm's founder, George Eastnam. He explained that "the letter 'K' had been a favourite with me – it seemed a strong, incisive sort of letter". The origins of Nipper the Dog, the trade mark of the His Masters Voice (HMV) records, lie in a painting by Francis Barraud of Nipper, his dead brother's fox terrier. His 1899 painting was admired by William Owen, the owner of The Gramophone Company, who paid Barrauld to redo the painting featuring his company's 'Improved Gramophone'. Adopted by the firm as its trade mark in 1909, this is one of the many creative associations between well known painters and advertising.

Advertising Media

Advertising is now a major area of economic and business activity in the richest and most diverse economies in the world. The USA and Japan spend more on advertising than any other countries while Germany spends relatively little given the size of the German economy.

The largest advertising nations

Country	Advertising and promotional expenditure (1994)	GNP%
USA	$112Bn	1.6
Japan	$46Bn	0.8
UK	$17Bn	1.4
Germany	$17Bn	0.9
France	$11Bn	0.8
Italy	$8Bn	0.7
Canada	$8Bn	1.6
Spain	$7Bn	1.2
Austria	$5Bn	0.8
Netherlands	$4Bn	1

Posters

The first collaborations between corporations and artists in advertising go back to the earliest of the modern advertising forms – posters. Artists as diverse as

George Eastman (1854-1932), founder of Kodak.
Eastman, an American inventor, developed a flexible roll film system of photography. His cameras were cleverly marketed under the slogan 'You press the button - we do the rest'.
(Image Select/Ann Ronan/Kodak).

Toulouse Lautrec, Norman Rockwell and David Hockney have used their art to support advertising. **The earliest evidence of the use of posters** for promoting or selling products or services dates from the period following the invention of movable type in 1450.

These early posters showed the key features of today's posters and were placed in prominent sites where passers-by could see the advertisement. Typically, they communicated a simple message backed by a clear and powerful image. They sought out a 'passing trade' so the information communicated was often specific and easily acted on, and they asked the reader to stop and note a key piece of information or image. Contemporary poster campaigns often reinforce a message communicated by other means.

Newspapers and leaflets

Posters are a limited advertising medium. Their strengths may not meet the needs of advertisers wishing to reach people in their homes. Posters are also not always suitable for people seeking specific information or if the advertiser has a complex message. Written advertisements such as pamphlets, brochures, newspapers or magazines provide many of these features. **The oldest written advertising existent** is from Thebes in 1000 BC. It advertised "a whole gold coin" for the return of a slave called Shem. There is no evidence about the effectiveness of this advertisement or where it fell in the old advertising maxim – "I know that 50 per cent of my advertising works, I just don't know which 50 per cent". In this case, which half worked depended on your point of view.

In the Middle Ages, the high cost of written materials, the smallness of markets and limited surpluses restricted most advertising to the work of town criers. However, the availability of paper and the invention of movable type around 1450 by Johannes Gutenberg created the conditions for the development of newspapers, leaflets, pamphlets etc. **The earliest regular newspapers** were in Germany. The oldest was probably the weekly *Aviso Relation oder Zeitung* first published in January 1609. These weekly newspapers spread across Europe over the next fifty years.

The first British newspaper appeared in 1621. Its publisher, Thomas Archer, was promptly imprisoned – establishing another all too common precedent. No copies of his paper survive. The earliest newspaper with surviving copies was the *Weekly Newes* published between 1622 and 1625. Newspapers became increasingly popular after this. Like many publishers after them, these pioneers found that advertising revenues were an invaluable supplement to other income. **The first advertisement** appeared in the French weekly *Journal Générale d' Affiche* or *Petites Affiches*. This was primarily an advertising medium and carried little news. An untitled Dutch news sheet contains **the first integration of advertisements in a paper devoted primarily to news**. In Britain, this example was followed by Samuel Peck's *Perfect Diurnall* which carried book advertisements from November 1646 for 6 pence (2½p) per insertion. Other early UK advertisements were for coffee (1652), chocolate (1657) and tea (1658).

The earliest classified advertisements were in Thomas Newcome's *Publick Adviser*, which was the earliest newspaper devoted solely to advertising and operated between 19 May and 28 September 1657. Fifty years later, E. Everingham's *Generous Advertiser* took the rather ungenerous step of introducing **fees for classified advertisements for the first time** on 28 January, 1707.

The earliest daily newspaper was the *Einkommenden Zeitungen* published at Leipzig, Germany, between July and September 1650. In the UK, E. Mallet's *Perfect Diurnall* followed between February and March 1660, but it was not until the next century that a daily newspaper managed to sustain itself much beyond a few months. *The Daily Courant* was introduced in 1702 and survived until issue number 6002 in June 1735.

 The earliest illustrated advertisement in an English newspaper – the *Faithfull Scout*, April 1652 – offered a reward for two jewels stolen from Hugh Clough, a London goldsmith.

The London Gazette introduced **the first advertising supplement** in June 1666. **The earliest illustrated trade advertisement for a specific product** was for a patent chocolate maker: it appeared in the *Daily Courant* on 17 March 1703. Advertising had prospered to such a degree that by 1758, Samuel Johnson felt forced to comment in *The Idler* that: "Advertisements are now so numerous that they are very negligently pursued, and it is therefore become necessary to gain attention by magnificence of promise and by eloquence sometimes sublime and sometimes pathetick".

 The first advertising agent of whom a reliable record exists is William Tayler of London. In 1786, he advertised himself as "Agent to the Country Printers, Booksellers &c". It was, however, twenty years before **the first advertising agencies** were founded: James White's agency established in London in 1800. Reynell and Son was founded by J. Reynell in London (1812); William Tayler went into partnership with Mr Newton in the 1820s to form Newton and Company.

 The earliest US advertising agency was established in 1841 in Philadelphia by Volney Palmer. The early agencies acted as true 'agents' for the newspapers. They bought space from the publishers and took on the task of selling the space, or sold the space for commission. These origins explain two peculiar feature of modern agency practice. First, the commission system by which agencies are paid through a 'commission', about 15 per cent on the amount billed rather than fees for work undertaken. Second, it is the agency that is the principal in law for the space booked. This means that it is the agency not the advertiser who is liable for any debts to the media owner.

George Newnes and *Titbits*

The trail had been blazed for the proprietors of the new generation of newspapers by a traveller in fancy goods in Manchester named George Newnes (1851–1910) who, sitting by the fire one evening with his wife, remarked, of a paragraph he had just read, "Now that is what I call an interesting titbit. Why doesn't someone bring out a whole paper of titbits like that?" "Why don't you?" asked his wife. Under her urging *Titbits* was started and the new journalism launched.

Titbits proved to be exactly what a new semi-educated public, in search of easily assimilated, potted information, wanted. Within three months of its launch in 1881 this penny weekly magazine had a sale of 900,000 and George Newnes, to his own amazement, was a rich man. Newnes went on to found *The Strand Magazine* (1881), *Country Life* (1897) and numerous other magazine. He was knighted and elected MP for the Newmarket division (Suffolk).

Alfred Harmsworth (1865–1922), later Lord Northcliffe, was among the first contributors to *Titbits* and as soon as he could rake enough money together started his own competitor to it, *Answers* in 1888. With *Answers* as a foundation, he built up an empire of cheap popular magazines before he was 30, and was ready to try out the same formula in daily newspapers.

Display advertising emerged during the 19th century. *The Times* ran **the earliest full page advertisement** on 1 January 1829 for Edmund Lodge's *Portraits and Memoires of the most illustrious Personages of British History.*

The first illustrated full-page advertisement appeared in the *Courier and West End Advertiser* on 10 July 1842 for British Cornflour.

 The surge in production capabilities, the emergence of mass markets, revolutions in news gathering techniques, and changes in newspaper production and distribution during the second half of the 19th century transformed newspaper advertising. Innovators like Northcliffe in Britain and Hearst in the USA saw that prices could be forced down by using advertising revenues. This, in turn, opened new markets for their newspapers and the products promoted on their pages. The earliest use of advertising to subsidize a newspaper was London's *City Mercury* in 1620. This free sheet existed solely on revenues from advertisements.

 The communication revolution in the second half of the 19th century shaped the current link between newspaper income from cover prices and advertising revenues. The Daily Mail in Britain and the New York Evening Journal in the USA were founded by Alfred Charles William Harmsworth (Lord Northcliffe) and William Randolf Hearst

The UK's daily newspapers (1995)

Newspaper	Daily circulation (M)
The Sun	4.1
Daily Mirror	2.6
Daily Mail	1.8
Daily Express	1.3
Daily Telegraph	1.1
Daily Star	0.7
The Times	0.6
Evening Standard	0.5
The Guardian	0.4
The Independent	0.3
The Financial Times	0.3

Source: *ABC,* Jan-Jun 1995.

Top 10 daily newspapers in the world (1994)

Rank	Newspaper	Country	Average daily circulation (M)
1	Yomiuri Shimbun	Japan	8.7
2	Asahi Shimbun	Japan	7.4
3	People's Daily	China	6.0
4	Bild Zeitung	Germany	5.9
5	Wall Street Journal	USA	1.9
6	USA Today	USA	1.4
=7	Los Angeles Times	USA	1.2
=7	New York Times	USA	1.2
=7	New York Daily News	USA	1.2
10	Washington Post	USA	0.8

respectively. Just like today, the biggest advertisers were drawn from the soaps and food producers. Thomas Beecham was the first person to spend more than £100,000 on advertising in the UK (1890), and William Lever used newspaper advertising to project brands like Sunlight Soap and Lifebuoy to prominence. These brands provided an assurance of quality in the new mass market. This commitment to quality existed at the start of Lever Bros. when William Lever supplied his mother with soaps for her wash house in Wigan, Greater Manchester. Lever filtered out the impurities and found demand soon exceeded supply.

Soap wars

The extent of competition in markets and between businesses prompted one writer to describe the rivalry between Procter and Gamble and Unilever in North America as the Soap Wars. This is probably a fair description especially as the total amount spent on competition between these two giants could probably finance a medium size war. Their fifty

years' rivalry has involved a gross expenditure by both parties of about $10Bn in the UK since the end of World War Two and a further $50Bn worldwide over the same period Two – at current prices. Their expenditures in the detergent market have driven virtually all other competitors from the market.

Brand leaders

The persistent strength of the reassurance and reliability of brands is seen by the ability of brand leaders like Persil and Ivory to hold their market leadership over decades.

The UK's oldest continuing brand leader among significant, advertised consumer brands is Rowntree's Pastilles while Singer Sewing Machines holds that position in the USA. These brands established their initial dominance through a skilled use of newspaper advertising, posters and retail promotion.

An 1889 advertisement for Sunlight Soap, which appeared in The London Illustrated News. (Ann Ronan Picture Library).

Decades of leadership – today's oldest brand leaders

USA Brand	Achieved leadership	UK Brand	Achieved leadership
Singer sewing machines	1890s	Rowntree's pastilles	1880s
Coca-Cola	1890s	Cadbury's chocolate	1880s
Wrigley chewing gum	1900s	Brooke Bond tea	1890s
Kodak	1900s	Kodak	1900s
Ivory soap	1900s	Johnson's floor polish	1900s
Gillette razors	1900s	Gillette razors	1900s
Nabisco biscuits	1900s	Schweppes mixers	1910s
Hershey chocolate	1900s	Hoover vacuum cleaners	1920s
Sherwin Williams paints	1910s	Kelloggs corn flakes	1920s
Ever Ready batteries	1910s	Stork margarine	1920s
Life savers (candies)	1910s	Persil	1920s
Campbell's soups	1920s	Heinz soups	1920s

Total advertising expenditure (including direct mail) £M (UK)

	1990	1991	1992	1993	1994
National newspapers	1187	1121	1155	1220	1336
Regional newspapers	1715	1628	1640	1715	1871
Consumer magazines	541	506	466	448	499
Business & professional	790	708	746	714	828
Directories	492	504	523	551	589
Press production costs	412	417	427	438	478
TOTAL PRESS	**5317**	**4884**	**4957**	**5085**	**5600**
Television	2325	2295	2472	2605	2873
Direct mail	979	895	945	90	1050
Outdoor & transport	282	267	284	300	350
Radio	163	149	157	194	243
Cinema	39	42	45	49	53
TOTAL	**8925**	**8532**	**8859**	**9140**	**10,169**

Source: *Advertising Association*

Newspapers remain a major advertising medium. In 1989, total newspaper advertising in the USA exceeded $10Bn for the first time. The same year saw British newspaper advertising – of all kinds – exceed £100M ($165M). Classified advertising makes up the largest category of total newspaper advertising. In 1994, the total advertising expenditure in the UK exceeded £10 billion for the first time.

Total advertising expenditure (including direct mail) percentage of total (UK)

	1990	1991	1992	1993	1994
National newspapers	13.3	13.1	13.0	13.3	13.1
Regional newspapers	19.2	19.1	18.5	18.8	18.4
Consumer magazines	6.1	5.9	5.3	4.9	4.9
Business & professional	8.9	8.3	8.4	7.8	8.1
Directories	5.5	5.9	5.9	6.0	5.8
Press production costs	4.6	4.9	4.8	4.8	4.7
TOTAL PRESS	**57.6**	**57.2**	**55.9**	**55.6**	**55.1**
Television	26.0	26.9	27.9	28.5	28.3
Direct mail	11.0	10.5	10.7	9.9	10.3
Outdoor & transport	3.2	3.1	3.2	3.3	3.4
Radio	1.8	1.7	1.8	2.1	2.4
Cinema	0.4	0.5	0.5	0.5	0.5
TOTAL	**100.0**	**100.0**	**100.0**	**100.0**	**100.0**

Source: *Advertising Association*

The Newhouse Family

Magazines are among the most dynamic and profitable areas of text-based publishing and hard copy advertising. No family has made a greater success in this sector than the Newhouse family. Si and Douglas Newhouse regularly appear among the richest people in the world. They achieved this position through the success of their large and profitable 'stable' of magazines. This includes *Parade* which is probably the most profitable magazine in the world with total weekly circulation of 35M as a supplement to 330 Sunday newspapers. A full colour advertisement costs just under $400,000.

Newhouse was founded by Samuel I. Newhouse between 1910 and 1920. When Samuel left school he worked for a magistrate who took over a newspaper – *The Bayonne Times* – as settlement of a debt. Samuel was asked to look after the paper, and he turned the paper to profit while learning the business. In the 1920s and 1930s he acquired other newspapers, mainly in the New York area.

Today Newhouse newspapers are often monopolies in their local areas. This has produced a powerful sales and profit base. The move into large-scale magazine production occurred in the 1970s and 1980s. Their most successful magazines include *Brides*, *The New Yorker*, *GQ*, *Vanity Fair* and *Vogue*.

The Newhouse Group has been called the largest family business in the world. Almost seventy family members work for the company. When asked why they did not buy the *Chicago Sun Times*, the reply was that there were "no relatives available to run it".

The biggest press advertisers in the UK are Gallaher Tobacco with a total press advertising spend during the first half of the 1990s of £140M ($200M). Many of the largest newspaper advertisers are drawn from the retail sector.

 The world's largest newspaper advertiser is the US retailer May Department Stores with an average spend during the early 1990's of $200M. They are followed by R. H. Macy & Co. and Sears Roebuck. The New York Times has **the largest newspaper advertising revenue of any single newspaper in the world** with an annual average of $775M, and an average advertising volume of 4.5 million inches per year. The largest UK newspaper in terms of pages carried is the *Daily Express* with an annual average of 4700 pages. *The Financial Times* has **the largest advertising revenue in Britain** at £165M.

Britain's **largest consumer magazine** in terms of display advertising revenue is the *Radio Times*. The largest selling French magazine is *Femme Actuelle*, which is also probably the largest selling magazine in Europe. The biggest selling German magazine is *Horzu*.

Britain's largest magazines by advertising revenue (1994)

Rank	Magazine	Advertising revenues (£M)
1	Radio Times	27.551
2	Economist	19.197
3	TV Times	18.228
4	Woman's Own	16.112
5	Cosmopolitan	14.982
6	Good Housekeeping	14.014
7	Woman	13.372
8	Vogue	12.743
9	Bella	11.801
10	Reader's Digest	10.404

Electronic media

 The dominance of newspapers as an advertising medium was challenged in this century by the emergence of electronic media such as radio, film and television. **The first radio advertisement**

The world's largest magazines by advertising revenue (1994)

Magazine	Country	Advertising revenues
Time	USA	$540M
Sports Illustrated	USA	$510M
People	USA	$500M
TV Guide	USA	$480M
Parade	USA	$450M
Business Week	USA	$380M
Newsweek	USA	$360M
Fortune	USA	$270M
Forbes	USA	$250M
US News and World Report	USA	$240M

was transmitted by station WEAF, New York on 28th August 1922. It was a 10 minute talk about properties for sale. The success of this initiative – two apartments were sold – encouraged others to advertise on radio. Among these pioneers were American Express, R. H. Macy & Co., Metropolitan Life and Colgate. **The first UK radio advertisements** were in 1923 for Selfridges department store. The creation of the BBC and the embargo on advertising stopped radio emerging as a major UK advertising medium until the 1970s. London Broadcasting was **the first commercial radio station** (i.e. funded by advertising revenues) in the UK. Its first advertisement was for Birds Eye Fish Fingers on 8 October 1973. **The largest UK radio advertiser** in 1994 was McDonalds, with a total spent on advertising of £3.7M.

The **earliest use of television for advertising** was at the Hairdressing Fair of Fashion in November 1930 when Messrs Eugene Ltd of Dover Street, London used closed-circuit television to promote their permanent waving technique.

The first, open, public broadcast advertisement was for a Bulova watch. It was shown on NBC's WNBT station in New York on 27th June 1941.

The first commercial shown on television in the UK was for Gibbs SR Toothpaste. It was transmitted at 09:01 on the opening day of Independent Television, 22 September 1955. **The first colour advertisement shown on UK television** was for Bird's Eye Peas. It was transmitted in the British Midlands, at 10:05 am on the 15th November 1969.

The use of film to promote products and services predated television by over half a century. The New York firm of Huhn & Webster were making films for Haig Whiskey, Pabst Milwaukee Beer and Maillard's Chocolate in 1897. The same year saw Arthur Melbourne Cooper make the first British advertising film – for Bird's Custard Powder – in 1897. Bird's custard continues to use film and television as a key element in its advertising

Bird's Custard has used similar brand colours and symbols for very many years, a practice that helps to encourage brand loyalty.
The company was the first to use film for advertising in Britain, as long ago as 1897. *(Kraft General Food Ltd).*

mix.

Cooper made **the oldest surviving advertising film** – for Bryant and May, calling for donations to supply the troops in South Africa with matches. **The oldest surviving US advertising film** is for Admiral Cigarettes and was made by Edison & Co. and is copyrighted August 5, 1897.

Television and film came together once again in 1995 when Walt Disney Corporation acquired Capital Cities/ABC for $19Bn to create **the largest media corporation in the world** with a combined value of £40Bn. Merger, acquisition and joint venturing has led to six major corporations achieving a major share in the Western media.

Europe's largest media company is Bertelsmann of Germany, with a total annual revenue from all media sources of $2.4Bn.

The world's largest media corporations

Company	Value (market capitalisation $Bn)
Walt Disney	40
Time Warner	32
Viacom	27
News International	19
Tele-Communications Inc	17
Seagram	14

Advertising Agencies

The largest advertising agency in the world is the Japanese agency Dentsu, whose worldwide income was $1.5Bn in 1994. Dentsu is significantly larger than its closest rivals McCann-Erickson World and Euro RSCG with total incomes of just above and just less than $1Bn respectively. Their income comes from a variety of sources but is primarily based on a mixture of commission on advertising billings and fees.

The world's top 20 agency brands

Rank	Agency	Worldwide gross income (US$M) 1994	Worldwide capitalized billings (US$M) 1994
1	Dentsu Inc.	1568.7	12,325.4
2	McCann-Erickson worldwide	1063.4	7,092.9
3	J. Walter Thompson Co.	881.4	6,077.3
4	Hakuhodo	774.2	5,766.5
5	BBDO worldwide	736.5	5,832.3
6	Grey Advertising	700.7	4,689.2
7	Leo Burnett Co.	677.5	4,592.0
8	Lintas worldwide	665.5	4,438.9
9	Euro RSCG	639.6	4,391.3
10	DDB Needham worldwide	629.1	4,886.6
11	Ogilvy & Mather worldwide	611.1	5,302.6
12	Saatchi & Saatchi Advertising	602.4	4,820.7
13	True North Communications	549.1	4,674.9

14	Publicis Communication	529.3	3,601.8
15	Young & Rubicam	506.6	4,114.1
16	D'Arcy Masius Benton and Bowles	500.2	4,493.5
17	Bates worldwide	494.1	3,952.5
18	Lowe Group	300.3	2,074.1
19	Bozell worldwide	229.7	1,750.0
20	Tokyu Agency	212.1	1,629.3

Source: *Advertising Age*

Top US agency brands ranked by gross income (1994)

Rank	Agency	Gross income ($M)
1	Leo Burnett Co.	322.1
2	J. Walter Thompson Co	317.4
3	Grey Advertising	302.2
4	McCann-Erikson Worldwide	261.4
5	BBDO Worldwide	245.9
6	Saatchi & Saatchi Advertising	241.5
7	True North Communications (FCB)	236.8
8	DDB Needham Worldwide	228.2
9	D'Arcy Masius Benton & Bowles	219.3
10	Young & Rubicam	184.7

Source: *Advertising Age*

Top US agency brands ranked by billings (1994)

Rank	Agency	Gross income ($M)
1	True North Communications (FCB)	2589.2
2	BBDO Worldwide	2423.2
3	D'Arcy Masius Benton & Bowles	2247.2
4	Leo Burnett Co.	2226.3
5	J. Walter Thompson Co.	2218.8
6	Grey Advertising	2015.7
7	Saatchi & Saatchi Advertising	1932.2
8	DDB Needham Worldwide	1919.1
9	Young & Rubicam	1885.6
10	Ogilvy & Mather Worldwide	1776.2

11	McCann-Erikson Worldwide	1743.9
12	Bozell Worldwide	1315.0
13	Bates Worldwide	1083.3
14	N.W. Ayer & Partners	861.2
15	Campbell Mithum Esty.	850.6
16	Wells Rich Greene BDDP	840.6
17	Chiat/Day	820.0
18	TMP Worldwide	784.8
19	Ammirati & Puris/Lintas.	753.3
20	Messner Vetere Berger McNamee Schmetterer	708.0

Source: *Advertising Age*

Top 10 ad organizations (1994)

Rank	Organization	Worldwide gross income ($M)
1	WPP Group	2768.2
2	Interpublic Group of Cos.	2211.0
3	Omnicom Group	2052.6
4	Dentsu Inc.	1641.7
5	Cordiant	1431.5

Source: *Advertising Age*

The largest advertising agencies in the USA and UK ($M billings)

USA (1994)	$M billings	UK (1994)	$M billings
True North (FCB) Communications	2589.2	Saatchi & Saatchi Advertising (now Cordiant)	1008.9
BBDO Worldwide	2423.2	J. Walter Thompson (London)	802.7
D'Arcy, Masius Benton & Bowles	2247.2	Ogilvy & Mather	771.3
Leo Burnett	2226.3	D'Arcy Masius Benton & Bowles	620.1
J. Walter Thompson	2218.8	Bates Dorland	515.8
Grey Advertising	2015.7	Grey Communications	510.8
Saatchi & Saatchi Advertising	1932.2	Young & Rubicam	448.6

DDB Needham Worldwide	1919.1	McCann Erickson UK	427.5
Young & Rubicam	1885.6	Lowe Howard-Spink	380.0
McCann Erickson Worldwide	1743.9	Abbott Mead Vickers/BBDO	373.1

Source: *Advertising Age*

Europe's largest advertising agencies, by country

Country	Advertiser	Billings ($USM)
Austria	GGK Vienna/Salzburg	103.176
Belgium	McCann-Erickson Belgium	122.046
Bulgaria	GGK Sofia	2.3
Croatia	McCann-Erickson Croatia	5.804
Cyprus	D'Arcy Masius Benton & Bowles	2.773
Czech Republic	Mark/BBDO	21.049
Denmark	Grey Communications Group	204.423
Estonia	Bates AGE Reklam	8.0
Finland	AS & Grey	137.626
France	Euro RSCG France	1,747.3
Germany	BBDO Group Germany	677.055
Greece	Spot Thompson Group	171.765
Hungary	McCann-Erickson Hungary.	29.990
Iceland	YDDA Advertising (Bozell)	2.706
Ireland	Wilson Hartnell Group	57.143
Italy	Armando Testa Group	394.208
Netherlands, The	BDDO Nederland	267.560
Norway	Bates Gruppen	182.025
Poland	Bates Poland	31.0
Portugal	McCann-Erickson/Hora	105.462
Romania	Bates Centrade S&S	5.6
Russia	Young & Rubicam	22.493
Slovakia	Soria & Grey	15.534
Slovenia	SMS/Bates/SSA	64.0
Spain	Bassat, O&M	252.951
Sweden	McCann Erickson AB	101.908
Switzerland	Young & Rubicam	164.906
Turkey	Cenajans Grey	164.906

Source: *Advertising Age*

Barbie

Advertising has played an important role in the history of the most successful toy in history – The Barbie Doll. Almost 600 million Barbies have been sold since the doll was first introduced in 1959. At its peak in 1988, 54,000 Barbies were being sold every day in the USA. Copies have been tried but not one has come close to matching the sales of the original.

The originator of the idea for Barbie was Ruth Handler, who was the wife of Elliott Handler, one of the founders of Mattel – the second largest toymaker in the USA and now the owners of Barbie. She explained her thinking to the New York Times. "If a little girl was going to do role-playing of what she would be like at 16 or 17, it was a little stupid to play with a doll that had a flat chest. So I gave her beautiful breasts".

The success of Barbie has extended to a partner, Ken, clothes, accessories and related products. Demand for clothes made Mattel the fourth largest clothing manufacturer in the USA – using almost 100 million yards of fabric by 1995. Almost 100 new costumes are produced each year with the wedding outfit the most popular.

The links with the founders and originators was broken in 1980 when the Handlers sold most of their stock. At the time Mattel was the largest toymaker in the USA.

Barbie, the most successful toy in history. (Norton and Company).

Japan's top advertising agencies in 1994

Rank	Agency	Billings (US$M)
1	Dentsu Inc.	11,070
2	Hakuhodo Inc.	5327
3	Tokyu Advertising	1557

Source: *Advertising Age*

The distinctive nature of advertising with its strong dependence on an understanding of local culture and acceptable image, means that the largest agencies vary considerably between countries.

Japan's advertising industry has grown to reflect the success of the Japanese economy.

Public relations

The biggest launch of a product or brand in UK business history was the introduction of Britain's national lottery in 1994. Saatchi and Saatchi was given a media budget of £35M in the first year. This renewed an old relationship between advertising and lotteries. James White, one of the first advertising agents, made part of his reputation by writing lottery puffs – or at least commissioning his friend Charles Lamb to write them at the start of the 19th century. One of these blurbs read:

A SEASONABLE HINT – Christmas gifts of innumerable descriptions will now pervade this whole kingdom. It is submitted whether any present is capable of being attended with so much good to a dutiful son, an amiable daugher, an industrious apprentice, or a faithful servant, as that of a SHARE of a LOTTERY TICKET, in a scheme in which the smallest share may gain near two thousand pounds. Advertising is only part of an ever wider mix of mar-

keting techniques used to communicate with markets. Public relations (PR) is especially important in conveying complex yet subtle messages to diffuse modern markets. Public relations work extends from efforts to reach communities that cannot easily be reached by traditional means (e.g. politicians) to managing a firm's response to specific positive and negative events. Burson-Marsteller is **the largest PR firm in the world**, with net fees of $192M in 1994. Shandwick have more employees, but a smaller gross fee income. Smith & Harroff have the highest net fee income per employee, at $224,508.

Shandwick was **the UK's largest PR company** with a fee income of $36,656,880 in 1994. The highest fee income per employee is earned by Financial Dynamics, at $111,000 per employee.

The top PR firms in the world

Rank	Company	1994 Net Fees ($000)	Employees
1	Burson-Marsteller	191,999	1 700
2	Shandwick	160,100	1 813
3	Hill & Knowlton	139,300	1 227
4	Communications International	111,720	1 183
5	Edelman Public Relations Worldwide	74,909	819
6	Fleishman-Hillard	73,898	775
7	Ketchum Public Relations	55,405	467
8	Ogilvy Adams & Rinehart	39,055	411
9	Robinson Lake/Sawyer Miller/Bozell	37,800	250
10	The Rowland Co.	35,000	301

Source: *The J. R. O' Dwyer Company, Inc.*

The turbulence in the PR industry is vividly illustrated by the changes over the last decade in the top ten rankings.

Rank (1985)	Rank (1995)	Company	Fee income ($) (year ending 84/85)	Where are they now?
1	–	Good Relations	5,100,000	Now part of Lowe Bell.
2	12	Charles Barker	4,551,000	Under new ownership.

3	1	Shandwick	2,900,000	Second largest agency in the world.
4	6	Burson-Marsteller	2,848,000	Sixth in 1995 league.
5	3	Dewe Rogerson	2,114,000	Third in 1995 league.
6	–	Welbeck PR	1,895,000	Bought by Shandwick.
7	5	Hill & Knowlton	1,784,00	Fifth in 1995 league.
8	17	Daniel J Edelman	1,610,000	Down to number 17.
9	–	Kingsway Group	1,460,000	Part of the Rowland Company.
=10	–	Carl Byoir & Associates	1,400,000	Part of Hill & Knowlton.
=10	–	Harrison Cowley Group	1,400,000	Bought by Management in 1994.

The Top 10 market research companies in Britain, 1994

Rank	Company	Turnover (£000)
1	Taylor Nelson AGB plc	58,052
2	NOP Research Group	43,703
3	Research International (UK) Ltd	40,009
4	Millward Brown International	34,300
5	BMRB International Ltd	20,227
6	RSL – Research Services Ltd	17,804
7	The Research Business Group	13,343
8	MORI	12,799
9	The MBL Group plc	8297
10	The Harris Research Centre	7755

Source: The Market Research Society

At the other extreme of marketing activity, direct marketing and sales promotion work is typically linked closely with sales and purchasing. **The UK's largest direct marketing company** is WWAV Rapp Collins. The largest sales promotion company is IMP.

Market research

Market research is a vital feature of modern marketing. **The oldest UK market research firm** is Campden and Chorleywood Research Association founded in 1919. The next oldest are BMRB founded in 1933 and Mass Observation established in 1937. **The largest Market Research Agency in Britain** is Taylor Nelson AGB with a turnover of £55M in 1994.

Imports and exports

The internationalization of markets has increased sharply in the post World War

Gross Domestic Product (GDP) of Major Nations

Country	GDP in US$ (1995 estimates)	per head
USA	7,379,000,000,000	27,600
Japan	5,075,000,000,000	40,390
Germany	2,436,600,000,000	30,400
France	1,558,000,000,000	26,340
United Kingdom	1,168,500,000,000	20,000
Italy	1,167,300,000,000	20,100
Brazil	837,300,000,000	5.000
Canada	599,300,000,000	19,700
China	580,000,000,000	500
Spain	522,400,000,000	13,300
South Korea	478,900,000,000	10,600
Russia	438,000,000,000	3,000
Netherlands	420,500,000,000	26,900
Australia	357,700,000,000	19,600
Mexico	321,000,000,000	3,400
India	305,900,000,000	300
Argentina	296,000,000,000	8,600
Switzerland	293,200,000,000	41,300
Taiwan	291,300,000,000	13,600
Belgium	261,400,000,000	25,600
Austria	242,000,000,000	30,200
Sweden	218,300,000,000	24,600
Indonesia	193,700,000,000	1,000
Turkey	175,900,000,000	2,800
Thailand	175,100,000,000	2,900
Denmark	173,400,000,000	33,200
Hong Kong	158,800,000,000	25,900
Norway	147,100,000,000	33,600
South Africa	138,900,000,000	3,300
Saudi Arabia	131,800,000,000	6,800
Poland	125,000,000,000	3,200
Finland	123,200,000,000	24,100
Greece	117,000,000,000	11,300
Venezuela	98,000,000,000	4,500
Malaysia	90,000,000,000	3,900

Country	GDP in US$ (1995 estimates)	per head
Israel	89,400,000,000	15,500
Colombia	86,600,000,000	2,400
Portugal	86,400,000,000	8,700
Singapore	85,500,000,000	28,100
Philippines	70,900,000,000	1,000
New Zealand	61,300,000,000	16,900
Ireland	60,600,000,000	16,800
Chile	60,000,000,000	4,200
Iran	59,800,000,000	900
Pakistan	59,400,000,000	500
Egypt	53,600,000,000	900
Czech Republic	49,100,000,000	4,700
Algeria	48,200,000,000	1,700
Hungary	47,100,000,000	4,600
Ukraine	46,000,000,000	900

Two era. The world's largest importers and exporters, however, have remained broadly the same over the last decade. The USA is both **the largest exporter of goods and services and the largest importer.**

Failure and Success

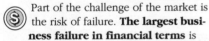 Part of the challenge of the market is the risk of failure. **The largest business failure in financial terms** is probably still the Ford Edsel. The introduction and subsequent withdrawal of the Edsel cost Ford an estimated $350M in 1953. At current prices this equates to a loss of about $3Bn. Du Pont's imitation leather product – Corfam – lost over $700M a decade later equating to a contemporary deficit of around $2Bn. It is harder to arrive at an accurate estimate of the real losses associated with Concorde but they are unlikely to less than $1.5Bn at current prices.

 These vast losses are linked with the failure of new product introductions. Some experts argue that the biggest real loss was caused by the decision of

Xerox to give Rank the licence to develop the Latin American market. Eventually, Xerox bought these rights back for a mixture of fee and royalty. This eventually meant that Xerox were giving Rank Xerox a royalty on sales they made themselves. The gross cost of this has been put at over $6Bn.

The film industry has seen some of the most public loses of money in a relatively short time.

Films recording the greatest losses

Rank	Film	Gross Loss (estimated)
1	Inchon (1981)	$100M
2	Hook (1991)	$80M
3	Hudson Hawk (1991)	$65M
4	Heaven's Gate (1980)	$50M
5	The Adventures of Baron Munchausen (1988)	$45M

6	1941 (1979)	$40M
7	Ishar (1987)	$35M
8	Alien (1992)	$30M
9	Memphis Belle (1990)	$25M
10	Caligula (1979)	$25M

The same industry has seen spectacular earnings from successful films. The biggest grossing films for their eras set standards their rivals strive to match. In real terms *Gone With the Wind* is the biggest grossing movie in history with total revenues (at current values) of $750M.

The all-time movie blockbusters

Rank	Film	Theatrical rentals, $M (In real dollars, not adjusted for inflation)
	The Teens/20s	
1	The Birth of a Nation	10.0
2	The Big Parade	5.1
3	Ben Hur (MGM)	4.6
	The 30s	
1	Gone with the Wind (MGM)	79.4
2	Snow White and the Seven Dwarfs (Disney)	61.8
3	Pinocchio (Disney)	33.0
	The 40s	
1	Bambi (Disney)	47.3
2	Cinderella (Disney)	41.1
3	Song of the South (Disney)	29.2
	The 50s	
1	The Ten Commandments (Paramount)	43.0
2	Lady and the Tramp (Disney)	40.2
3	Peter Pan (Disney)	37.6
	The 60s	
1	The Sound of Music (Fox)	79.9
2	Love Story (Paramount)	50.0
3	Doctor Zhivago (MGM)	47.3
	The 70s	
1	Star Wars (Fox)	193.5
2	The Empire Strikes Back (Fox)	141.6
3	Jaws (Universal)	129.5
	The 80s	
1	E.T. The Extra-Terrestrial (Universal)	228.6
2	Return of the Jedi (Fox)	168.0
3	Batman (Warner Bros)	150.5

Source: *Variety,* 2 May, 1990

E.T. The Extra-Terrestrial
(Universal Pictures) was the most successful film
of the 1980s in terms of theatrical rentals.
(The Kobal Collection).

Top 10 films of the 1990s

Rank	Film	Year
1	Jurassic Park	1993
2	Forrest Gump	1994
3	The Lion King	1994
4	Home Alone	1990
5	Mrs Doubtfire	1993
6	Ghost	1990
7	Aladdin	1992
8	Terminator 2: Judgement Day	1991
9	Dances with Wolves	1990
10	The Fugitive	1993

Source: British Film Institute

Aspirin wars

Analogies between market competition and warfare are common. The analogy with war was used to describe the struggle for dominance of the global market for aspirin. At its heart is the curious and unique case of rivalry between Bayer of Germany and Bayer (USA). These two firms have a common root, a bitter rivalry for many years and eventual rapprochement when they were remerged. The rivalry centred on aspirin.

This painkiller was originally developed by Felix Hoffmann for Farbenfabriken Bayer (A. G. Bayer) in 1897. The new drug – acetylsalicylic acid (ASA) – became **the most commercially successful drug** in modern pharmaceutical history. In the USA alone almost $1Bn worth of aspirin and its branded versions were consumed every year in the late 1980s. This is roughly one third of the analgesics market or seven per cent of the total over-the-counter drugs market. Worldwide sales are roughly four times that figure. The identification of a link between aspirin consumption and the reduced risk of certain types of heart disease during the 1980s stimulated demand at the start of the 1990s by over 50 per cent.

Aspirin originally emerged as an alternative to another product developed by

143

Bayer. This was a derivative of morphine which was originally developed by an English chemist C.R.Wright. The head of Bayer's drug testing laboratory rediscovered and tested it on Bayer workers. Their reaction was favourable. One comment was that it made them feel 'heroic', and from that observation came the drug's brand name, Heroin.

Aspirin was one of the main products of the Farbenfabriken Bayer business in the USA. It was especially important as it was the only significant market in which Bayer had both a trademark and a patent on aspirin. Just before the start of the First World War, aspirin accounted for a third of Bayer's North American sales and almost half its profits. The war was a disaster for Bayer especially as in 1918 the US government expropriated the business, goods and assets of Bayer and sold them in public auction to Sterling Products Inc. for $5.3M.

Over the next 70 years competition between the two firms would move from the high moral tone adopted by Carl Duisberg who argued that Sterling's use of the Bayer name was wrong ("you will be a fake Bayer") to raw competition for market share across the world. It reached its depths with the integration of Bayer into I.G. Farben AG – the notorious Nazi-controlled industrial conglomerate. It extended to include virtually all the key players in the world drugs industry and drew to a close only when the two firms were formally merged in the 1990s.

The battle for dominance in oil

The competition for local, national and global success has waged more fiercely in the oil industry than in virtually any other sector. As early as 1870, John D. Rockefeller's brother William defined relations with their rivals as "war or peace". The description of Rockefeller as a 'robber baron' reinforced this image of fierce competition, and it was a competition which extended far beyond the nor-mal confines of commerce.

The first of many wars over the control of oil supplies was fought by Imperial Russia to gain control of the independent Khanate of Baku in the 1820s. Its conquest led to the creation of the first oil industry in Russia by 1829. It was, however, fifty years before Russia has its own Oil King – Ludwig Nobel – to rival Rockefeller. For much of the next half century, the oil industry saw the first true globely competitive market. The pattern of this rivalry was finally set with the emergence and consolidation of Western European oil interests in firms like Royal Dutch Shell, Anglo-Persian Oil and others. Each had its spheres of interest: Standard in the USA, the Nobels and the Rothschilds in Russia, and Royal Dutch Shell in the Near and Far East. Attempts were made to enter and undermine each other's local interests, but efforts were also made to establish alliances.

The wealth and power of the oil industry made its operations a focal point for debates on competition and attempts to change the patterns of ownership and control. Ida Tarbell's articles in *McClure's* magazine in 1902 was one of the first attempts to use public opinion to rein in, reform and, eventually, control competition in a major US industry. Three years later, in the Baku oilfields of Russian-controlled Azerbaijan, a more extreme attempt was made to change the nature and form of industrial comptition. These oilfields were at the centre of the 1905 Russian Revolution and the oil workers of Baku were the first major group to elect Bolshevik deputies to the Russia Duma.

It was the naval rivalry between Britain and Germany and the First World War that highlighted the new dimension to competition that oil added to world affairs. Oil was at the heart of the technological and trading revolution that fuelled the naval race. Oil-burning warships were faster, more spacious and easier to man – especially in battle – than their coal-burning rivals. Maintaining her lead in naval power forced the UK to rebuild and re-equip her fleet. Germany fought to catch up and overtake this position. The shift to oil had a second effect. The fleet could not rely on a raw material – coal – available in vast quantities at home. The main sources were across seas in other continents; securing these supplies and maintain the supply routes further stimulated this competition.

💲 Oil played a major part in the First World War. Some commentators suggest the failure of Germany to secure adequate oil supplies – especially from the Baku region – eventually forced the German army to surrender. The armistice saw, perhaps, the first claim that access to a specific raw material led to victory. The director of France's Comité Générale du Petrole claimed that oil – "the blood of the earth" was the "blood of victory". The war virtually eliminated one the the key players in the prewar competition for dominance – Russia. The Revolution and nationalization of the oilfields reduced output and shifted attention to domestic issues. The postwar era saw the emerge of vast new oilfields in the Middle East.

💲 The decade after the end of World War One saw the first examples of two other features of competition in the oil industry. The first was exaggerated claims about impending shortages. In 1920, John Cadman, who was director of the US Petroleum Executive, claimed that US stocks would be exhausted by 1940. The second feature of this competition was misguided hopes about alternative substitutes. In 1919, the National Geographic was among those looking forward to the early available of large amounts of cheap oil from oil shale. President Carter saw the same hopes dashed 60 years later.

World War Two was very much an oil war. The role of motorized transport, the vast distances and the dominance of oil-based machines on land, sea and in the air forced that position. Several key events during the war turned on oil. The failure of the Japanese at Pearl Harbour to destroy the 4.5 million barrels of oil in the Pacific

A gusher in the Baku oilfields in Azerbaijan, from a print published in London in 1886. At the beginning of the 20th century the Azeri oilfields were a centre of revolutionary activity: the oil workers of Baku were the first group to elect Bolshevik deputies to the Russian Duma. Today independent Azerbaijan is an increasingly important oil producer with an output of over 85,000,000 barrels in 1993. (Ann Ronan).

Fleet's fuel reserves was probably as important as their failure to sink aircraft carriers. The Allies' use of high octane petrol added speed, manoeuverability and power to their aircraft. Victory confirmed the link between competition between oil companies and competition between nations. More revolutions have been stimulated and undermined to serve this interest than any other. From Suez in 1956 to The Gulf War in 1991, 'police actions' have been fought to protect oil interests and supplies. After a century of competition, the same key players, albeit in different guises – Exxon, Shell, BP etc. – continue to dominate the world's markets.

Industries and advertising

There are many links between the struggle for market position in the car industry and the oil industry. These extend beyond the parallel history of the industries to common themes and images in their advertising.

Car producers often dominate corporate rankings of the largest advertisers. In the USA, the automobile industry spends almost twice as much on media advertising as any other major industry grouping.

Advertising expenditure in the USA by major industries

Industry	Total ($Bn) 1990–1994
Automotive	17.00
Retail	8.70
Food	7.00
Restaurants	6.40
Entertainment and media	5.50
Telecommunications	3.30
Beverages	3.30
Drugs and remedies	2.80
Beer, wine and liquor	2.76
Toiletries and cosmetics	2.45

Ⓢ This level of advertising is a far cry from Henry Ford's early notions that cars sold on their price and reliability. His maxim – any colour so long as it's black – brought him vast success. In 1923, Ford reached its peak with sales of 2,120,898 cars and a US market share of over 57 per cent. Henry Ford's resistance to media advertising was legendary. It took the collapse of the Model T's sales and the year-long closure of his factories across the USA to force Ford to match the commitment of his rivals. The introduction of the Model A Ford was linked with **the biggest launch advertising expenditure in history** to date – $1.3M. Personality advertis-

ing was used extensively. Film stars like Douglas Fairbanks were photographed with the car.

Ⓢ The model for using advertising to support car sales had been established by General Motors, Chrysler and Ford's other US rivals. General Motors used posters and newspapers extensively from its early years, and was **one of the first companies to introduce corporate advertising** to build up the image of the firm beyond that of its individual products and brands.

> I had had some consumer studies made in 1922, and we found that people throughout the United States, except at the corner of Wall and Broad Streets, didn't know anything about General Motors. So I thought we should publicize the parent company
>
> Alfred P. Sloan *My Years with General Motors, 1963*

In the USA, Ford now spends more on media advertising for its brand than any of its rivals in the car industry. The strength of its brand image and the focus this permits reinforces this impression of dominance. General Motors, in its different guises, spend more but these are distributed across different 'brands'.

Major car producers and their advertising

Brand	Total ($M) 1990–1994
Ford	1776
Toyota	1535
Chevrolet	1433
GM	929
Buick	806
Dodge	744
Nissan	972
Mazda	835
Honda	685

General Motors total expenditure on its automobile brands in the USA was almost $4Bn during the first half of the 1990s.

Car production around the world

Rank	Country	Production
1	Japan	7.5
2	USA	5.4
3	Germany	4.3
4	France	3.2
5	Spain	1.8
(7)	UK	1.2

Source: *The Guinness Book of Answers* (10th edition)

Media advertising in the UK by industry

Rank	Industry code	Total $M (1990–1994)
1	Automobile	$3016
2	Retail	$1982
3	Food	$1804
4	Confectionary	$1543
5	Detergents	$1407
6	Financial services	$758
7	Telecommunications	$540
8	Media	$104

Advertising and information technology

The largest area of growth in advertising expenditure over the last few years is in computing and telecommunications. The recent growth in this industry is closely linked with sharp increases in media advertising. In the UK, British Telecom increased its media expenditure faster than

Car ownership around the world: the lowest number of persons per car

Rank	Country	Persons per car
1	San Marino	1
2	USA	1.3
3	Andorra	1.4
4	Monaco	1.4
5	Liechtenstein	1.5
6	Canada	1.6
7	Australia	1.8
8	Luxembourg	1.8
9	Iceland	1.9
10	Italy	1.9

Source: *The Guinness Book of Answers* (10th edition)

any other major company during the 1990s.

 Perhaps the most well known, single television advertisement ever shown was for the Apple Macintosh. At its time, it was **the most expensive television advertisement to produce**, and the commercial was shown only once. However, its impact was so great, and recall so high, that it is one of the most cost effective ads ever. It was produced by Ridley Scott and was based on the George Orwell novel, 1984. The commercial featured a dimly lit hall in which large numbers of workers are sitting on benches watching a huge screen. They are surrounded by guards and a Big Brother-like figure is talking to them in a version of George Orwell's Newspeak about the Informational Purification Directive.

Suddenly, a young, brightly dressed athlete runs towards the screen. She is wearing a Macintosh T-shirt and carries a sledgehammer. When she gets close to the screen, she hurls the hammer into the screen and it explodes. The voice over then says "On 24th January, Apple Computer will introduce Macintosh. And you'll see why 1984 won't be like 1984". The advertisement cost $600,000 to produce and $1,000,000 to show. It was shown only once.

More recently, the most intense competition in the computer industry has shifted from rivalry between hardware producers to competition between software producers. The user friendliness of the Apple Macintosh operating system has been matched in many key features by MicroSoft's Windows operating environment running on IBM-style personal computers. There are currently about 140 million people using IBM-style pcs compared to less than 10 million Macintosh systems. The dominant operating environment is DOS which operates on virtually all IBM-style machines. It is estimated that 35 million users have adopted MicroSoft's Windows environment.

Worldwide information technology market by region, 1993.

Region	Market value ($B)
US	158.92
Western Europe	140.36
Japan	64.96
Four Tigers: S Korea, Taiwan, Hong Kong, Singapore	5.80
Eastern Europe	3.48
Rest of World	32.48
Total	**406.00**

Source: *Financial Times*

The most expensive, and probably the most famous, television commercial ever shown was for Apple Macintosh.
The advertisement, which echoed Orwell's 1984, featured a young athlete and cost $600,000 to produce and $1,000,000 to show. It was shown only once. (BBDO/Los Angeles).

Advertising and retailing

In both Britain and the USA, the retail sector is the second largest advertising medi-

um. Retailers compete for market position in a host of ways that extend beyond media advertising. It is said that there are three keys to success in retailing – location, location and location. Purchasing policies, display, service and quality are just some of the elements of marketing success for retailers. Marks & Spencer is **Britain's most successful retailer.** It is the only retailer in the world with an AAA rating. It was probably **the first significant retailer to build its business around buying direct from manufacturers**. It is the only retailer to be voted 'Europe's most respected company' by the *Financial Times.*

The highest sales per square metre of any retailer in the world was earned by Richer Sounds. Their London Bridge Walk shop earned sales of £1630,73 per sq. metre (£17,553 per square foot) in the year ending January 31st 1995.

The largest department store is R.H.Macy & Co Inc of Herald Square New York City, USA. It covers 50.5 acres (20.3 hectares) and employs over 10,000 staff handling 400,000 tems. **The largest store in the UK** is Harrods. It has a total selling area of 25 acres (10.5 hectares) and employes just over 3000 people handling 200,000 items. Woolworth Corporation has **more outlets than any other** with 9000 stores worldwide. Oxfam operates **more shops than any other UK retailer** with roughly 600 outlets open at any time in the UK.

Design plays a major part in the presentation of products, services and the total marketing effort. **The world's largest design company** is WPP Group, which

Rank	Company	Fee income (£M)
1	WPP Group	84
2	Landor	45
3	Fitch-RS	39
4	Addison	21
5	Siegel & Gale	18

had revenues of £739M in 1994. **The UK's largest design group** is the Building Design Partnership, with 752 employees.

Sales staff are a vital part of the marketing effort of most firms. The Prudential has **the largest full-time sales force in the UK** with 7000 sales staff. **In the USA**, the Fuller Brush Company employs **the largest full-time sales force** with over 20,000 men and women selling brushes door to door. **The largest sales force, including full-time and part-time staff** was employed by Avon Products Inc. At its peak, the Avon sales force totalled just under half a million. This has now declined to under 400,000.

Much sales activity is linked with exhibitions and fairs. **The largest exhibition centre in the world** is the International Exposition Centre in Cleveland, Ohio, which is situated in a building which measures 232,258 sq metres (2.5 million ft^2). The National Exhibition Centre (NEC) in Birmingham is **the UK's largest exhibition centre**; the NEC consists fifteen exhibition halls covering 157,935 sq metres (1.7 million ft^2).

New forms of promotional activity

Sponsorship income may also be raised via charity credit cards. The charity credit card to raise the most money for beneficiaries is the Leeds Permanent Building Society Visa affinity credit card, which has raised over £5M since its launch in 1988.

The diversity of marketing activity is vividly illustrated by the growth of new forms of promotional activity that capitalize on new technologies and new forms of communication. Telemarketing – using telephones and other electronic media to make direct contact with customers – grew rapidly during the 1980s and early 1990s. **The world's largest telemarketing company** is Pioneer Tele-Technologies with total annual revenues of $400M. In the UK, BT operates the largest telemarketing com-

The top theme parks in the world

Theme Park	Location	Number of visitors
Walt Disney World	Orlando (USA)	32 million
Disneyland	Anaheim (USA)	14 million
Universal Studios	Universal City (USA)	5.5 million
Disneyland Tokyo	Tokyo (Japan)	5.2 million
Knotts Berry Farm	Buena Park (USA)	4 million
Sea World of Florida	Orlando (USA)	4 million
Sea World of California	San Diego (USA)	3.5 million
Kings Island	Kings Island (USA)	3.2 million
Cedar Point	Sandusky (USA)	3.2 million
Six Flags Magic Mountain	Valencia (USA)	3.2 million
Pleasure Beach	Blackpool (UK)	3 million
Busch Gardens	Tampa (USA)	3 million
Disneyland Paris	Paris (France)	3 million

Main Street at Walt Disney World (Orlando, Florida), the most successful theme park in the world in terms of visitors received: 32,000,000 per annum. (Spectrum Colour Library).

pany – BT Direct – with total revenues of $60M pa.

The more traditional direct marketing companies have generally held on to their market position by using new technologies and thinking to focus on more exact and detailed markets. Ogilvy and Mather Direct is **the world's largest direct marketing organization** with total billings of $450M. The development of marketing has seen it move into new industries as diverse as leisure and recreation and the promotion of economic development.

Major leisure developments like theme parks use their image, and the advertising assocated with their image, to boost incomes and revenues.

Marketing techniques are being used to boost the images and marketing positions of politicians and political parties, and even communities. Cities like Pittsburgh, Glasgow and Liverpool have used advertising and promotion to change their image and boost their reputation among business leaders and the general public. During the 1980s and early 1990s, Pittsburgh's image changed from being one the the the USA's least regarded cities as a place to do business in and live to one of the most highly rated. Similar research in the UK found that Glasgow and Liverpool had shown a similar sharp improvement in their standing.

The diversity of marketing activity and its power to influence behaviour continues to grow and with it its importance to modern business in good times and bad.

7

Risk and Exploitation

....

Risk is an integral feature of business activity. It counterbalances and in some ways justifies the rewards won when the entrepreneur, inventor or explorer succeeds. The costs of failure can be vast. Albert, Paul and Ralph Reichman experienced **the largest and quickest collapse in personal wealth in history** when their joint wealth dropped by $12Bn between 1991 and 1993. They had risked their wealth on the successful development of London's Canary Wharf. Delays, high interest charges, economic slowdown and worried bankers caused major problems for the gamble they took on this huge project. In 1991, *Fortune* magazine calculated that they were the fourth richest people in the world. By 1993, they were down to their last billion.

The oddest and perhaps the greatest collapse occurred to the Hunt brothers in their attempt to corner the silver market. In the course of their speculation the 'Silver Bears' wealth went from around $3Bn in 1970 to a peak of over $16Bn in 1980 to bankruptcy in 1987.

The British record for a short term collapse in wealth is probably held by the Duke of Westminster. The collapse in property values in the early 1990s saw his estimated wealth drop by $3Bn between 1992 and 1993. There is no evident link with risk taking in his case – just a change in market conditions. Robert

Maxwell took risks throughout his life. The accumulated effect of these gambles was seen after his death when estimates of his personal fortune were rapidly reduced from the peak in 1991 of $1.8Bn to nil or negatives.

Canary Wharf, Britain's tallest building at 243.5 m (800 ft). Delays on the development in London's Docklands, plus high interest rates and economic slowdown, contributed to the Reichman brothers record loss of $12Bn in their joint wealth during the period 1991-93. (Canary Wharf Ltd).

Many of these problems are closely linked with shifts in economic conditions and the values placed on assets. Confidence is a key factor. The Reichmans were probably confident that the economic confidence of the late 1980s in Britain would continue long enough for them to capitalize on their risk.

The greatest cash loss on a single day on the stock market is probably still the $65M that Ray A. Kroc of McDonald

Corporation experienced on 8 July 1974. There is some evidence that in real terms, i.e. bearing in mind contemporary circumstance the Du Pont family lost significantly more on 'Black Tuesday', the day the US stock market crashed in 1929 precipitating the great recession, when it is estimated that they lost just under $50M on the day. The decision by John D. Rockefeller in October 1929 to try to peg Standard Oil of New Jersey stock prices at $50 probably cost the company a similar sum.

The Silver Bubble

The attempt by Bunker Hunt and his brother Herbert to corner the world market in silver was one of the most dramatic near successes and total failures in 20th century business history. The brothers were sons of H. L. Hunt who in 1957 ranked second to John Paul Getty as one of the richest men in the world. His sons were determined to outdo him - at least in their willingness to speculate. Bunker was said to want to be the richest man in the world, just like Pa.

He had become involved in commodity speculation before he embarked on his sil-

ver dream. In 1973, he saw the value of his investment in beef treble in value when prices increased from 25c a pound to 60c in just eight months. Bunker almost managed a major coup in the mid 1970s from speculation in soya beans. The Hunts' move into silver prices occurred after a period of thirty years when the price of silver hardly shifted from the $1.29 per ounce 'cap' that the US Treasury placed on silver prices – this cap meant that the Treasury intervened when the price went below $1.29 per ounce. In 1967, the US Treasury dropped its intervention policy and in 1970

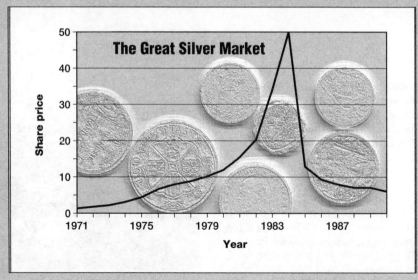

ceased selling silver. At the end of 1970, the world price of silver was $1.70 per ounce. The Hunts' first moves into the silver market saw prices increase gradually to $2 per ounce in March 1973 and $3 per ounce by July 1973.

The Hunts' holdings in 1973 were 35 million ounces. A year later they had pushed these up to 50 million ounces. Within two years they had doubled their holdings. The real pressure on the market occurred when the Hunts started working in concert with a group of Middle Eastern speculators. Together, they massively increased both their stocks and their futures trading. In August 1979 alone they acquired almost 50 million ounces.

The Hunts' holdings and futures options were put at almost 300 million ounces with a paper value of around $10.5 billion at the end of 1979. The other members of the cartel held similar amounts. Together they controlled three-quarters of the world's privately owned silver. The Hunt's profits on the 100 million ounces they had accumulated by the end of 1975 were approximately $3Bn. Early January 1980 saw another surge in silver prices until they peaked at just over $50 per ounce boosting the book value of the Hunts' silver assets to $15Bn.

The collapse started soon after, precipitated by the New York Silver Exchange's decision to confine trading in silver "for liquidation only". From then on, no new buyers could enter the market. The collapse in silver prices started soon after. On the 21st January prices fell to $44 per ounce, the next day to $34. The two days had cost the Hunts almost $5Bn. This is the largest private loss in such a short time in business history. The price continued to drop while the Hunts' futures market commitments to purchased silver started to come up. The Hunts' debts of $1.35Bn in the middle of March were the largest personal debts in history. At the end of March 1980, their options to purchase 30 million ounces at $35 on the London market were due. Simultaneously, the market price dropped temporarily to $10 an ounce. Other personal assets were sold to meet their liabilities. A recovery in silver prices in the middle of the year gave the Hunts a chance to reduce their liabilities but they failed to act. The price stared falling again so that by 1986 it was back down to $5 an ounce. The Hunts eventually declared themselves bankrupt in 1987. Bunker Hunt, the man who had declared" – If you know how much money you have got - you can't have very much" – now knew how much money he had.

Source: Derived from Beckman, R. *Crashes*

Futures Markets

Most financial, commodity and trade goods markets can be divided into 'spot' or 'futures' markets. In a spot market, the buyer is expected to pay 'on the spot', or now for immediate delivery. In a futures market, buyers enter a contract to sell or buy at a specified date for a price agreed now.

In a futures market the main items traded are the contracts to buy and sell. The contract may be for a commodity, e.g. silver or cocoa, a currency or even a financial deal. A seller might know

that at a fixed time in the future, say three months when the harvest arrives, he or she will have available a fixed amount of the commodity, e.g. cocoa. Today's price is $200 a tonne. He or she faces a choice. If they enter a futures contract now at a price of $200, that means the commodity is sold at $200 regardless of prevailing prices. If the price in three months is $150, the sellers have done well; if it is $250, they have done badly. Buyers face the same dilemma.

Balancing out these risks and seeking speculative advantage leads to the creation of markets in futures options. Traders take up options in order to resell them before they become due. The trader in cocoa futures buys a contract for cocoa at $200 a tonne believing the price will rise. The trader pays a deposit of $25. Over the next three months, information on the overall direction of prices improves. Assuming prices increase, the trader hopes to sell the option to buy at, say, $250 which gives a profit of 50 dollars. When prices move downwards trader faces the risk of comparable losses.

Boom and bust recur in business history.

The South Sea Bubble

 The sharpest changes in share values probably occurred with the South Sea Island Company between September 1719 and October 1720. Shares were initially issued with a nominal value of £100. The company's proposal in September 1790 to take over Britain's National Debt saw shares surge in value by around 400 per cent. Values rapidly increased to a peak of £1050 in September 1720 only to collapse to £150 in October and, then, to nothing.

The original purpose of the Company was to exploit a monopoly of trade in the South Seas. This area included the whole of South America, the West Coast of North America and the entire

Pacific Region up to the boundaries of the East India Company's territories in the Far East. The South Sea Company was one of only three companies then traded on the London Stock Exchange. The others were the Bank of England and the East India Company. Shares in both these latter companies were held by only a few people and there was pent-up demand for new opportunities to invest and speculate.

The South Sea trade was generally seen at the time as the most choice commercial prize in the world. In part, this was because of the wealth associated with South America and the scope to trade traditional English manufactures like broadcloth and iron for precious metals found in the region. It was even more attractive because of the Spanish policy of restricting South American trade to specific concessionaires. The growth of Britain's maritime power and her commercial strength convinced many that the South Sea Company could enter and dominate this trade. The Company offered to take over the National Debt in return for a monopoly over this trade. This proposal was generally welcomed especially after the increase in debt during the War of Spanish Succession (1702–1713).

The South Sea Company's shares were initially issued in 1714 with a further offering in 1717. The promise

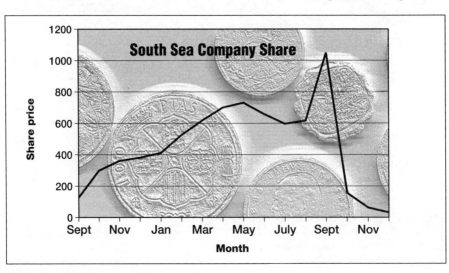

South Sea Company Share

A company for carrying on an undertaking of great advantage, but nobody to know what it is

The speculative frenzy that surrounded the South Sea Bubble saw a host of bizarre ventures started in London. These ranged from the company created with a £1M capital to build a perpetual motion wheel to the company for carrying on an undertaking of great advantage, but nobody to know what it is. The promoter of the latter company promised anyone buying a £2 share an income of £100 per annum. He collected £2000 in five hours – then disappeared.

of the monopoly and the offer to take over the National Debt saw shares soar in price in late 1719; their value grew rapidly during the first half of the year. A brief fall back was followed by heightened speculation despite the directors' decision to issue two further tranches of shares. The collapse of the share prices in October had effects right across London.

The South Sea Company never fulfilled the hope for profits and it was formally wound up in 1807 when Parliament withdrew its exclusive trading rights.

Wall Street Crash

The Wall Street Crash of 1929 showed many of the same features as the South Sea Bubble. The value of shares grew through most of the 1920s. In 1923, the New York Times Share Index stood at 106 and by the end of 1928 had increased to 331.

(S) **It was during 1929 that the sharpest increases and eventual "crash" occurred.** Prices increased from an index value of 360 points to a peak on the 3 September of 542, only to collapse to just over 200 in December. The greatest percentage increase occurred on 3 September 1929. The market went up by five per cent on the day. This eclipsed the previous peak of three per cent on 16 November 1928. On 'Black Tuesday' a then record 16,410,030 shares were traded on the US exchanges. This record lasted until April 1968. On 8 July 1932, the Dow Jones Share Index reached its lowest point at 41.22.

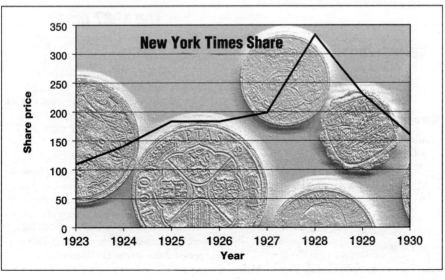

Figure: New York Times Share — Share price vs. Year (1923–1930)

The Wall Street Crash was heralded by The New York Times.
The paper's confidence that bankers were optimistic proved to be misfounded.
(Peter Newark's Western Americana).

Individual stocks fared even worse. The Goldman Sachs Trading Company's shares were valued at $104 when launched in 1929. Two years later their price was 1.75 dollars. The associated Shenandoah Trading Company's shares dropped from a peak of 36 dollars to 50 cents two years later. Major corporations saw their share values slump. Share values had lost $125,000 million in the course of the crash.

Collapsing share values during the Wall Street Crash

Corporation	Peak	Bottom
American Telephone and Telegraph	304	72
US Steel	262	22
Montgomery Ward	138	4
Otis Elevator	89	26
Standard Oil of New Jersey	76	20
General Motors	73	8

The 1987 crash

The most recent major stock market crash – October 1987 – saw share values on the New York Stock Exchange drop even more in cash terms that the 1929 Crash. This was **the largest loss ever on a stock exchange.** The total lost was $500,000,000,000 dollars. The market dropped by 508 points.

October 1987 saw record highs and lows on the US stock market. The record daily rise of 186.84 points was achieved on 21 October. This went some way to 'correct' the record day's decline which occurred two days earlier. **The record daily drop in share prices** occurred on the 19 October 1987 when

Share Price Index

The share price index is an index number computed from the average prices of a sample of company shares. This index is used to indicate general share price movements.

Index numbers are calculated from a fixed year, which is usually given the value of 100. If in ten years, average prices are calculated as having increased by 80 per cent, the price index is put at 180. Index numbers provide a facility to measure increases against a fixed point of time. They, also, allow the wide variations in cash amounts, e.g. between shares, to be accommodated within a standard figure.

In the UK, *The Financial Times* Share Index records movements on the London Stock Exchange. In the USA, share movements are monitored by the Dow-Jones Index. *The*

Financial Times Ordinary Share Index was started in 1935 with a base of 100. The index illustrates how much share prices have increased since that time. The Ordinary Share Index is calculated from the share prices of 30 blue chip companies.

The Financial Times-Stock Exchange Index (FT-SE or Footsie index) started with a base of 1000 in December 1983. It is calculated from the share price movements of the 100 largest companies on the stock exchange. The most comprehensive *Financial Times* index is the all shares calculated from the full 700 plus companies listed.

Changes in the prices are usually described as change in the index number, or points, on the market. An increase or decline of ten points means that the index number has risen or dropped by ten points.

The greatest drop in the Dow Jones Index on October 19, 1987 was dramatically recorded by The Times on the following morning. (The Times).

shares plunged by 22.6 per cent – 508 points. **The record drops and rises on the London exchange** coincided with the turbulence in New York. The greatest drop was on 20th October 1987 when the *Financial Times* Share Index dropped 250.7 points. The following day the market saw the greatest increase when shares went up by 142 points.

The overall percentage drop was far less than during the 1920s. Values slumped by 24 per cent in New York and by almost 30 per cent in London between the peak of September and a low point in November. The most dramatic change took place on the first day.

This was **the largest collapse in share values in the post-World War Two era**. Major corporations suffered alongside minor ventures. Marks and Spencer saw the sharpest ever drop in its share price – by 55 per cent – from £280 to £156.

The ten largest falls in the FT-SE 100 Index

Date	Index	Change
20 Oct 1987	1801.6	-250.7
19 Oct 1987	2052.3	-249.6
26 Oct 1987	1684.1	-111.1
22 Oct 1987	1833.2	-110.6
5 Oct 1992	24,446.3	-103.4
19 Aug 1991	2540.5	-80.5
24 Feb 1994	3267.5	-74.4
30 Nov 1987	1579.9	-71.7
16 Oct 1989	2163.4	-70.5
26 Jun 1995	3309.2	-70.2

Source: London Stock Exchange

Drops in the Dow Jones Industrial Average

Date	Per cent drop
October 19, 1987	22.61
October 28, 1929	12.82
October 29, 1929	11.73
November 6, 1929	9.92
August 12, 1932	8.4
October 26, 1987	8.04
July 21, 1933	7.94
October 18, 1937	7.75
October 5, 1932	7.15
September 24, 1931	7.07

The ten largest rises in the FT-SE 100 Index

Date	Index Value	Change
21 Oct 1987	1943.8	142.2
l0 Apr 1992	2572.6	136.2
17 Sep 1992	2483.9	105.6
18 Sep 1992	2567.0	83.1
7 Jul 1955	3462.9	74.5
5 Oct 1990	2143.9	73.5
31 Dec 1991	2493.1	73.1
3 Sep 1992	2381.9	68.9
30 Oct 1987	1749.8	67.8
1 Dec 1993	3233.2	66.3

 The continuing strength of companies like General Motors and Marks and Spencer shows that sound businesses will survive this kind of market turbulence and move on to greater successes. The collapse of specific businesses or commercial fortunes seldom offers the same opportunity for recovery except for the very largest organizations or where failure is largely a technical matter.

Bankruptcy

 The world's biggest bankruptcy was declared by Texaco was under the terms of the US Chapter 11 legislation which allows the company to con-

Tulipomania

Robert Beckman in his fascinating book *Crashes* states that the very first market crash that is well-documented occurred in the Dutch tulip market in the 1630s. Tulips had grown in popularity since their introduction into Europe in the 1570s. It was, however, the creation of a range of specialists in 'exotic' blooms that boosted the market. The 1620s saw demand for exotics like the Royal Queen Magenta, the Van Tromp and the General Bol increase steadily. Regular markets in bulbs were created in Amsterdam, Rotterdam, Leiden, Alkmaar and Hoorn. A futures market was created to cope with the surge in demand during the 1630s. Prices were doubling and trebling almost monthly during most of 1636 but the collapse started late in that year. Prices dropped even more quickly. In just three weeks at the end of the year prices dropped by 40 per cent.

tinue trading while the immediate causes of the financial difficulties are resolved. Texaco's immediate problems derived from the decision by Judge Solomon Casseb Jnr. on 10 Dec. 1985 that Texaco had used unethical practices to break up the proposed merger between Pennzoil and Getty Oil. This judgement required Texaco to pay $11,120M to Pennzoil. The dispute was eventually resolved out-of-court on the 10 Dec. 1995 when Texaco agreed to pay $5,500M.

The largest financial services bankruptcy was filed by the US securities firm Drexel Burnham Lambert in February 1990. Drexel Burnham Lambert declared itself bankrupt with liabilities of $3Bn, following the $650M fine imposed on the firm in December 1988 for insider trading. This was **the largest ever fine**. Drexel's employee Michael Milliken shared this dubious honour when he faced **the greatest ever fine imposed on an individual** – $200M on 24 April 1990. The largest fine

The world's largest public bankruptcies

Company	Bankruptcy date	Assets before bankruptcy ($Bn)	Adjusted for inflation 1995 ($Bn)
Texaco	1987	35.89	47.5
Penn Central	1970	6.85	24.9
Baldwin United	1983	9.38	14.4
Federated Department Stores	1990	7.91	9.8
Continental Airlines Holdings	1990	7.66	9.1
LTV Corp.	1986	6.31	8.6
Olympia & York Development Ltd	1992	7.02	7.6
Maxwell Communication Corp.	1991	6.35	7.0
Columbia Gas System	1991	6.19	6.9
R. H. Macy & Co. Inc.	1992	4.81	5.3

Source: *The 1995 Bankruptcy Year Book,* New Generation Research

Insider Trading

Insider trading occurs when people with privileged information use this to trade in stocks and shares. The classic example of insider trading occurs when directors of companies use 'inside' information to trade in shares of the company. A director may be aware that another firm is making a takeover bid for the firm. This will push the share price up so the directors, or their agents, buy shares at the current, low price to sell them at a higher price in the future. Similarly, directors might know of major problems facing the company. This will force share prices down. Directors selling their shares at such a time will get a better price than others who sell later when the crisis is exposed.

In the UK and the USA, the responsibilities of directors are being specified with increasing rigour following a series of cases where directors used their 'inside' information to gain special advantages. The Business Roundtable in the USA and in the UK, a series of reports first by Sir Adrian Cadbury and later by Sir Richard Greenbury, have sought to identify 'rules' to govern the behaviour of directors.

ever imposed on an individual in Britain was the $7.5M fine imposed on Gerald Ronson. This was, however, subsequently overturned on appeal.

Europe's largest bankruptcy was Maxwell Communications which crashed in December 1992. Prior to its collapse,

Maxwell Communications had stated assets of $6.35Bn.

Japan's biggest bankruptcy was Sanko Steamship. Sanko was the world's largest operator of oil tankers when it failed in

Wall Street, New York, the world's financial heart. (Gamma).

Public companies and assets filing for bankruptcy (USA) 1980–1994

Year	Number of companies	Assets ($M)	Average assets ($M)
1980	62	1671	27
1981	74	4703	64
1982	84	9103	108
1983	89	12,523	141
1984	121	6530	54
1985	149	5831	39
1986	149	13,033	87
1987	112	41,503	371
1988	122	43,488	356
1989	135	71,371	529
1990	115	82,781	720
1991	125	83,202	666
1992	91	54,283	597
1993	86	16,752	195
1994	70	8336	119
15 Year Total	**1584**	**455,110**	**272**

Source: *The 1995 Bankruptcy Yearbook,* New Generation Research

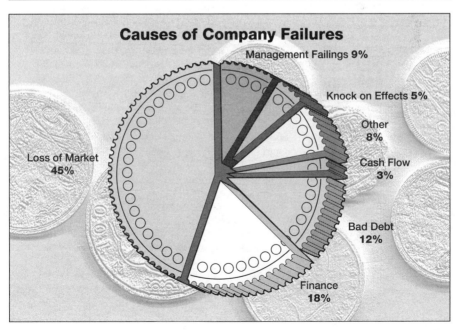

Causes of Company Failures

Management Failings **9%**

Knock on Effects **5%**

Other **8%**

Loss of Market **45%**

Cash Flow **3%**

Bad Debt **12%**

Finance **18%**

August 1985 having accumulated losses of $715Bn between 1983 and 1985. At the end of July 1985, its total debts to banks and finance companies exceeded $2.2Bn.

The largest fine imposed on a British company was the $32M imposed on British Steel by the European Community on 16 February 1994 for colluding in price fixing during the 1980s.

The causes of corporate failure are often a mixture of commercial and legal factors. The commercial conditions are typically a mixture of depressed markets and high interest rates hitting a company which has grown rapidly through acquisitions, which, in turn, have stretched the firm's financial reserves beyond their ability to service their debts. Shrewd observers often quote the rhyme – turnover is vanity; profits are sanity; cash is reality – in the aftermath of these failures.

The legal environment also has an effect. In some countries, e.g. the USA, it is relatively easy to declare a business or person bankrupt, and the penalties are mild. In contrast, countries like Germany have harsh penalties and strict rules.

Risk of bankruptcy by occupation or business sector (UK)

Sector	Per cent total bankruptcies
Self-employed / unemployed	26.2
Retailing	23.1
Construction	16.0
Road haulage	7.6
Hotels & restaurants	3.2
Company directors	3.1
Garages	2.9
Professional services	2.7
Other	15.2
Total	**100**

Britain's biggest bankrupts

Individual	Year	Debt ($M)
Kevin Maxwell	1992	$633
Asil Nadir	1991	$590
George Walker	1993	$281
William Stern	1978	$267
Rajendra Sethia	1985	$246
Selig Waldman	1992	$179
Safiye Nadir	1991	$114
Paul Bloomfield	1992	$94
Roger Levitt	1992	$78
Ali Farhani	1990	$53

The worst years in the postwar era for bankruptcies among public companies in the United States were 1985 and 1986, when 149 public companies, with combined assets of $5.8Bn and $13.1Bn respectively, failed. These figures for assets were dwarfed in 1991 when 125 public companies with total assets of $83.2Bn failed.

The worst year for all types of bankruptcies was 1993 when there were almost 500,000 bankruptcies in the industrially developed world. The USA accounted for the largest number of these failures with over 200,000 bankruptcies, and the same year saw 50,000 bankruptcies in the UK. This is ten times the record for prewar bankruptcies, which was 5048 bankruptcies in 1923; this record stood for fifty years until 1974 when 5,608 bankruptcies were recorded.

The main stated reason for company failure is loss of market followed by financial problems.
Bankruptcy is closely linked with the failures of individuals. **The world's greatest bankrupt** seemed to be Donald Trump, whose business seemed to be on the point

Asil Nadir

Asil Nadir (b. 1941) founded the Polly Peck Corporation, which had the highest performing share on the British Stock Market during the 1980s, but collapsed in 1991. In a short period of time, Nadir moved from being listed as one of Britain's richest men, with an estimated fortune in 1990 of over $1.5Bn, to a defender in a series of bankruptcy suites.

Asil Nadir's story is hard to separate from the history of Polly Peck, the firm he built into a global enterprise. Nadir was born in Lefke, Cyprus, the son of Turkish Cypriot parents. After his education in Cyprus and Turkey, he followed his father to Britain where he had migrated to escape ethnic conflict in Cyprus. Nadir founded Nadir Fashions in 1965 but merged it into a larger enterprise, Wearwell Clothing in 1967. He acquired Polly Peck, a small clothing company, with an offer of 9p per share in 1980. In subsequent publicity, Polly Peck claimed that anyone buying $150 worth of shares in 1980 would have held shares worth $1.5M in 1990 – one of the fastest capital gains in modern stock market history.

During the 1980s, Polly Peck was one of the most popular shares on the UK Stock Market. The price of its shares grew until they peaked at 462p (720c) on 8 June 1990. Its portfolio of activities expanded to include textiles, fruit growing, processing and distribution, domestic appliances, electronics, hotels and leisure interests. Sharp increases in its share prices were characteristic of the company even when it became heavily burdened with debt and was seeking new shareholder support. From the end of 1979 to late 1980, for example, shares increased in value by 2708 per cent. During the 1980s, the price of Polly Peck shares and its range of activities increased despite a series of crises of which the most notable were in 1982/83 and 1985.

The crisis which destroyed the group was precipitated by a series of internal and external events including the Gulf War and Nadir's failed attempt to take the Group off the Stock Exchange and turn it into a private company. The scale of the Group's debts were exposed by these events.

Problems were heightened by a series of interventions by the UK's regulatory, fraud and tax authorities. Initially, Nadir seemed determined to fight these claims. In 1993, however, he fled to Northern Cyprus claiming a massive international conspiracy to ruin him and destroy his company. Many of the major parts of the former Polly Peck group were eventually sold off.

of collapse when his Taj Mahal Casino in Atlantic City (New Jersey) filed for bankruptcy on August 28th, 1991. His total debts were estimated at $2.5Bn. Despite that, his business affairs seem to have recovered. If he succeeds, this will probably be **the greatest, personal financial recovery in history.**

Trump has apparently added a new dimension to the maxim – if you owe a banker a hundred dollars, you have a problem. If you owe a banker a million dollars, he has a problem. Now it seems if you owe your bankers a billion dollars, the banking system has a problem.

Britain's biggest bankrupt is Kevin Maxwell. The collapse of Maxwell Communications and its associated businesses left him with over $600M of debt. It had taken only a year for the previous greatest bankrupt – Asil Nadir – to be overtaken. Before them, the greatest British bankrupt was William Stern. His businesses failed in 1974 leaving him with personal debts of $250M.

The Maxwell family saw **the sharpest drop in the value of personal assets in the UK** when the value of their holdings in Maxwell Communications and Mirror Group

Newspapers slumped from $1.5Bn to nothing between 1989 and 1992. This drop was four times that experienced by their nearest rival Tiny Rowland, whose shares in Lonrho declined in value by $300M during the same period. Since then, the recovery in share values have eliminated most of Rowland's losses.

The risk of bankruptcy varies considerably by industry and location. In the UK, more bankruptcies occur among the self-employed than any group. The most 'at risk' commercial sector is retailing, while the London and the South East of England dominate the regional rankings.

Profits can be made from recovery. **The sharpest profit speculation in UK business history** came after the collapse of Rolls-Royce, whose collapse in 1971, was associated with a record estimated cash shortfall of $250M. On 4 October 1971, the Rolls-Royce accounts showed debts of $240M and $120M in assets for unsecured creditors. Share dealing was suspended when the share price dropped to 0.5p, but those shareholders who hung on saw a dramatic turnaround. The British government paid $100M for the aero engine developments and $35M was realized by floating Rolls-Royce Motors. An additional $140 was received from debtors, producing a surplus of $75M for ordinary shareholders. Anyone buying the shares at 0.5p was paid 58.1p, making an 11,600 per cent profit in less than five years.

The Barings collapse

There is little hope of this kind of improvement after the collapse of one of Britain's oldest banks. Baring Brothers and Co Ltd faced losses of $1.3Bn after Nick Leeson – a Singapore-based derivatives trader – wildly miscalculated movement on the Japanese markets. At the heart of the Barings collapse are some familiar prob-

Derivatives

Derivatives are financial instruments that are derived from other financial instruments e.g. shares, options or futures. Derivatives trading occurs between two parties when they enter into trading arrangements based on their assumptions about the future performance of the underlying assets, such as movements in the stock market.

lems of failed companies. There was rapid growth during the 1980s, which had been based on an experienced team of derivatives traders which broke up at the end of the decade.

Despite that, the bank still pressed on with its growing derivatives business in the Far East and its operations grew rapidly during the early 1990s.

Nick Leeson
on the flight back to
Singapore to face trial.
(Rex Features London).

History repeats itself?
Barings and the River Plate
loan crisis of 1889–90

The Barings crisis of 1890 resulted from the bank's overexposure in loans to the countries bordering on the River Plate – notably Argentina – with whom Britain's trade had boomed during the late 1870s and 1880s. This boom was fuelled by the exploitation of raw material deposits and demand for British-made manufactured products. Argentina with its vast natural resources seemed to be an especially attractive source of opportunity for speculators. The country rapidly increased its indebtedness to meet the new demands on its exchequer. Debts increased sevenfold in the decade up to 1889 when they stood at the unprecedented level of £70M. Barings' liabilities were over £21M, which was far more than the firm could support.

On this occasion, William Lidderdale, the Governor of the Bank of England, intervened to avert a crisis that he believed would undermine the credibility of the British banking system. He immediately raised £1.5M in gold by selling Exchequer bonds to the State Bank of Russia. He then borrowed £3M from the Bank of France, using the Rothschilds as his agent. Lidderdale ignored the refusal of the Chancellor of the Exchequer to support Barings and organized a consortium of banks and other financial institutions led by Rathbones of Liverpool. This raised a guarantee fund of £7M. Lidderdale managed this between close of business at 5 p.m. on Friday and noon on Saturday – this was perhaps the fastest and most effective intervention in a UK banking crisis by a Governor of The Bank of England.

Barings was reconstructed as a joint stock bank. By 1894, every advance made to Barings by the guarantee fund was paid off and the guarantors were released from all responsibilities.

Disappearing banks

The US banking crisis of the early 1930s saw the destruction of more banks than at any other period in history. These collapses were linked with the crash of 1929, but the epidemic of closures was affected by a mixture of falling farm prices, declining confidence and international speculation.

Over five hundred banks failed during 1929 but the problems grew in 1930 and 1931 as farm prices remained low and investors remained wary of any risk. Federal government intervention through the Reconstruction Finance Corporation (RFC) seem to improve things in 1932, but the real crisis occurred when the extent of RFC loans in its first six months exposed the problems facing the banking sector.

The initial crisis was confined to small towns and local banks, but soon spread to bigger cities like St Louis and Cleveland. Initially the largest cities seemed immune but in February 1933 Detroit was hit by the combined effect of a sales slump for cars and the banking crisis. The Governor of Michigan ordered the closure of all banks in the state on 14th February 1933. This precipitated a national crisis. Between the Governor's decision and the end of February, nine states called banking holidays to stem the haemorrhage of funds, and in the first few days of March sixteen states took similar steps.

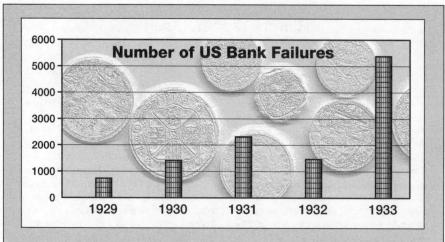

By the inauguration of President Roosevelt (in March 1933), only ten US states had a banking system that was operating normally. On Sunday, 5 March 1933 Roosevelt closed every bank in the USA for the first time in history. It took a week to sort out the situation and the banks started reopening on the 13th March.

The mid 1980s saw the most recent emergency in the US banking system. The collapse of Continental Illinois and then ESM Government Securities was part of an emergency that saw 138 US banks fail in 1985 and 126 banks fail in 1986. The difficulties of the savings and loans banks in the USA are estimated to have cost the US taxpayer billions of dollars.

Source: Derived from Beckman, R. *Crashes*

The worst six months in modern international banking

Date	Event
November, 1994	George Soros announces losses of $600M through miscalculating the strength of the Japanese yen
December, 1994	The Municipality of Orange County, California announces losses of $1.7Bn on derivatives
February, 1995	Barings, a 233 year old institution, is forced into bankruptcy following $1.3 Bn losses on derivatives
March, 1995	Procter & Gamble announces losses of $102M on derivatives bought from Bankers Trust Co.
April, 1995	Kidder Peabody broken up and sold by General Electric amid claims that the actions of one member of staff led to a shortfall of $210M

Problems occurred when Nick Leeson shifted his stance from arbitrage – buying futures on one exchange and hedging the risk by selling them on another – to speculation.

With arbitrage, the returns are relatively small. They occur on the margin between the price paid and the price obtained in deals that take place almost simultaneously. Instead, Mr Leeson speculated that the Japanese market would move consistently in a specific direction i.e. upwards. This was against the recent trends on the Tokyo exchanges and offered scope for massive gains if Leeson was right. Instead, the exchange stayed weak and slumped badly after the Kobe earthquake.

Barings was left with major commitments which inevitably meant huge losses as

prices in the Tokyo market dropped. The second feature of a likely disaster showed itself in the poor management controls which failed to identify likely problems in time and respond quickly. The bank's failure was almost inevitable under these circumstances.

The Mississippi Bubble

At the start of the 18th century, France had its own version of the South Sea Bubble. The 'Mississippi Bubble' centred on the efforts of John Law to solve France's financial problems by creating a central bank and a trade in paper money. The effects of its collapse had a far greater effect upon France than the failure of the South Sea Company did upon England. It meant, for example, that France lacked a central bank for a crucial period of its economic rivalry with Britain, and left the French financial system highly fragmented with centres at Lyon, Rouen and elsewhere vying for leadership. It is also said to explain the traditional reluctance of the French peasant to put much faith in paper money.

John Law was a Scottish financier and gambler who persuaded Philippe, Duke of Orléans and regent of France during the childhood of Louis XV, to let him tackle the problems of the massive deficits in royal finances. The total deficit, at the time, was 3 billion livres – today's equivalent is about $200Bn. This is probably the largest peacetime debt ever accumulated by a national government and it is certainly comparable with the US national debt during the late 1980s.

Law's solution or 'system' was to create a national bank that would offer paper money capable of being redeemed on demand by silver coins at the value on the note at their date of issue. The notes were thus a perfect hedge against inflation besides acting as a means to improve national liquidity and stimulate economic growth. The Banque Générale was an immediate success when

it opened in May 1716. Inflation dropped from 30 per cent per annum to 4 per cent. Branches of the bank were opened in Amiens, La Rochelle, Lyon and Tours.

The Banque Générale rapidly expanded its activities especially through its monopoly of trade with the French possessions in North America. Despite opposition, the bank continued to prosper and it became the world's first central bank when Banque Générale's assets were absorbed by the newly created Banque Royale in 1718. A year later, the 'system' was extended to include the newly formed Companie des Indes and a monopoly over national tax collection for the next nine years. Law, also, offered to repay the French national debt.

Share prices began to surge: during 1719, prices increased tenfold. The area around the bank's headquarters in Rue Quincampoix became a major commercial centre. The first dividend was declared at 40 per cent, which pushed share prices even higher until they was a gain of 4000 per cent on the 1716 price. The collapse was precipitated by the decision of two members of the royal family to exercise their rights under the system and convert their paper money to gold and silver coin. A run started and the resources did not exist to meet the promises. Law responded by a massive devaluation in the value of the notes. Share prices dropped by seventy five per cent in three months. The Banque Royale eventually suspended trading and closed its door on 10 October 1720.

Source: Beckman, R. *Crashes*

A third common feature of a commercial failure is a reluctance to learn from the problems of others. Four years earlier, Allied Lyons had suffered the, then, greatest loss by a UK company from currency speculation – $220M from "dealings in currency instruments". Only a year before Barings faced its difficulties, the German industrial group Metallgesellschaft reported the largest foreign exchange losses by a European company when it reported a deficit of $1Bn on derivatives trading in international markets. The collapse of Barings saw the demise of **the UK's oldest independent investment firm.**

The failure of Barings following disastrous overseas trading is an unusual example of history repeating itself. In 1890, Barings came close to collapse after becoming over exposed through large-scale lending to Argentina. On that occasion, the Bank of England organized a consortium of banks led by Rathbone Brothers of Liverpool to rescue Barings. In 1995, no such rescue was possible. It required the Dutch bank ING to take over the bank to keep much of its operations intact and keep the losses of investors to a minimum.

Banking crises

Orange County's losses (see p.168) led to **the biggest municipal bankruptcy in history.**

The line between failure and success in business can be very fine. Perhaps the earliest victim of this delicate balancing act in the postindustrial world was Samuel Crompton (1753–1827). His invention of the 'spinning mule' was one of the most important developments of the first Industrial Revolution, but Crompton had little money to exploit his invention and sold the patent for £67. Later, Parliament made him an award of £5000. Despite that, his business failures led him to die a very poor man.

 In the third quarter of the nineteenth century, the collapse of the Crédit Mobilier de Paris ruined the Péreire brothers. The brothers had played a key part in the industrialization of France: Emile developed some of the most important early French railways; Isaac Péreire was instrumental in reorganizing the supply of gas to Paris. The entire Crédit Mobilier structure collapsed when the brothers overstretched their resources by, among other things, investing in the creation of the Russian railway system. At the same time, they alienated both the Rothschilds and the Bank of France. Shortly before the Industrial Exhibition of 1867, the Péreire brothers' credit collapsed. The brothers were ruined and the bank's shares dropped from 1,982 francs a share to 140 francs in **the most spectacular financial crash in 19th century France.**

Losses

Railway 'fever' during the 19th century was closely linked with individual and corporate success and failure. The ruin of George Hudson, one of the most important English railway promoters during the 1830s and 1840s, brought to an end the

Famous bankrupts

Individual	Cause of loss	Debts
Charles Goodyear	Battle to protect patents on vulcanized rubber	$200,000
Mark Twain	Investments in failed inventions	$250,000
Phineas Barnum	Swindled	$400,000
Walt Disney	Failure of his Laugh O Gram Co. of Kansas City	$15,000

first phase of railway building in Britain. In North America, Jay Gould, the 'prince of railway, robber barons', was said to have "compromised or ruined" every enterprise with which he was associated. His attempt to corner the gold market prompted the 'Black Monday' stock market collapse of September 1869. Despite this, Gould was worth $100M when he died in 1892.

Gould's fortune rivalled that of his contemporary – Cornelius 'Commodore' Vanderbilt. His life and that of his descendants vividly illustrates the extent to which business creates both opportunities for wealth and the attendant risks. The Commodore is said to have told his son William that "any fool can make a fortune. It takes a man of brains to hold on to it after it is made". His son William evidently learned the lesson. In **the most spectacular improvement in a great fortune**, he doubled the $100M he was left within 10 years. The truth of the Commodore's saying was confirmed within three generations. When his grandson Neily died, in perhaps the most dramatic example of the collapse of a great fortune, the net value of his estate was $150.

The law and damages

Highs and lows were seen as integral parts of commercial life in the last century. The law was seldom seen as a major source of redress. In perhaps the best summary of this philosophy Commodore Vanderbilt once wrote to a rival "You have betrayed me. I will not sue you – I will ruin you". On another occasion he is said to have commented "What do I care about the Law. H'aint I got the power". This disdain for the law and lawyers is no longer sustainable in a world in which lawyers play a major part in an increasingly litigious business community.

Vanderbilt was one of a generation of notorious robber barons. Along with John D Rockefeller, Jay Gould, Washington Duke, James J. Hill and Leland Stanford, he was not only one of the richest men in history but one of the most notorious.

Fortune magazine recently identified Robert Maxwell as the most notorious of today's business people.

Only two years before the crisis at Barings, another established London financial institution faced a comparable crisis. In this case, the crisis was provoked not by speculation but by a legal decision. In October 1993, Mr Justice Gatehouse made the largest ever commercial award against a UK bank when he ordered Samuel Montague to pay $300M to the creditors of the collapsed British and Commonwealth Holdings. The award seemed set to make Ian McIntosh the author of the five most expensive words in the English language. The suit turned on his comment to Richard Heley of British and Commonwealth's Merchant bank BZW. Heley had asked whether Samuel Montague's clients – Quadrex – could fund their $400M bid for British and Commonwealth Holdings. McIntosh replied that "They're good for the money". When Justice Gatehouse made his award these five words had a face value of $60M each.

The scale of these and other business losses has increased the interest and involvement of the legal profession. This is especially true in the United States where a tradition of litigiousness and allied specific legislation, such as that on product liability, makes businesses' legal costs the highest in the world. The tort system, i.e. the rules governing product liability, medical malpractice and other personal injuries, costs US business roughly $180Bn per year. This figure has increased by almost a third over the last decade.

US industry faces **the highest insurance bills in the world** – $24Bn a year. **The largest civil damages ever awarded** were the $11.12Bn awarded against Texaco, but it was eventually agreed that Texaco would pay the plaintiffs, Pennzoil, $5.5Bn.

The largest damages against a private individual were the $2.1Bn awarded against Charles H Keating Jnr. on 10 July 1992. Keating was ordered to pay this sum

Bhopal

Bhopal, a city of just over 1,000,000 people, is the capital of the state of Madhya Pradesh in India. The city was governed for almost a hundred years by a series of women rulers, or begums, and had a good reputation for advancing women's rights and education. Bhopal sprang to international prominence in December 1984 when it was the scene of the world's most deadly chemical accident: the disaster killed 2500 people and left over 200,000 maimed and injured.

The factory involved in the accident was operated by the US chemical giant Union Carbide. The plant produced an essential component, called Sevin (part of the chemical family of carbamates) in a type of insec-

ticide. In the course of the Bhopal disaster the accidental injection of water into a tank of methyl isocyanate, the chemical used to make Sevin, produced a cloud of toxic gas which killed and injured many living around the plant.

The problems were made worse by previous failure to clear away the shanty town that had been set up around the factory. This meant that the worst tragedies hit the poorest members of the local community. Poor communication and lack of prior warning of the potential hazards were, also, claimed as major contributory factors in the tragedy. In 1989, the Indian Supreme Court imposed the largest civil fine ($470M) in Indian history on Union Carbide.

to 23,000 small investors defrauded by his company – Lincoln Savings and Law of Los Angeles, California. **The largest international award against a company** was the $470M that Union Carbide agreed to pay the Indian Government to compensate the people of Bhopal.

The largest law suit ever sought to date is the $675 trillion action brought by I. Walton Bader in 1971 against General Motors for polluting all 50 US states. In March 1994 a group of US lawyers presented a class-action lawsuit "on behalf of everyone who has ever been addicted to

Texaco and Pennzoil – the largest civil settlement

The early 1980s saw an increase in the business pressures on the oil industry and a spate of mergers and acquisitions. This prompted several oil companies to approach the larger shareholders of Getty Oil, mainly members of the Getty family, about merging or acquiring the company. It appears that a deal was done between Gordon Getty, J. Paul Getty's son, and Pennzoil, a large independent oil company led by Hugh Leidtke.

Shortly afterwards, it seems that Texaco gained some information on the deal agreed between Getty and Leidtke and made a superior counter offer. Getty accepted this proposal which gave the

shareholders $10.2Bn for their holdings. It was, at the time, the largest takeover offer in history.

Pennzoil reacted by accusing Texaco of adopting unethical tactics to prevent its merger with Getty. Its case was successful when Judge Solomon Casseb, Jnr., ruled in favour of Pennzoil at his court in Houston in December 1985. The decision provoked a major crisis in Texaco as the firm was in the process of renegotiating its relations with the government of Saudi Arabia, a major source of its supplies. Eventually, an out-of-court settlement was produced in which Pennzoil won $5.5Bn in compensation but Texaco retained its holdings in Getty Oil.

The world's most expensive lawyers

Nation	Billing $ per hour (1992)
UK	585
Germany	510
Switzerland	445
Liechtenstein	400
Austria	385
Sweden	373
Japan	350
Macao	350
Hong Kong	325
Belgium	313

Despite the scale of the US settlements, North American lawyers are not among the highest paid in the world.

Increasingly the financial advisors, accountants and audits of companies are being challenged in the courts over their roles in ensuring proper stewardship and reporting. **The largest award in history against accountants and auditors** was the $400M awarded against Ernst & Young for its role in various savings and loans banks in Tennessee and others. The figure awarded against Ernst & Young is tiny when compared with the estimated industry losses of between $75–$100Bn in the Savings and Loans crisis in the USA (1985–86), which is **the largest domestic financial failure in history**. These are estimates put before the US Congress of the likely costs of resolving this failure. The failure of the Bank of Credit and Commerce International cost UK local authorities $150M.

smoking". This action seeks over $100 trillion. The largest delayed action award for product liability was made in 1891. A press manufactured in 1890 for embossing book covers crushed the fingers of a young printer. Harris Corporation of the USA, which had taken over the original producers, were made to pay the injured person $700,000 in compensation.

The greatest bank fraud in history occurred in the Atlanta (Georgia, USA) branch of the Banca Nazionale del Lavoro. On the 6th September 1989, the bank admitted that it had been defrauded of $3Bn through unauthorized loan commitments to Iraq.

Tiny Rowland and the Al-Fayeds

What was probably the longest row in British business history ended in 1993 when Tiny Rowland of Lonrho and Mohamed al-Fayed of Harrods made peace. The row had lasted the best part of a decade and cost Lonrho around $60M and Fayed a similar sum.

The original battle started over control of the House of Fraser Store Group which owned Harrods. It extended to raise questions about the financial status of the different parties and their credibility as business leaders. It was alleged that Rowland seemed at times to use his control of The

Observer newspaper to extend the battle while the Fayeds hung a model shark in the Harrods Food hall to symbolize the battle.

Eventually, the conflict was resolved at a ceremony in the Food Hall. Both sides explained that their differences were resolved. Together they took down the stuffed shark called Tiny and the smaller one it was eating, and dispatched it to the Harrods museum.

Source: *Sunday Times*

Computers make frauds on this scale much easier than in the past. **The largest admitted lost** was acknowledged by Equity Funding of America, which confessed that it had lost $2Bn (current value $7Bn) on fake insurance policies issued between 1964 and 1973. Many of the biggest losses are covered by insurance.

Catastrophes

The world's worst catastrophe of insured damage was Hurricane Andrew, which passed over the Bahamas, South Florida and Louisiana, and cost an estimated $15Bn in 1992. The second largest was the Californian earthquake of 1994. **The largest British loss** was the South Coast storm of 1987 which cost £2.6Bn

The largest marine insurance loss was $836 million for the Piper Alpha disaster in the North Sea, July 6, 1988. **The largest terrestrial loss** was the Union Carbide methylisocyanate plant explosion in Bhopal, India. The total insured loss was $780 million. **The most costly disaster in real terms** was the Exxon Valdez oil spill which eventually cost around $20Bn.

World's worst catastrophes (by insured damage)

Event	Cost	Year
Hurricane Andrew	$15.5Bn	1992
Californian Earthquake	$11.2Bn	1994
Florida Floods	$8.5Bn	1994
Hurricane Gilbert	$6Bn	1967
Hurricane Hugo	$5Bn	1989
Exxon Valdez Oil Spill	$4.75Bn	1990
Typhoon Mireille	$4.5 Bn	1988
Daria Winter Storm	$4.5 Bn	1990
Enchova Oil Platform	$4Bn	1989
South Coast Storms	$3.8 Bn	1987

Oil pollution at sea off Kuwait: an estimated 816,000 tonnes of oil were deliberately released in January 1991 during the Gulf War. The oil, which was up to 432 mm (17 in) thick in places, spread over some 644 km (400 miles) of coastline. (Gamma).

The Valdez Principles

The Valdez Principles (unveiled in September 1989) were drawn up by an alliance of environmental groups, bankers and investment fund managers known as the Coalition for Environmentally Responsible Economies, which came together after the Exxon Valdez oil spill. The Principles are guidelines for corporate conduct to protect the environment. The Coalition's main aim is to monitor corporate compliance with the principles, publicize their findings and encourage others to invest only in, and buy from, such companies whenever possible.

The real cost of the Exxon Valdez oil spill

Item	Cost ($M)
Clean up	2250
Fines	2000
Loss of market share	1750
Disruptions to supplies	750
Compliance with new regulations	500
TOTAL	**7250**
Discount on Exxon shares	10–15,000
Grand Total	**$17,500-11,500M***

* Shares were trading at a premium of $2–4 before the spill and a discount of $6–8 after the spill

Increasing numbers of awards, costs and fines are linked with environmental pollution. The US Oil Pollution Act gave the US government the power to award unlimited liability on tanker owners for the harm done by spills – this followed the Exxon Valdez disaster (see above).

In Britain, British Coal heads the league table of prosecutions by the National Rivers Authority for environmental damage.

8

The Key Sectors

The primary industries – agriculture, fisheries, forestry, hunting, mining and other extractive industries – are **the oldest forms of commercial activity.** The first farmers who exchanged surpluses from their farms for meat or skins from hunters, were engaging in a system of trade that persists to today. **The largest barter trade in history** – between Royal Saudi Arabian Airlines and Boeing – was part of the same basic system of trading. Royal Saudi Arabian Airlines exchanged 36 million barrels of oil, each valued at $1300 for ten Boeing 747s in July 1984.

The past

The earliest form of manufacturing – of handmade tools – about 600,000 BC was the production of flint tools and arrowheads to meet the needs of hunters and farmers. The emergence of the earliest craftsmen coincided with the first sustained agricultural surpluses in the Mesopotamian Delta. **The earliest reliable evidence of harvesting of cereal crops** dates from around 9000 BC around Jericho in Palestine.

A Boeing 747. Boeing made the biggest barter deal in history in 1984 with Royal Saudi Airlines. (Lufthansa/Ann Ronan at Image Select)

The earliest crops and livestock

Item	Location	Date
Cereals	Palestine	c. 9000 BC
Peas and lentils	S. Iran, Syria, Palestine	c. 8000 BC
Beans and squashes	S. America	c. 7500 BC
Taro	New Guinea	c. 7000 BC
Sheep and goats	Syria	c. 7000 BC
Rice	China	c. 7000 BC
Cattle and pigs	Turkey	c. 6500 BC
Potatoes	Peru	c. 6000 BC

Source: James, P. and Thorpe, N. Ancient Inventions

Successful farming was linked with the growth of other business activities and invention. There is evidence that **the first ploughs** were in relatively widespread use by around 3000 BC by which time livestock were already being used to pull both ploughs and carts, to help with cultivation and harvest as well as for their wool, fur, skin and meat.

The earliest evidence of farming in mainland Britain is at Freshwater West, Pembrokeshire, which dates back to around 5000 BC. Land ownership records are difficult to prove, but the Swedish firm Atvidaberg Industries is better known for its mining interests but was involved in farming for some time before 1419 when it started to mine copper.

 The oldest continuing agricultural enterprise is the Reichsgraph von Kesselstatt vineyard near Trier, Germany, which has been in the same family since 1377. The Burgerspital zum Heiligen Geist vineyard near Würzburg in Germany claims a longer history but it is owned by a hospital not a family. Even greater age is claimed for the producers of the Cyprus Commanderie wines which are said to come from a vineyard that supplied wine to King Richard I of England (1157–99). **The oldest vineyard in North America** was founded at the Mission San Diego in 1769. Two years later the oldest surviving US vineyard was established. **The oldest Australian vineyard** is B. Seppelt and Sons Pty, Ltd which was founded in 1851.

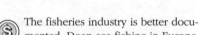 The fisheries industry is better documented. Deep-sea fishing in Europe dates back to around 5000 BC. There is evidence from Stone Age sites in Ireland and Scotland of large quantities of deep-sea fish such as cod. **The oldest paddle for a boat** was found at Star Carr, North Yorkshire, and dates back to 8500 BC. The Faversham Oyster Fishery Company (Kent, England) is oldest company in this sector for which reasonable records exist. Existing data suggests that the firm was founded around 1189, but for much of its history it was more of a guild than a company. **The oldest continuing North American fisheries enterprise**, the Hudson's Bay Company, was established in 1670 primarily to exploit the fishing and trapping opportunities in Canada.

The commercial exploitation of timber was initially linked with its use for other processes. The ancient Swedish company Stora Kopparbergs Aktiebolag was primarily involved in the mining and processing of copper but exploited the local forests to meet its needs. Another Swedish company A-B Billingsfors-Langed is **the oldest timber company in the world**. It was founded in 1738 near Lake Väner in central Sweden. **The oldest North American timber company** is the Price Company of Quebec, founded in 1816.

Evidence of hunting goes back to the origins of humanity. Commercial hunting on land peaked during the eighteenth and nineteen century with the exploitation of the animal stock of North America. William Cody (1846–1917), also known as Buffalo Bill, is reported to have killed 5000 buffalo in 18 months as part of his contract to supply meat to the Kansas Pacific Railway. The oldest company with a major historic involvement in hunting is the Hudson's Bay Company.

The Hudson's Bay Company

The Hudson's Bay Company owes its origins to two French Huguenot fur traders, Pierre Esprit de Radisson and Médart Chouart de Groseilliers, who were among the first to open up the north and west of Canada and bought a fortune in furs from the Indians. On their return to Quebec most of their furs were confiscated by government officials and they returned to France to plead their case. However, the French court refused to hear their appeals. They, then, went to England, where they told King Charles II of the riches to be won in Canada.

The king granted a charter to his cousin, Prince Rupert of the Palatinate, and 17 associates including de Groseilliers to open up Canada for England. Charles II granted this charter despite England conceding to France all rights to Canada at the Treaty of St. Germain-en-Laye (1632). The charter created the "Governor and Company of Adventurers of England trading into Hudson's Bay" and gave them sole rights of trade in the "Great Lone Land" – the lands drained by rivers and streams flowing into Hudson Bay. At the time no-one realized the vast extent of what became known as Rupert's Land, a territory covering Ontario, Quebec (north of the Laurentian Mountains and west of Labrador), all of Manitoba, most of Saskatchewan, and the southern half of Alberta.

The Company, which was incorporated by Royal Charter on 21 May 1670, was set up to trade in furs with the indigenous people of North America. Its early years were marked by fierce struggles with the French and later with its Canadian rival, the North West Company.

The Hudson's Bay Company operated out of trading forts such as the Albany, the Nelson, the Churchill and the Severn. Typically these were at junctions of rivers such as the Moose River. The North West Company's main centre was at Fort William on Lake Superior. Between them these corporations administered the land as well as holding monopoly trading rights over a vast part of Canada, including part of the northwestern United States, and up to the Arctic Circle.

The two companies were eventually merged by Act of Parliament which still gave the new company sweeping trading rights over virtually all of Canada excluding the Great Lakes area and the Maritime Provinces. This made it the largest private landowner in history. It was eventually forced to give up its rights by the Deed of Surrender of 1869 (confirmed by an Act of Parliament in 1870), selling its chartered lands to the new Dominion of Canada in return for a one-off payment of $1.5M and 1.42 million hectares (3.5 million acres) of farmland in the western prairies. At the time it was the largest farming concern in the world. Subsequently all the Company's land was sold, but it retained some mineral rights and was for many years the world's largest single dealer in furs.

In the early years of the 20th century, the Hudson's Bay Company began to expand

Canadian fur trappers working for the Hudson's Bay Company,
from an illustration published in Paris in 1879.
(Ann Ronan).

its wholesale and retail activities to operate large modern department stores in major cities and suburban areas. In 1970 it received supplemental charters as a Canadian company, and its headquarters were transferred from London to Canada. In 1987 it sold off its Arctic stores, and in 1991 stopped selling furs in its stores. Today, the Company is primarily involved in real estate management and natural gas and oil production.

Evidence of mining goes back to the Stone Age. **The earliest evidence of mining** is from Nazlet Sabaha Garb, Egypt, around 100,000 BC. These mines, like many of the earliest mines, were exploiting sources of silica and flint. The skeleton of a Stone Age flint miner – dating back to c3500 BC was found at Obourg in Belgium. **The earliest evidence of mining in Britain** is flint mining at Church Hill, Findon, West Sussex.

The earliest mining for metal, especially copper, dates from about 4500. There is evidence of copper mining at Rudna Glava in Serbia around the middle of the fifth millennium BC. Many of the ancient peoples of the Middle and Far East were expert at mining. The Egyptians mined turquoise, copper and gold from around 2600 BC. The Greeks mined silver and lead from 2000 BC. The Hittites were **the first to mine iron ore** and produce iron goods around 1600 BC, while the Chinese were mining coal during the first millennium BC. The Romans operated some of the largest and most sophisticated mining projects of the ancient world: their mines in Spain were especially vast and, at Las Herrides, they left 270,000 tonnes of slag from their silver mines after 350 years of mining. The Romans were able to drain flooded mines by complex series of water wheels. The Romans were, also, **the first to install bathhouses in mines** by an order of the Emperor Hadrian.

There is evidence of iron mining and working in Northern Nigeria around 500 BC.

Perhaps the oldest company in the world – Stora Kopparbergs Aktiebolag (in Sweden) – is also the **oldest continuing mining operation**. It originally mined and processed copper but has since diversified into a wide range of mining and processing industries. The company was in existence for some time before 1288 when a Swedish bishop bartered an eighth share in the enterprise. By the start of the next century the king of Sweden had shares in the venture.

Continuous copper mining in Germany can be dated back the origins of the Salzdetfurth Company in 1199. **The first use of steam engines** to drain mines (mainly coal) was in Britain in the 1830s.

The earliest extraction of oil and natural gas dates back to Mesopotamia c.3000

The world's first oil well:
Drake's Well at Titusville, Pennsylvania (USA).
Edwin Laurentine Drake (1819-80), centre,
talking to his engineer while the labourers who
sank the well stand in the background.
Oil was struck on 29 August 1859.
(Ann Ronan at Image Select).

BC. Hit, on the Euphrates near Babylon, was an especially famous source of oil and bitumen. Greek fire, a mixture of petroleum and lime, was seen as one of the most terrible weapons of the ancient world. Natural gas was used in ancient Iran and China. The earliest evidence of organized drilling for natural gas is in China around AD 300. The gas was used to boil brine and distil salt.

Large-scale exploitation of oil and natural gas reserves dates back to the middle of the 19th century. **The first company set up specifically to exploit oil** was the Pennsylvania Rock Oil Company, which was established in 1855 by George Bissell, a New York lawyer, and James Townsend, a New Haven banker. They developed **the world's first oil well** in Titusville, Pennsylvania, in 1859. There is, however, evidence that oil wells had been drilled in the 12th century at Pozzuoli, near Naples (Italy), and at Baku in Azerbaijan.

The oil companies with the longest history of continuous operations are those that were created from John D. Rockefeller's Standard Oil company such as Exxon, Standard Oil of New Jersey etc.

Agriculture, forestry, and fisheries today

Agriculture is by far **the world's largest source of employment**. Half the world's population is engaged in agriculture, but this figure has dropped significantly over the last 50 years. However, agriculture remains the major area of economic activity in most parts of the world.

The largest farms in the modern world are the kolkhozy collective farms of the former Soviet Union. Despite being reduced in numbers since 1988 they still account for 169 million hectares or 417 million acres.

The largest farms in terms of land masses are the cattle stations of Brazil and

A collective farm in the former Soviet Union.
The largest farms in the modern world,
collectives still account for 169 million
hectares (417 million acres).
(Rex Features London).

Top meat producers in the world

Rank	Country	Meat production (tonnes p.a.)
1	China	19,538,000
2	USA	17,831,000
3	Russia	9,300,000
4	Germany	6,693,000
5	Ukraine	4,300,000
6	France	3,912,000
7	Argentina	3,196,000
8	Brazil	3,029,000
9	Poland	2,461,000
10	Italy	2,404,000
11	Mexico	2,369,000
	UK	*2,287,000*

Australia. **The largest station** is the Anna Creek cattle station of South Australia, which covers 30,000 km² (11,600 sq mi). Anna Creek is the equivalent to about one quarter of the land mass of England. Sheep stations can sometimes be as large as the biggest cattle ranches. **The largest sheep station in the world** is the Commonwealth Hill Station in Australia, which covers 10,567 km² (4080 sq mi). Between 50,000 and 70,000 sheep graze on the farm plus about 24,000 kangaroos. Sir William Stevenson's sheep station in New Zealand accommodates more sheep – 127,406 – in a smaller area.

The largest arable farm in the UK covers 4,500 hectares (11,000 acres) and is operated by the Earl of Iveagh at Elvenden, Suffolk. **The largest chicken farm** in the world is owned by the Agrigeneral Company LP in Ohio, USA. It has 4.8M chickens producing 3.7M eggs daily. **The largest piggery** in the world is the COMTIM unit near Timisoara, Romania. It houses 70,000 sows producing 1.2M piglets per year. **The largest turkey farmer** in the world – the British company Bernard Matthews Plc – produces 10M turkeys per year. **The largest individual turkey farm** is at North Pickenham,

Norfolk (England) and produces 1M turkeys per year. **The largest farm business in the UK** is the Co-Operative Society's CWS Agriculture, which manages farms in excess of 21,000 hectares, approximately 11,000 hectares of which are wholly owned by the Society. The two largest enterprises are the dairy herd, which runs to 4400 cows, and the growing of wheat which extends to 7000 hectares.

China is the world's largest agricultural nation, producing almost 20 per cent of world output.

World cereal production

Crop	Producer	Amount in 1993 (Million tons)
Maize	USA	165,145,008
Oats	Russia	9,916,000
Rice	China	180,000,000
Barley	Russia	23,500,000

Source: *FAO*

At the turn of the century, agricultural, food, mining and other raw materials companies were among the greatest corporations of their era: firms like Armour and Company of Chicago ranked in the top ten US corporations. During the ensuing century, many of these corporations have merged with others, broadened their sphere of operations or disappeared. The largest agricultural concerns are now parts of much larger ventures – often in related areas. **The largest true 'agribusiness'** (i.e. a firm with its primary activities centred on agriculture) is ConAgra with gross revenues in 1994 of $23,512M and profits of $413M.

The forestry products industry shows some of the same features but the close links with the paper industry makes it easier to identify the very largest corporations. Early in this century Weyerhaeuser Timber Co was one of the largest primary producers

in the world and easily **the largest timber company** with assets of $153M in 1917. Only Standard Oil of New Jersey and Standard Oil of New York were significantly larger.

In the UK, The Forestry Commission is the largest producer of domestic forest products. The Hanson Group, however, has major international holding making it **the largest UK forestry company. The largest forest and paper products company in the world** is International Paper of New York. For a time, Sir James Goldsmith was the largest individual owner of exploitable forest reserves.

The largest forest in the world is the Northern Forest which covers much of the Great Lakes states, the Appalachian Mountains, and the New England states in the United States extending into Canada, Alaska, northern Russia and Scandinavia. **The most profitable and commercially developed forest** is the softwood forest of the Rocky Mountains (Canada). This contains 36.4 million hectares (90 million acres) of commercial forest. **The largest forest in Britain** is Kielder Forest in Northumberland.

The fisheries industry is as old as agriculture. Many different fish are hunted and farmed for consumption and pleasure across the world.

The largest fisheries industry is in North America. **The largest and most fertile fisheries stocks** were those in the Grand Banks off the coast of Canada and the USA, but these stocks have plummeted, with a drop of 95% in the most valuable commercial sea fish – cod – in just a few years. The attempt by the Canadian government to conserve stocks by banning fishing in the early 1990s led to **the largest drop in employment in the fishing industry** when 27,000 fishermen lost their jobs.

The seas around Northern Europe were also among the most fertile in the world but stocks collapsed earlier this century.

The herring fleet at Hull (East Yorkshire) in the 1930s. The North Sea fish stocks have declined drastically during the last half century, largely owing to overfishing. (Popperfoto).

This pattern is being repeated across the world with haddock, cod and flounder being so scarce off Cape Cod that much of America's oldest fishing area is now off limits. Pacific, Caribbean and Indian Ocean stocks are dropping. The annual marine-fish catch, peaked at 86 million tonnes in 1989, dipped to 82.5 million tonnes in 1992 and just under 80 million tonnes in 1994. This was the lowest level for over a decade. In addition there 13.5 million tonnes of freshwater fish landed in 1989 and roughly the same in 1994.

The people of Iceland are **the largest consumers of fish** with an average annual consumption of 203.7 lbs (92.4 kilos) followed by the Japanese at 157 lbs (71.2 kilos) and the people of Hong Kong 112.2 lbs (50.9 kilos). The USA is **the largest exporter and second largest importer of fish** in the world. Russia is **the largest importer of fish.**

The largest fishing port in the UK, by value of fish landed, is Peterhead, in Scotland, where £73M of fish were landed in 1994.

Extractive industries

The largest recoverable coal reserves in the world (about 45 per cent of the world's total) are in China. The United States has the world's second largest estimated recoverable coal reserves about 15 per cent of the total, with Russia coming third with about 14 per cent.

Recoverable coal reserves

Country	Recoverable reserves (Bn metric tonnes)
China	720
USA	240
Russia	230
Others	320
Total	**1510**

The United States reserves are sufficient for around 250 years' consumption at present rates. Total world reserves could last about 300 years.

The oil industry is **the world's largest primary industry** and has held this position since Black Gold replaced King Coal as the primary energy source in the world. Today the primary fuel energy sources are: liquid fuels (gasoline, kerosene etc.), coal and coke, natural gas, nuclear energy, wood, water, wind and geothermal energy.

The world's deepest penetration into the Earth's crust is the exploratory borehole near Zapolarny in Russia. The drilling started in May 1970 and by early 1995 was close to its target of 15,000 m or 49,212 ft. The Glomar Challenger has recorded **the deepest recorded drilling into the sea bed** at 1740m (5709ft). **The deepest drilling in the North Sea** is the 795.8 metres (2611ft) depth reached by the Sovereign Explorer operated by Scotdrill Offshore Co., Aberdeen and contracted to Chevron.

As early as 1910, oil companies accounted for fourteen of the hundred largest corporations in the world.

Half a century later the scale and influence of the oil industry was, perhaps, even greater. Ten of the top hundred corporations in the world were from the oil industry. This situation is paralleled today.

Oil giants at the start of the century

Company in top 100 firms in world

Standard Oil of New Jersey

Standard Oil of New York

Royal Dutch Shell

Burmah Oil Co., Ltd

Texas Co.

Gulf Oil Co.

Anglo Persian Oil

Standard Oil of Indiana

Standard Oil of California

Nobel Brothers Petroleum Producing Company

Magnolia Oil Company

Pure Oil Company

Sinclair Oil and Refining

Pan American Petroleum & Transport

Mid and late 20th century might for the oil giants

Companies in top hundred corporations in world

The 1950s	The 1990s
Standard Oil Co. (New Jersey) (4)	Exxon (8)
Standard Oil Co. (Indiana) (9)	Royal Dutch Shell (10)
Royal Dutch Shell (14)	Mobil (22)
Anglo-Iranian Oil Co. (25)	British Petroleum (31)
Socony-Vacuum Oil (46)	Elf Aquitaine (46)
Texaco (35)	Texaco (57)
Gulf (49)	ENI (63)
Standard Oil of California (69)	Chevron (68)
Burmah Oil (78)	RWE Group (81)
Cities Service Co (89)	Pemex (83)
	Amoco (86)
	Total (98)

Figures in brackets are world ranking

For most of the history of the oil industry, the processors of oil – firms like Standard Oil – dominated the market. Standard Oil was **the first company in history to totally integrate the four primary business activities of production, distribution, marketing and management.** Standard Oil achieved major breakthrough in production economics to obtain "entirely new scale in plant and still size" cutting prices from over five to less than three cents a gallon. Standard went on to link these production economies with savings in distribution costs. Initially, these were through deals with the railways, later pipelines were laid to reduce cost even more. More recently, the supertanker played a similar role in slashing the costs of shipping oil from the Middle East to the USA.

The OPEC oil crisis of the 1970s shifted power temporarily in favour of the oil producers. Since then awareness of both the limits on oil reserves and the cost of oil has reduced OPEC's power and the influence of the oil-producing countries. The term 'oil reserves' describes the amount of crude oil that is expected to be produced in the future from wells in known oilfields. It is estimated that **the world's total recoverable oil** in the world's conventional oilfields is 1 trillion barrels and that about 50 per cent of this will be consumed the year 2000.

The annual world consumption of refined petroleum is about 23 billion barrels. **The world's largest refinery** is the Petroleos de Venezuela oil refinery in Judibana, Falcon, Venezuela. It had a peak capacity of 571,000 barrels per day in 1990 and a current output (1995) of 525,000 barrels. **The largest refinery in the UK** is the ESSO refinery at Fawley (Hampshire) with a capacity of 15.6 million tonnes per annum.

Russia is **the largest producer of oil** with a peak production of 12.5M barrels in 1988 and a current production of 10M barrels a day; this compares with the 8M barrels per day produced by Saudi Arabia and the 7M barrels a day produced by the USA – the next largest producers. UK production is 2M barrels a day under normal conditions.

The USA consumes more oil and oil related products than any other country. The known oil reserves of the world are

Oil Giants after World War I

Company in Top 100 firms in World	Assets $M (1917- 1919)
Standard Oil Co of New Jersey	574.1
Standard Oil Co of New York	204.3
Texas Co	144.5
Gulf Oil Co	142.9
Standard Oil Co of Indiana	126.9
Standard Oil Co of California	126.9
Magnolia Oil Company	122.8
Pure Oil Company	110.0
Sinclair Oil and Refining	93.8
Pan American Petroleum & Transport	83.0
Burmah Oil Co Ltd	62.8
Anglo Persian Oil	29.1
Shell Transport & Trading Company Ltd	18.2

around 137Bn tonnes with Saudi Arabia, Iraq, Kuwait, Iran, the United Arab Emirates, Venezuela, Russia, Azerbaijan, Kazakhstan, Mexico, the United States, China, Libya, Nigeria, Indonesia, Algeria, Norway, Canada, India, Oman, Qatar, and Yemen holding the largest reserves. Over three quarters of these reserves are in the Middle East.

The world's largest oil field is the Ghawar field in Saudi Arabia developed by ARMACO. It stretches for 240 x 35 km (150 x 22 miles). **The largest field in Europe** is the area of the UK continental shelf designated for oil exploration, covering 651,650 km2 (252,000 square miles).

Shell is **the largest offshore oil operator** in the world with 68 installations. This compares with 50 for Elf and 38 for Mobil the two next largest operators. BP is **Europe's largest offshore operator** with 16 installations in Europe. Oil reserves and deposits of natural gas are closely related.

In 1821 the town of Fredonia, New York State, was **the first city in the world to**

be lit by natural gas, but natural gas uses remained localized because there was no way to transport gas over long distances; now, however, it is an increasingly important fuel source. **The world's largest producer of natural gas** is Russia with 613Bn m^3 . The USA is the second largest producer with 503Bn m3. The UK is a major world producer – currently the sixth largest producer – with 53.9Bn m^3.

The largest gas deposit in the world is at Urengoi, Russia, with an eventual production of 200,000 million m^3 and proven reserves of 7,000,000 million m^3. **The greatest gas fire** occurred at Gasi Touil in the Algerian desert from noon on 13 November 1961 to 9.30 a.m. on 28th April 1962. The pillar of flame reached 137 m (450 ft) and smoke 182 m (600ft). For a fee of $1M, it was finally extinguished by Paul Neal (Red) Adair using 245 kg (540 lb) of dynamite .

Oil spills

Some reports claim that the Siberian Oil spill of 1994–95 is **the world's greatest oil spill.** Some estimates put the total loss at almost 2M tonnes of oil; most estimates put the figure much lower but data from this region remains poor.

The wider environmental impact of spills depends as much on local environmental conditions as on the amount of oil spilt. The Exxon Valdez oil spill involved 34,000 tonnes, far less than the 87,000 spilt off the Shetland Islands, north of Scotland, but the Exxon Valdez spill killed almost half a million birds while seas around Shetland recovered very quickly. Even the vast losses into the seas around Kuwait did not have the long-term effect predicted. *Nature* magazine reported that within two years certain parts of the marine ecosystem seemed cleaner and healthier now than before the Gulf War, and the levels of petroleum hydrocarbons in sediments and some molluscs was lower than recorded before the war. This probably reflects the sharp reductions in small-scale, casual

---

European Economic Community gas consumption

Rank	Country	Gas consumption (M tonnes oil equivalent)
1	UK	44.9
2	Germany.	44.9
3	Italy.	37.0
4	Netherlands	30.8
5	Belgium	9.3
6	Spain	4.5
7	Denmark.	1.7
8	Ireland.	1.4
9	Greece	1.0

Source: *Panorama of EC Industry 1991--1992, 1991, p.1–25, from BP Statistical Review*

The world's worst oil spills

Date	Location	Description	Tons spilled
Jan 25 1991	Sea Island, Kuwait	Iraq deliberately dumped oil into the Gulf	1,450,000
Jun 3 1979	Gulf of Mexico	Ixtoc 1 oil well explosion	600,000
Feb 1983	Persian Gulf	Nowruz oil field explosion	600,000
Jun 1942	East coast of USA	German U-boat attacks on US tankers	590,000
Jul 19 1979	Trinidad and Tobago	Collision between Atlantic Empress and Aegean Captain	300,000
Aug 6 1983	Cape Town, South Africa	Fire aboard Castillo de Beliver	250,000
Mar 16 1978	Portsall, France	Grounding of Amoco Cadiz	223,000
Mar 18 1967	Land's End, Cornwall, England	Grounding of Torrey Canyon	119,000
Dec 19 1972	Gulf of Oman	Collision of Sea Star with another ship	115,000
Mar 20 1970	Tralhavet Bay, Sweden	Collision of Othello with another ship	100,000
May 12 1976	La Coruna, Spain	Grounding of Urquiola	100,000

dumping from ships cleaning ballast tanks or other sources. Large spills account for less than 10 per cent of the oil dumped into the sea every year.

Oil spills have effects that go far beyond the immediate destruction of the local environment. They can have a disastrous effect on fishing, tourism and other sea-related economic and social effects. Local wildlife suffers very badly. Sea birds, for example, die in vast numbers. Even when 'saved' and 'cleaned' their survival rates are low because petroleum dissolves the protective waxes and oils in bird feathers. When birds, and other animals in the sea, are coated in oil they have little hope of survival as their buoyancy, flight and respiration are destroyed by oil. Shellfish in the vicinity became inedible with direct effects for the wildlife that live off them and those commercial activities that rely on them.

The long-term effects are equally bad as the toxic elements in oil persist in the food chain. After the Amoco

Cadiz spill death rates among bottom-dwelling species such as sea urchins were very high, and some species seemed to disappear altogether. Experts believe that oil-tainted environments probably recover eventually, although not all species may return to their pre-spill status. Some oceans are more vulnerable to long-term damage than others, however. The waters of the Mediterranean Sea change relatively slowly, and an oil spill such as the Troodos shipping incident in the Gulf of Genoa could have incalculable consequences.

Consumption of minerals

Industrial societies use a vast array of extracted materials. The major types or groups of minerals are: native elements; sulfides; sulfosalts; oxides and hydroxides; halides and borates; carbonates; nitrates and iodates; phosphates, vanadates, and arsenates; sulfates; tungstates and molybdates; and silicates. The USA is **the largest user of mined**

materials using roughly 4Bn tonnes of mined material each year or about 18,000 kilograms (40,000 lbs) per person. Japan is the next largest total user with about 1.7 billion tonnes or 13,500 kilograms (30,000 lbs) per person. In the UK 9000 kilograms (20,000 lbs) of mined material is used per head.

Annual value of non-fuel raw materials consumed per head for major industrial countries

Country	Value per consumer ($Bn)
USA	326
Japan	152
Germany	104
Russia	49
China	34
UK	31

The typical citizen of a prosperous, advanced industrial society will consume vast quantities of the major minerals. The volumes of these minerals consumed vary considerably. The heaviest users of industrial raw materials are in the USA where the average individual lifetime consumption is 360 kilograms (800 lb) each of lead and zinc, 680 kilograms (1500 lb) of copper, 25,000 kilograms (56,000 lb) of steel and more than 25,000 kilograms (500,000 lb) of coal. In China, in contrast, individual consumption is 90 kilograms (200 lb) each of lead and zinc, 68 kilograms (150 lb) of copper, 5,000 kilograms (11,000 lb) of steel and less than 22,680 kilograms (50,000 lb) of coal.

Working the face in a gold mine near Johannesburg (Gauteng, South Africa). (Spectrum Colour Library).

Consumption of major minerals per capita of major industrial societies

Mineral	Consumption (lbs)	Consumption (kilograms)
Lead	600	270
Zinc	600	270
Copper	120	688
Aluminium	3000	1333
Clay	20,000	8800
Salt	21,000	9333
Steel	42,000	18,750
Coal	400,000	180,800
Stone, sand, gravel, and cement	750,000	334,500

Top Western mining companies

Rank	Company	Share of total value of production of non-fuel minerals in 1990 (%)
1	Anglo American (South Africa)	8.5
2	RTZ (UK)	4.2
3	State of Chile (Chile)	3.0
4	State of Brazil (Brazil)	2.6
5	Brascan/Noranda (Canada)	1.8
6	Inco (Canada)	1.8
7	Broken Hill Pty (Australia)	1.5
8	State of Zaire (Zaire)	1.5
9	Phelps Dodge (USA)	1.4
10	Hanson (UK)	1.4
11	Gencor (South Africa)	1.3
12	Asarco (USA)	1.3
13	Western Mining (Australia)	1.2
14	MIM Holdings (Australia)	1.2
15	Placer Dome (Canada)	1.0
	Others	17.1

Source: *Financial Times.*

The top ten suppliers of gold

Rank	Area	1993 tonnes
1	South Africa	584
2	United States	348
3	Russia	241
4	Australia	232
5	Canada	155
6	China	121
7	Brazil	78
8	Papua New Guinea	60
9	Colombia	36
10	Chile	36
	Others	279
	Total	**2,170**

Source: The Gold Institute

Iron is the most extensively mined metal with almost a 973.0 million tonnes mined annually. It is followed by aluminium at 18 million tons, copper at 11 millions tones and zinc at 7.2 million tons.

The Freegold Company is the largest producer of gold with a total annual production of 3630 million ounces per annual. South Africa is the largest national producer of gold.

The top ten consumers of gold (1993)

Rank	Area	tonnes
1	Europe	745
2	Middle East	390
3	India	300

4	Japan	.235
5	North America	.240
6	China	.220
7	Taiwan	.190
8	Thailand	87
9	Hong Kong	57
10	South Korea	73
	Others	351
	Total	**2,888**

Source: *The Gold Institute*

The utilities

The utilities cover a wide range of business sectors including: postal services; telecommunications; gas, electricity and water, production, processing and/or distribution, and, in some senses, railways.

The largest utilities are in the telecommunications sector. AT&T has a total turnover of $75Bn; British Telecom is Britain's largest utility with a turnover in 1994 of $22Bn. The **largest gas or electric utility company in the world** is Tokyo Electrical Power with total revenues in 1994 of $50Bn. The **largest gas or electric utility** is British Gas with a turnover of $15Bn.

Traditionally, utilities have employed very large numbers of people. The US Postal Service **employs more people than any other utility in the world** with 728,944 employees during 1994. The Post Office is **the largest employer among British utilities** with 189,000 employees in 1994.

 The USA is **the largest user of nuclear energy in the world**. Its installed capacity of 106,098 megawatts in 112 power stations is larger than the installed capacity of next two largest countries (France and Russia) combined. France is **Europe's largest user of nuclear energy** in terms of both the percentage of energy generated by nuclear power and the consumption of millions of tonnes of oil equivalent. France gets 75 per cent of its energy from nuclear genera-

The nuclear power plant at Bugey (France).
Over 72% of the electricity generated in France is from nuclear power plants. This is the highest contribution by nuclear power to the power requirements of any major industrial nation.
(Sipa Press/Rex Features).

Employment in utilities

World		UK	
Company	**Employees**	**Company**	**Employees**
US Post Office	728,904	British Post Office	189,000
Deutsche Bahn	357,324	British Telecom	137,500
Deutsche Post	340,000	British Rail	127,890
Deutsche Telekom	223,000	British Gas	81,397
SNCF	215,787	Nuclear Electric	13,180
Nippon Tel & Tel	194,700	Scottish Power	8,300
British Post Office	189,000	Eastern Electric	8,019
France Telecom	152,886	Midland Electric	7,413
Japan Postal Service	143,331	E. Midland Electric	6,484
British Telecom	137,500	Southern Electric	6,141

tors (compared with 20 per cent in the UK) and consumes 61 million tonnes of oil equivalent of nuclear energy.

Manufacturing

The manufacturing sector is at the heart of industrial and business activity. The largest firms in the world General Motors and General Electric are fundamentally manufacturing concerns. At the start of the century, the largest company in the world was the United States Steel Corporation with total assets of $2,449.5M. The steel sector dominated the manufacturing giants of that era with four of the largest corporations in the USA operating in the steel sector.

In the middle of the century the industrial base of the largest firms was dominated by automotive, steel and chemical concerns. US hegemony seemed firmly established. As the century draws to a close, Japan's challenge to the USA is clear.

Large manufacturers are generally massive employers of labour especially related to their total revenues. In 1994 Mitsubishi had **the largest total revenues of any corporation in the world**: this diversified financial and commercial services company had

gross revenues of $178Bn but employed only 36,000 people. In contrast, General Motors, with total revenues of $155Bn employed 692,800 people.

The motor vehicles industry has been overtaken in recent years as **the largest industry in the world** – at least in terms of employment – by the electronics and electrical equipment sector.

The growth of the electronics and electrical equipment industries is driven by a mixture of public and private interest. The convenience of electricity has often outweighed price and other considerations: when battery-powered electric motors were first introduced in the middle of the 19th century, the editor of the *Philosophical Magazine* pointed out that power from this source was twenty five times as expensive as power from steam.

In 1882, Octavius Coope's home – Berechurch Hall near Colchester (Essex) became **the first house in Britain to be lit throughout by electricity.** Coope calculated that building his own electricity generators, instead of a private gasworks, provided him with lighting for £200 p.a. instead of the £400 p.a. cost of gas.

The largest manufacturers in the world

The 1900s	The 1950s	The 1990s
US Steel (steel, USA)	General Motors (automotive, USA)	General Motors (automotive, USA)
Bethlehem Steel (steel, USA)	US Steel (steel, USA)	General Electric (electronics, USA)
Armour & Co. (food, USA)	E. I. du Pont Nemours (chemicals, USA)	Marubeni (engineering, Japan)
Swift & Co (food, USA)	General Electric (electronics, USA)	Ford (automotive, USA)
Midvale Steel (steel, USA)	Ford (automotive, USA)	Toyota Motor (automotive, USA)
International Harvester (machinery, USA)	Bethlehem Steel Corp. (steel, USA)	Hitachi (electronics, Japan)
E. I. du Pont Nemours (chemicals, USA)	Imperial Tobacco (tobacco, UK)	Matsushita (engineering, Japan)
Lever Brothers (chemicals, UK)	Western Electric (electronics, UK)	General Electric (electronics, USA)
Friedrich Krupp (metals, Germany) Germany)	Union Carbide (chemicals, USA)	Daimler-Benz (automotive,
J & P Coats (textiles, UK)	ICI (chemicals, UK)	IBM (computers, USA)

World's Largest Industries

Industry sector	Revenues ($M)	Employees
Electronics & electrical equipment	781,085	3,868,784
Motor vehicles and parts	971,925	3,328,151
Food	261,906	1,211,188
Chemicals	277,483	1,103,905
Metals	258,647	1,056,586
Aerospace	121,706	751,316
Computers & office equipment	184,533	730,353
Industrial & farm equipment	148,567	659,979
Engineering	202,154	615,357
Pharmaceuticals	109,904	565,436

These figures in the accompanying table are based on the payroll and performance of companies in the *Fortune* 500 largest companies in the world and are probably a good indicator of size for industries which are dominated by large-scale production like motor vehicles and aerospace. They probably underestimate the size of sectors like food production.

The largest firms in the largest industries

Industry	Largest in world	Largest in Europe
Electronics & electrical	Hitachi (Japan)	Philips Electrical equipment (NL)
Motor vehicles and parts	General Motors (USA)	Daimler-Benz (Germany)
Food	Philip Morris (USA)	Unilever (UK/NL)
Chemicals	E. I. Du Pont de Nemours (USA)	Hoechst (Germany)
Metals	IRI (Italy)	IRI (Italy)
Aerospace	Boeing (USA)	British Aerospace (UK)
Computers & office equipment	IBM (USA)	ICL (UK)
Industrial & farm equipment	Mitsubishi Heavy Industries (Japan)	INI (Spain)
Engineering, construction	CIE Générale Des Eaux (France)	CIE Générale Des Eaux (France)
Pharmaceuticals	Johnson & Johnson (USA)	Sandoz (Switzerland)

The growth and significance of the automobile and vehicle industry is well documented. Car and other vehicle production remain at the heart of most significant industrial economies. Japan is **the largest producer of automobiles in the world.** In 1993, Japan's total output was 7,450,000 cars. The next two largest producers in

1993 – the USA and Germany – produced 5,400,000 and 4,270,000 cars respectively.

The **best-selling car in Europe today** is the Volkswagen Golf. **The largest selling car ever** is considered to be the Volkswagen Beetle, which overtook the Model T which was previously considered to be the best-selling car, in the world.

Germany is **the largest producer of cars in Europe** with 4,660,657 vehicles produced in 1994. The next largest producers are France, Spain, UK, Belgium, and Italy. Britain's car industry is **the fastest growing in Europe** – albeit primarily through Japan manufacturers.

The **largest single automobile plant in the world** is the Volkswagernwerk at Wolfsberg, Germany, which employs almost 60,000 people and can produce 4000 vehicles a week. The factory build-

The beetle-shaped Volkswagen
(the 'People's Car') being launched by Hitler in 1936. The Volkswagen works at Wolfsburg, Lower Saxony, Germany, is the largest single automobile works in the world. (Peter Newark's Military Pictures).

Motor vehicle production in selected countries

Year	United States	Britain	France	Germany	Japan	World Total
1955	9204	1237	725	909	69	13,743
1965	11,138	2177	1642	2976	1876	24,542
1975	8987	1648	2186	3186	6942	33,263
1984	10,925	1134	3062	4009	11,465	41,772
1990	9783	1566	3769	4977	13,487	48,345
1993	10,684	1568	3155	3990	11,227	

ings cover 150 ha (371 acres) and the entire site is 760 ha. (1878 acres).

Vehicle manufacturers dominate European rankings of the largest employers. Three of the five largest employers are drawn from the vehicles' industries.

The electronics and automotive industries have gained prominence during the 20th century. The third key manufacturing industry which grew to dominate world markets during this century is the chemicals industry.

The largest chemicals company in the world is E. I. du Pont de Nemours, which is the largest in terms of revenues ($39,680M) and profits ($2,727M) but trails

Europe's largest business employers

Company (nationality)	Employees in 1994
Siemens (G)	391000
Daimler Benz (G)	371107
Unilever (UK/NL)	294000
Fiat (I)	260951
Volkswagen (G)	253108
Philips (NL)	252214
Nestle (Swiss)	209755
ABB (Sweden)	206490
Alcatel (F)	196500
BAT Industries (UK)	190308

Brunner and Mond

The origins of ICI and Zeneca lie in an unusual partnership between the son of a Unitarian schoolmaster and a Swiss scientist. John Brunner (1842–1919), from Liverpool, started his chemicals company in Widnes in 1863. Ten years later he established his partnership with Ludwig Mond (1939–1909) to build a giant alkali producing plant at Winnington, near Northwich, in Cheshire. The success of their enterprise established a tradition of chemicals production in the locality that continues today.

Their profits prompted Ludwig Mond to comment "we are no longer making chemicals, we are making money". Although their company, Brunner-Mond, was one of the largest in Britain, it was dwarfed by their German rivals. During and after World War One, the British government encouraged large-scale merger and acquisition to build up a large and internationally competitive, UK chemicals industry. Eventually, this led Mond's son, Alfred (1868–1930), to conclude a merger with the other large British chemicals company, Nobels, to form the Imperial Chemical Industries in 1930.

the German giants Hoechst, BASF and Bayer in terms of employees. Du Pont employs 107,000 people compared with the 172,483, 115,000 and 153,866 employed by Hoechst, BASF and Bayer respectively. Britain's largest chemicals company is Imperial Chemical Industries (ICI).

The discovery of mauve by William Perkin (1839–1907) led to **the first synthetic dyes** and ultimately the modern chemicals industry. After making this discovery at the age of 18 Perkin went on to make other discoveries: he was, for example, the first to develop a synthetic perfume. His discoveries were, however, seldom taken up in his home country. Germany was at the fore in developing a chemicals industry while France led the way with perfumes and cosmetics – L'Oreál is still **the largest cosmetics company in the world**.

The largest cosmetics companies

Company	1994 ($Bn)
L'Oreal	8.2
Unilever	4.8
Procter & Gamble	4.8
Shiseido	4.6
Avon	2.7
E Lauder	2.3
Kao	2.3
Revlon	2.1
Wella	1.9
Sanofi	1.8

Unilever is the only (part) British company among the world's largest cosmetics companies despite Perkin's role in its origins.

The pharmaceutical sector has **the largest return on investment of any industry sector**: in 1994, the industrial median return was 16.1 per cent. This was over twice that earned by the telecommunica-

tions sector – 7 per cent – the next largest sector. Pharmaceuticals, also, earned **the highest return on assets** with 12.3 per cent compared with the 5.1 per cent earned by the next highest – beverages. Johnson & Johnson is **the world's largest pharmaceutical company** with revenues of $15,734Bn and 81,500 employees. There are two UK companies among the largest pharmaceutical concerns: **the largest UK pharmaceutical company** is Smithkline Beecham with total revenues of $9,946M.

The service sector

The 19th and 20th centuries can be described as the centuries of extraction and manufacture. The 21st century looks increasingly like the century of business services. The 1995 *Fortune* 500 ranking of the largest companies in the world, identified trading as its largest category with twenty two companies with a total turnover of $1,311,937M. The size of this sector partly reflects the success of Japanese trading houses or Sogo Shosha: companies like Mitsubishi, Mitsui, ITOCHU and other trading companies had a large proportion of Japanese trade. Traditionally, they handled a vast array of services from banking and finance through to marketing research; they developed markets for Japanese products and handled the financing of new projects. Their role has shifted over the last decade as some Japanese producers have sought greater autonomy. Some trading houses have extended their operations to handle the goods and services of non-Japanese companies.

The largest non-Japanese trading company is the Veba Group of Germany. Several developing countries have tried to emulate Japan's success by developing their own trading companies: Ssangyong of South Korea is the largest of these.

The size of the trading houses highlights the scale and impact of the service sector generally: it is estimated that over 50 per cent of the labour force in the industrially-developed world is now employed in the service sector. The

The largest trading companies

Company	Revenues in 1994 ($Bn)
Mitsubishi	176
Mitsui	171
ITOCHU	168
Sumitomo	162
Marubeni	150
Nissho Iwai	101
Tomen	70
Nichimen	56
Kanematsu	56
Veba Group	40

Travel and tourism is **the largest single service sector** with almost 10m people employed across the world. This makes travel and tourism the largest employer in the world after agriculture. Paris is **the most highly regarded travel and tourism destination in the world** according to the *Official Meeting Facilities Guide*. It is followed by Hawaii and Hong Kong. London is **Britain's most popular destination.**

Car travel is **the means of transport most often used domestically.**

Air is **the fastest growing means of international travel**. Chicago is **the airport which handles the largest number of passengers every year** with 65.1 million international and domestic passengers in 1994.

 The most profitable airline is Singapore Airlines with net profits over the past five years of $2Bn. Boeing is **the world's largest aerospace company** with British Airways carrying 30.5M passengers in 1994, more than any other airline in the world. United Airlines

highest proportion is in the United States where over 60 per cent are employed in services. Across the European Union, just under 45 per cent of the labour force is employed in services. The highest shares in services are in Britain and the Benelux countries where almost 55 per cent of the labour force now work in this sector.

Top airports by total terminal passengers

Rank	City/Country	Airport	Total passengers
1	Chicago, USA	Chicago O'Hare	64,441,000
2	Dallas/Ft Worth, USA	DFW International	51,944,000
3	Los Angeles, USA	LA International	46,965,000
4	London, UK	London Heathrow	44,968,000
5	Tokyo, Japan	Tokyo-Haneda International	42,639,000
6	Atlanta, USA	Hartsfield Atlanta International	42,033,000
7	San Francisco, USA	San Francisco International	31,789,000
8	Denver, USA	Stapleton International	30,877,000
9	Frankfurt, Germany	Frankfurt International	30,085,000
10	New York, USA	John F. Kennedy International	27,761,000
11	Paris, France	Orly	25,009,000
12	Paris, France	Charles de Gaulle	24,770,000
13	New York, USA	Newark International	24,287,000

Source: *Guinness Book of Answers, 10th edition.*

handles **the largest number of passenger kilometres** (that is the number of passengers by distance travelled) with 162,494M per annum. The Cessna Aircraft Company of Wichita, Kansas (USA) has produced more aircraft than any other: it has manufactured almost 180,000 aircraft since its formation in 1911. **The oldest airline in the world** is KLM, the national airline of the Netherlands, which operated its first scheduled service on 17 May, 1920 between Amsterdam and London.
Aeroflot employs more staff than any other airline. In 1990, its peak, it employed 600,000 people, that is, more than the total staff of the 18 largest US carriers.

 The air route with **the highest level of international passenger traffic** is London to Paris with over 3 million passengers a year. The next busiest international route is London to New York with just under 2.5 million passengers travelling each year.

The largest airport in the world is the King Khalid International Airport near Riyadh in Saudi Arabia. The airport covers 225 km² (55,040 acres).

Tokyo is **the most expensive airport.** Heathrow is **the largest airport in**

The UK's top hotel groups

Rank	Hotel group	Number of rooms in the UK
1	Forte Hotels/Granada	29,696
2	Thistle Hotels	14,300
3	Queen's Moat House	10,624
4	Hilton Hotels	8420
5	Accor Hotels	4205
6	Swallow Hotels	4037
7	Holiday Inn	3744
8	Stakis Hotels	3742
9	Jarvis Hotels	3200
10	De Vere Hotels	3117

The EC's top hotel groups

Rank	Hotel Group	Number of rooms
1	Accor	112,810
2	Forte/Granada	36,750
3	Louvre	25,576
4	Queen's Moat Houses	21,123
5	Ladbroke (Hilton)	15,164
6	BIL Mount Charlotte	14,170
7	Bass (Holiday Inn)	11,944
8	Saison (Intercontinental)	9530
9	ITT (Sheraton)	8038
10	Rank	6939

Source: *Kleinwort Benson*

Europe with over 47 million international and domestic passengers in 1993. Manchester is **Europe's fastest growing airport.**

The expansion of travel and tourism is closely liked with growth in other service sectors. The hotel trade is a major part of the service sector. **The largest hotel group in the world** is the Holiday Inn Group, which operates 1643 hotels as wholly owned, managed or franchised properties with 327,059 rooms. Granada is **the largest hotel and catering company in Britain.** It has over 344 properties in the UK with more than 29,696 rooms.

Accor is the **largest hotel group in Europe** with 112,810 rooms. Accor's merger with Carlson travel made it **the largest combined travel agency in the world.**

The largest single hotel in the world is the Hotel Izmailovo Complex in Moscow with 5000 rooms catering for 9500 people. The London Forum Hotel is **Britain's largest hotel** with 910 bedrooms accommodating 1856 guests. The Hotel Excalibur covers **the largest area of any hotel.** It is built on a 47.3 ha. (117 acre) site. It contains 4032 de luxe rooms, has seven themed restaurants and eleven food outlets.

The largest banking and financial institutions by sector

Sector	Firm	Revenues in 1994 ($Bn)
Brokerage services	Merrill Lynch	18.2
Commercial banks	Deutsche Bank	33.1
Insurance (Stock)	Allianz Holding	40.4
Insurance (Mutual)	Nippon Life	75.3
Savings	Halifax	13.4*

* includes merger with Leeds Permanent Building Society

Few industries are more closely associated with the service sector than banking and finance which extends from commercial banking to insurance and equity management.

Japan's postal service is **the world's largest single deposit taker** with total deposits of $350Bn.

Mitsubishi Bank is **the world's largest bank** on the basis of its market capitalization of $71,738M. **Europe's largest bank** in terms of market capitalization is the Hong Kong and Shanghai Banking Corporation with a market capitalization of $28,458M.

The UK bank with **the largest number of branches** is the Lloyds TSB Group, with 2948 branches nationwide.

The merger of Lloyds Bank and the Trustee Savings Bank (TSB) created Britain's second largest bank in terms of market capitalization. The combined market capitalization of $16,258M is second only to that of the Honk Kong and Shanghai Bank's $28,458 M. The combined bank will have **the largest market share of UK banking**, with 21% of the market.

The World Bank is **the single largest source of development**

The largest banks in the UK

Bank	No. of branches
Lloyds TSB*	2948
National Westminster Bank	2286
Barclays	2019
Midland Bank	1735
Royal Bank of Scotland	750
Abbey National	656
Bank of Scotland	424
Clydesdale	302
Ulster Bank	146

* Lloyds and TSB are scheduled to merge

funds and the largest single borrower on most financial markets. It has two major constituents – the International Bank for Reconstruction (IBR) and the International Development Association (IDA).

In the late eighties, its policy of making profits from its investments and the tendency for its income from loans to poor countries to exceed its disbursements came under fierce criticism.

The World Bank

The World Bank is a specialized agency of the United Nations. Created by the Bretton Woods Agreement in 1944, its initial goal of assisting European postwar recovery was soon subsumed in a wider role to provide loans and technical assistance to promote the balanced growth of international trade and economic development, especially in underdeveloped areas. The World Bank is now the single most important agency in the economic development of poorer countries.

Membership of the World Bank (which is based in Washington DC) consists of 159 countries. It makes loans to member countries for private concerns if a member government guarantees the loan, but the main focus of lending is long-term projects, especially those that improve the economic infrastructure and living standards of the country. The Bank's capital ceiling or authorized capital is $171Bn.

At the heart of the Bank's work is technical help for member countries. This means that it goes far beyond merely providing loans, and helps set up and oversee individual projects. There is criticism that the Bank is a 'rich nations' club'. This image is reinforced by the voting system on loans: votes are weighted according to a member's contribution. This means that major contributors, like the USA, have a major say in any lending. The Bank's board of governors meet annually to determine policies.

The top development banks

Company	Year end	Capital $M	Assets $M	Pre-tax profit $M
World Bank /IBRD	30/06/93	25,123	135,001	1,130
European Investment Bank	31/12/92	14,542	102,527	1,174
Export-Import Bank of Japan	31/03/93	11,135	72,905	317
Japan Development Bank	31/03/93	8,262	106,915	384
Asian Development Bank	31/12/93	7,966	25,111	570
Inter-American Development Bank	31/12/93	7,528	29,693	382
European Bank for Reconstruction & Development	31/12/93	3,329	7,888	5
African Development Bank	31/12/91	3,154	9,747	160
Korea Development Bank	31/12/93	2,440	41,092	261
National Financiera	31/12/92	1,536	30,842	244

Source: *The Banker, May 1994.*

Equity and bond markets play a vital part in the financial services sector. They provide a funding base for business while creating a framework for investment and financial management. The UK operates **the largest stock markets in Europe.** The London Stock exchange is the third largest in the world after New York and Tokyo. The Chicago Board of Trade is **the largest commodity futures exchange in**

How Europe's stock markets shape up

Domestic equities	Number of companies listed	Market value £M	1993 turnover £M
Amsterdam	319	44,573	161,084
Athens	150	1,730	8,462
Brussels	159	7,465	54,318
Copenhagen	246	13,747	28,587
Germany	426	377,983	313,027
Helsinki	57	5,492	16,147
Lisbon	183	418	2,193
Luxembourg	56	718	13,061
Madrid	376	26,358	99,002
Milan	218	49,638	91,888
Oslo	120	11,136	18,530
Paris	656	106,802	308,750
Stockholm	105	26,253	67,912
Switzerland	215	128,157	181,695
UK	1,927	281,983	810,102
Vienna	111	8,456	18,283

Source: London Stock Exchange

the world. It was established in 1848 and now sponsors futures trading in grains, soybeans, silver, gold mortgage interest rates, long-term US Treasury bonds and the major stock market index. In 1994 it dealt with 180M contracts.

 Since the collapse of the Soviet Empire in 1990-91, and the spread of capitalism in Central and Eastern Europe, stock exchanges have opened in a number of cities in the region including Moscow, St Petersburg, Warsaw, Budapest, Prague, Kiev and the capitals of the Baltic republics. It is a nice irony that more than one of these new exchanges has been established in a building that was formerly the property of the Communist Party. Stock exchanges have also been established in Communist China at Shanghai, Beijing and Shenzhen: the latter, a 'boom city' near Hong Kong, has had a somewhat tumultuous early history.

The sound and effective organisation of business across the world depends heavily on the personal and business services provided by lawyers, accountants and consultants. **The largest legal practice in Europe** is Clifford Chance.

Largest European law firms (by number of partners)

Firm	Country	Partners
Clifford Chance	UK	228
Eversheds	UK	209
Linklaters & Paines	UK	147
Lovell White Durrant	UK	140
Freshfields	UK	125

Simmons & Simmons	UK	122
Allen & Overy	UK	113
Norton Rose	UK	102
Slaughter & May	UK	101
Herbert Smith	UK	98

Source: *International Finance Law Review Sept. '93*

The **largest consultancy business in Europe** is Anderson with a European fee income of $935M in 1994. The **largest accountancy firm in Europe** is KPMG Peak Marwick with a European fee income of over $3bn in 1994. The UK's largest practice is Coopers & Lybrand.

The growing importance of the service sector is illustrated by the scale of service exports. The USA is the largest exporter of services with total export revenues in 1993 of $185Bn. This compares with the $110Bn and $87Bn earned by France and Germany respectively, the next largest exporters of services. The growth of the service sector at home, and internationally, highlights the impact that this sector will have as the world's economy moves towards the new millennium.

Top UK accountants (by fee income)

Rank	Firm	Fee income £M	Number of partners
1	Coopers & Lybrand	553.0	701
2	KPMG Peat Marwick	490.7	598
3	Ernst & Young	390.6	399
4	Arthur Anderson	388.6	247
5	Price Waterhouse	385.7	482
6	Touche Ross	345.5	370
7	Grant Thornton	113.8	208
8	BDO Binder Hamlyn	108.5	217
9	Pannell Kerr Forster	83.1	189
10	Stoy Hayward	74.7	169

Source: *Sunday Times 3/4/94*

Looking Forward, Looking Back

The business world is so closely linked with the wider society and environment that virtually all aspects of business affect and, are in turn, affected by business. From R&D expenditure to arts and entertainment there is an intimate link between commerce and most aspects of society. R&D expenditure shapes the future.

Edison's invention of the research laboratory at Menlo Park, New Jersey, in 1876 established a framework for organized research and development that has played an important part in shaping innovation, product and development for the last hundred years.

Research laboratories have produced such important commercial products as the electric lamp (Menlo Park, 1878), radar (US Naval Laboratory, 1922), foam rubber (Dunlop Latex Laboratories, 1929) stereophonic discs (Bell Laboratories, 1932), polythene (ICI Laboratories, 1933), nylon (Du Pont Laboratories, 1938), transistors (Bell Laboratories, 1948), video recorder (Bing Crosby Enterprises, 1952), Librium (Roche Laboratories, 1960), office fax (Xerox Laboratories, 1964), microprocessors (Intel Laboratories, 1969), Post-It Notes (3M Laboratories, 1979), laptop computer (Tandy Laboratories, 1983), and the personal colour videophone (Compression Laboratories, 1992).

This does not mean that individual inventors working on their own are unimportant. Individuals created the first telephone (Alexander Graham Bell, 1876), man-made fibre (Sir Joseph Swan, 1883), the snapshot camera (George Eastman, 1888), the brassiere (Herminie Cadolle, 1889), the safety razor (King Camp Gillette, 1901), the car radio (George Frost, 1922), Penicillin (Dr Alexander Fleming, 1928), soft ice cream (Thomas Carvelas, 1934), the Polaroid camera (Dr Edwin Land, 1948), the floppy disk (Dr Yoshiro Nakamats, 1950), Velcro (George de Mestral, 1957), the personal computer (Steven Jobs and Steven Wozniak, 1977), Rollerblades (Scott Olsen, 1980), and genetic fingerprinting (Dr Alec Jeffreys, 1985). The cost of research and development and introduction of new products and services makes it increasingly hard for individuals to make a wholly independent impact.

R&D

A symbiotic relationship between individuals and institutions is increasingly important. It might take the form of an individual like Arthur Fry spotting a use for a material which eventually produced Post-It Notes.

The R&D investments of large firms might be turned into important products by staff who leave like Steven Wozniak who left Hewlett Packard and eventually helped to create Apple Computers. Even when individuals start alone, perfecting a product like Velcro took George de Mestral 14 years from identifying the problem and possible solution to producing a viable product: his original idea came in 1941 from seeing the way burrs attached themselves by thousands of little hooks. It was not until 1957 that Velcro was ready for the market.

The scale of R&D is affected by the sector in which firms operate.

Survival in sectors like pharmaceuticals, chemicals and electronics is highly dependent on sustaining a competitive position through research and development. Industries like retailing and distribution are far less dependent on R&D; more money is invested in R&D in the electronics and electrical equipment sector than any

other. During the 1990s, total expenditure has topped $200Bn.

In the UK, the largest sector is pharmaceuticals with a gross investment of over $12Bn over the same period.

The largest R&D expenditures by industrial Sector Worldwide

Sector	Invested $M (1990–1994)
Electronics	203,775
Engineering (Vehicles)	117,367
Chemicals	84,601
Engineering	80,714
Pharmaceuticals	46,706

The biggest spenders on R&D during the 1990s

World Company	1991–1994 ($M)	Europe Company	1991–1994 ($M)	Company (UK)	1991–1994 ($M)
GM (USA)	24972	Daimler-Benz (Germany)	20688	Glaxo	4187
Daimler-Benz (Germany)	20688	Siemens (Germany)	20382	SmithKline Beecham	3333
Siemens (Germany)	20382	ABB (Swiss)	9384	Unilever	3058
Hitachi (Japan)	20074	Philips (NL)	8469	Shell Transport & Trading	3041
Ford (USA)	18360	Alcatel (France)	8263	Zeneca	2981
IBM (USA)	17961	Bayer (Germany)	8048	GEC	2600
Matsushita (Japan)	15948	Hoechst (Germany)	7885	Wellcome	1816
Fujitsu (Japan)	14466	VW (Germany)	7381	ICI	1799
Toshiba (Japan)	12472	Ciba Geigy (Swiss)	6814	BP	1543
AT&T (Japan)	12246	Hoffman-La Roche (Swiss)	6304	BT	1540

US and Japanese companies are **the most active investors in R&D**: between them they account for over two thirds of all companies represented in the top 200 companies spending on R&D.

The largest R&D expenditures by industrial sector UK

Sector	Invested $M (1990–1994)
Pharmaceuticals	12,544
Engineering	4980
Oil	4821
Electronics	3914
Food	3628

The returns from investment in R&D can be vast.

Glaxo is not only the UK's largest investor in R&D but it has probably earned the best return from previous investment. Glaxo's ulcer treating drug – Zantac – is **the world's best selling drug** with sales in 1994 of $3.9Bn worldwide.

The costs and potential returns from R&D are so great that the vast majority of firms cannot afford to keep up with the giants. Many smaller firms build their businesses by exploiting the opportunities which larger firms fail to identify. Steven Jobs developed the 'mouse' or 'graphical user interface' 'invented' in the laboratories of Xerox. He bought out the rights and converted the product to a universal addition to personal computers.

Even the largest firms struggle to sustain their R&D efforts during fallow times. The pharmaceutical sector during the 1990s turned to merger and acquisition in response to declining returns to R&D expenditure and increasing concern about healthcare costs. This change in strategy produced the largest spate of mergers in the industry's history.

Not all industries have adopted the same approach to R&D. Rapidly growing industries like the media and entertainment sector put much of their emphasis on the ability to manage diverse and complex enterprises, deal making and managing talent. Rupert Murdoch's career and the scale of his company – News Corporation – symbolizes all of these virtues. *Vanity Fair* magazine identified him as the most powerful private citizen in the world on the

The most powerful 'information age' business leaders

Individual	Scale of Ventures managed, owned or led ($Bn)
Robert Allen (AT&T)	74
Rupert Murdoch (News Corporation)	20
Bill Gates (Microsoft)	17
Gerald Levin (Time Warner)	16
Michael Eisner (Walt Disney Corp.)	14
Andrew Grove (Intel)	12
Sumner Redstone (Viacom Inc.)	11
John Malone (Tele-Communications Inc.)	7
Steven Spielberg (Amblin Entertainment)	4
David Geffen (Dreamworks)	2

basis of his influence on the media and entertainment industry. *Vanity Fair* ranked his corporation number one in the 'new establishment' of information age firms.

In the entertainment business, creativity counts for more than mere investment. **The longest running and most commercially successful television and film series** is Star Trek. The first episode – The Man Trap – was shown in 1966. Since then it has spawned off:

• Three other major TV series: Star Trek – The Next Generation, Deep Space Nine and Star Trek – Voyager

• Five films: Star Trek – The Movie, Star Trek II – The Wrath of Khan, Star Trek III – The Search for Spock, Start Trek IV – The Voyage Home and Star Trek Generations

• A host of product developments, endorsements and conventions

The crew of Starship Enterprise in Star Trek,
the longest running and most commercially
successful television series ever. (Image Select).

• The name for the first US space shuttle.

The original idea was developed by Gene Roddenbery who sold the idea to DesiLu Productions: this TV production firm soon lost faith in the idea and tried to sell it on to CBS.

Top earners

Profits in the entertainment industry are largely dependent on the talent employed. This makes artists among the highest paid people in business. Steven Spielberg is **the highest earner**, followed by Oprah Winfrey. The Beatles **earn the most of any music group** – despite breaking up as a band twenty five years ago in 1970.

Only two of the top earning artists are in the top selling LP records of all time. Michael Jackson's Thriller is the best selling album of all time with 40M sold while the Beatles Sgt Pepper's Lonely Hearts Club Band sold 26M. Steven Spielberg is associated with **the biggest selling film of the 1990s** (Jurassic Park), 1980s (ET: The Extra Terrestrial) and the second biggest seller of the 1970s (Jaws).

The Top Earners in the UK

Rank	Name	Company	Dividends £
1	D Sainsbury	J Sainsbury	37,635,924
2	Sir Andrew Lloyd Webber	Really Useful	19,209,148
3	R Hobson	National Parking Corp.	4,893,276
4	Sir Donald Gosling	National Parking Corp.	4,116,563
5	Lord Rothermere	Daily Mail & General	3,742,587
6	D Crossland	Airtours	3,642,421
7	T Hemmings	Scottish & Newcastle	3,157,561
8	P Johnson	Park Food Group	2,970,696
9	Hon Simon Weinstock	GEC	2,939,172
10	Sir David Alliance	N Brown	2,872,493

Source: *Labour Research*

Steven Spielberg directing Harrison Ford in Indiana Jones. Spielberg, who has founded his own company Amblin Entertainment, is one of the leading 'Information Age' business leaders. Spielberg is also the highest paid entertainer with estimated earnings in 1994-95 of $285,000,000. (Image Select).

The highest paid entertainers 1994/5

Entertainer	Earnings 1994/5 (Millions)
Steven Spielberg	$285
Oprah Winfrey	$146
Beatles	$130
Rolling Stones	$121
Eagles	$95
David Copperfield	$81
Pink Floyd	$70
Michael Jackson	$67
Barbra Streisand	$65
Sylvester Stallone	$58

Only a few corporate leaders, notably those with major share holdings, compare in earning power with the entertainment sector. David Sainsbury, for example, added a dividend cheque for £37,635,924 to his salary of £362,000. This made him **Britain's largest earner.**

Company reports

Information on the wider activities of corporations is more widely available today than in the past: this reflects the continuing pressure in most mature economies for greater disclosure by companies. This information is usually made available through annual reports and other public statements which vary considerably in quality and openness. **The most highly rated annual report in the world** is pro-

The top annual reports

(according to Certified Accountant)

Company (Country)

Sara Lee Corp. (USA)
Veba AG (Germany)
ICI / Zeneca (UK)
Sainsbury (UK)
Hoechst AG (Germany)
General Electrical Co (USA)
Tenneco (USA)
Unocal Corp. (USA)
Du Pont (USA)
Allied Signal (USA)

duced by the US company Sara Lee. The magazine *Certified Accountant* ranked annual reports against a set of criteria and rated the Sara Lee report as the best designed and most informative.

Environmental problems

 Some observers of modern business have reversed the old Yorkshire saying "where there's muck there's brass (money)" to say "where there's brass there's muck". This highlights the impact of industry and business on the environment. Environmental deterioration has accompanied industrial development since long before the industrial revolution.

The impact of pollution on rivers, the effects of oil spills and the risks of certain types of farming, fisheries and mining policies have already been identified. Many of the world's most endangered species are at risk because of commercial developments.

Commercial activities are linked with a range of environmental problems. Cigarette ends and sweet wrappers are the commonest forms of litter in Britain.

Industrial activity produces a range of

potentially harmful emissions. Germany is the top exporter of hazards, according to OECD. Carbon dioxide is one of the prime industrial gases. The US produces the highest output in terms of total emissions and per capita.

The quality of the natural environment is affected by gases which are produced as part of commercial and industrial activity. Carbon dioxide (CO_2) is emitted by operations which range from motoring to running many forms of industrial equipment. The USA is the world's largest producer of carbon dioxide in terms of CO_2 emissions per capita, producing 5.33 tonnes of carbon dioxide per capita in 1993 (or 1356M tonnes in total). Canada is the second largest producer of CO_2 on per capita basis with 4.15 tonnes per capita. China is the second largest in terms of total CO_2 produced with 694M tonnes produced.

Top 10 exporters of hazardous waste.

Rank	Country	Annual waste export (000s of metric tonnes)
1	Germany	522
2	Netherlands	195
3	Canada	175
4	USA	157
5	Switzerland	121
6	UK	83
7	Austria	68
=8	Hungary	25
=8	Sweden	25
10	Finland	24

Source: OECD

Environmental damage from acid rain has been reported in northern Europe and North America. High levels of acid rain have also been detected in other areas of

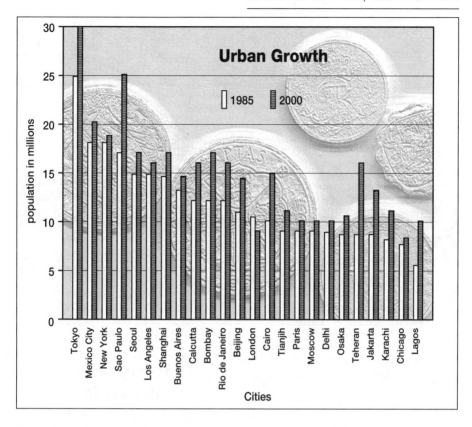

the world, such as above the tropical rain forest of Africa. Acid rain has destroyed plant and animal life in lakes, damaged forests and crops, endangered marine life in coastal waters, eroded structures, and contaminated drinking water.

(S) The sulphur dioxide (SO_2) produced by industry is the principle cause of acid rain. It is often associated with power generated by certain types of coal fired power station. Canada is the largest producer of SO_2 on a per capita basis with total emissions of 119 kg per head. The next largest on this basis are the USA and Germany with total emissions of 81 kg and 71 kg per capita. The USA is the largest overall producer with a total output of 20.5M tonnes.

(S) Some industries and companies have developed bad and good reputations for their effect on the natural environment. Sometimes, this is an apparently inevitable result of the nature of their industry. It is hard, for example, to build up a large, opencast mining industry without a negative effect on the natural environment, at least in the short term. Elsewhere, the impact is considerable, but there is little public awareness. For example, for a long time IBM were the largest users of CFCs – the gases thought to deplete the ozone layer – but there was little public knowledge.

Land deterioration is a growing problem across the world as the 'green revolution' slows down and environmental damage increases. Deterioration is worst in Central America.

The scale of this deterioration and the increased 'industrialization' of agriculture partly explains the dramatic growth in urbanization around the world.

The biggest cities are all major business centres. Urban growth is accelerating: Tokyo is **the largest city in the world**

Tokyo, *the world's largest metropolis with 25,000,000 citizens living in the city proper and the contiguous urban area. Nearly one half of the world's twenty largest cities are in the Pacific Rim, the fastest growing economic region of the globe. (Spectrum Colour Library).*

with a population of 25 million, set to grow to 30 million by the year 2000. In 1995 there were 300 cities with over 1,000,000 inhabitants including 13 with over 10,000,000. In 1900 there were only 16 cities with over 1,000,000 inhabitants.

Where to do business

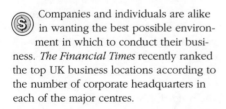 Companies and individuals are alike in wanting the best possible environment in which to conduct their business. *The Financial Times* recently ranked the top UK business locations according to the number of corporate headquarters in each of the major centres.

In Britain, Black Horse Relocation recently ranked Birmingham as the most attractive business location.

Each year, the US Heritage Foundation identifies the best countries in which to do

Top 10 UK business locations (1995).

Rank	Location	Number of corporate headquarters
1	London	207
2	Birmingham	17
=3	Edinburgh.	13
=3	Reading	13
5	Slough	12
6	Manchester	11
=7	Bradford	9
=7	Glasgow	9
=7	Kingston-upon-Thames.	9
=7	Leeds	9

Source: *Financial Times*

business. In 1995, Hong Kong was ranked by the Foundation as top of this list.

In sharp contrast to the best places in which to do business, Indonesia was identified by Transparency International and

Top 10 Office Rents

Rank	Location	Country	Rent ($ per m2)
1	Bombay	India	1,840
2	Tokyo	Japan	1,600
3	Hong Kong	Hong Kong	1,300
4	Beijing	China	970
=5	Shanghai	China	880
=5	New Delhi	India	880
7	London	UK	730
=8	Singapore	Singapore	670
=8	Paris	France	670
10	Frankfurt	Germany	570

Source: *The World in 1996 - The Economist Publications.*

World prosperity league – GDP per head at purchasing power parity

Rank	Country
1	Luxembourg
2	United States
3	Switzerland
4	Japan
5	Belgium
6	Norway
7	Denmark
8	Canada
9	Iceland
10	Austria
11	France
12	Germany
13	Italy
14	Netherlands
15	Australia
16	Hong Kong
17	Singapore
18	United Kingdom
19	Sweden
20	New Zealand

Source: OECD

Top London business areas (1995)

Rank	Location (by postcode)	Number of corporate headquarters
=1	London EC	55
=1	London W	55
3	London SW	50
4	London WC	16
5	London NW	12
6	London SE	9
7	London E	7
8	London N	3

Source: *Financial Times*

Göttingen University as the country most afflicted by corruption.

The powerful link between the health of the local business community and prosperity is vividly illustrated by OECD's 'world prosperity league'. Virtually all the countries identified by the Heritage Foundation (as the best places in which to do business) are in the 'prosperity league', while only one of the countries most afflicted by corruption is present.

Best options for the future

And for the future, what are the best jobs to opt for? According to *U.S. News & World Report* the future will be rosy for those in the following professions.

Sector	Job title	Average salary for top position ($)
Accountancy	International accountant	55,000 – 84,000
Architecture	Design/Build specialist	61,500 +
Consulting	Human resources pro	62,000
Education	Specialist in English as a second language	40,500
Engineering	Software engineer	60,000
Entertainment	Computer animator	80,000 +
Environment	Computer mapper	75,000 +
Finance	Investment manager	175,000 – 325,000
Health care	Information specialist	82,500
Hospitality	Food service manager	48,000
Human services	Residential counsellor	25,000 – 35,000
Information services	Web master	100,000 +
Law	Employment lawyer	173,000 – 194,000
Media	Online content developer	80,000
Medicine	Internist in infectious diseases	215,000
Sales	Wireless salesperson	70,000
Science research	Genetic researcher	80,000
Social Work	Geriatric case manager	45,000
Sports management	Corporate sales representative	80,000 +
Telecommunications	Computer security expert	90,000

Source: *U.S. News & World Report*

New jobs and new types of career are appearing; new industries are being established; new companies are being founded. And in these innovations, new business records are being set all the time. All that is constant is risk.

Index

3M 65, 68
ABB Asea Brown Boveri 101, 106, 195, 204
ABB Lumus Crest 31
ABN-Amro Holding 15
ADA 70
AEG 101
AEI 21
AFL-CIO 115
AMARCO 187
AT&T (American Telegraph & Telephone) 12, 13, 14, 19, 20, 24, 68, 73, 158, 191, 204, 205
ATLAS 70
Abbey National 15, 26, 95, 199
Abbott Mead Vickers 136
Aberdeen 36, 185
absenteeism 107-8
Accor 198
accountants 29, 173, 202
achromatic lens 76
acid rain 208-9
Adair, Red 187
adding machine 75, 77
Addison 149
Adidas 120
Admiral cigarettes 133
advertising 119-37; agents 126-7, 133-7
Aeroflot 198
aeroplane 69, 72
aerosol can 66, 79
Aerospaciale 101
Africa 55, 102, 209
Agnelli, Gianni/family 88, 91
agribusiness 183
Agricultural Industrial Complex Workers Union 109
Agrigeneral Co. LP 182
Agroprombank 16
aid and trade 96
air bag 67; brake 63; conditioning 78; cooled engine 64; pump 56, 57
airlines 197-8
airports, major 197
airship 78
Albany (NY) 44, 60
Alcatel Alsthom 73, 195, 204
al-Fayed, Mohamed 173
Algeria 24, 141, 187
Alldays Peacock & Co Ltd. 36
Allen & Overy 30, 202
Allen, Robert 205
Alley, William 90
Alliance, Sir David 207
Allianz Holding 199
Allied Domecq 26

Allied Lyons 170
Allied Signal 208
all-metal aircraft 78
alloys, development of 69
alternating current, first 63
aluminium 77, 189, 190
alum production 38
Amalfi Tables 36
Amalgamated Society of Carpenters & Joiners 111
Amalgamated Society of Engineers 49, 111
Amblin Entertainment 205
American Brands 90
American Declaration of Independence 42
American Express 90, 132
American Federation of Labour 49, 111, 115
American Smelting 20
American Stores 104
American Tobacco 20
Ammirati & Puris/Lintas 135
Amoco 20, 23, 185
Amsted Industries 118
Amsterdam 37, 39, 40, 161, 198, 201
Anaconda Copper 19, 20
anaesthetics 76
analog information 72
Analytical Engine 69
ancient world, business in 33-4
Andorra 147
Andreas, Dwayne 90
Anglo American 190
Anglo Iranian Oil/Persian Oil 21, 144, 185, 186
annual model changes (cars) 64
Ansaldo S.p.A. 31
antibiotics 65
anticoagulants 78
antiglare headlights 71
antihistamines 80
anti-knocking gasoline 66, 74, 78
anti-trades union legislation 49, 50, 110, 113
Antwerp 38, 94
Apple Macintosh Computer 68, 147-8, 204
aqualung 65, 80
aqueducts 35
Archer Daniels Midland 90
Archer, Thomas 125
Archibald Turner & Co.106
arc lamp 76
Argentina 140, 167, 170, 182
Argyll Group 26

Arkwright, Sir Richard 43, 58, 59, 88
Armando Testa Group 136
Armour & Co. 19, 183, 193
Armstrong Whitworth 21
ar-Rhazi 54
arts, sponsorship of 97-8
Arthur Anderson 29, 202
Asahi Bank 15; Mutual Life 30
Asarco 190
Asia 28, 39, 81, 93, 99, 101, 114, 208
aspirin 77, 142-4
assembly line production 78
assets, largest commercial 15
Associated Portland Cement 22
Athens 201
Atlanta (Ga.) 96, 121, 173, 197
Atlantic City 165
Atlantic Richfield 23
Atlee, Clement 114
atomic bomb 65, 80
Atvidaberg Industries 178
Australia 29, 50, 60, 107, 140, 147, 178, 181, 190, 211
Austria 60, 123, 124, 136, 140, 173, 208, 211
automated digital computer 80
automatic drive 74, 78; warehousing 72
automobile *see* car
Avis 118
Avon Products 20, 149
Avondale 118
Ayer, N.W. & Partners 135
Azerbaijan 144, 145, 181, 187
Azores 40
BAA 26
BASF 196
BAT Industries 14, 16, 21, 24, 25, 100, 107, 195
BBC 132
BBDO 133, 134, 135, 136
BCCI 173
BDO Binder Hamlyn 202
BET 100
BMRB International 140
BMW 120
BOC Group 26
BP (British Petroleum) 12, 21, 23, 24, 25, 31, 94, 96, 145, 185, 204
BT (British Telecom) 12, 14, 20, 21, 22, 24, 25, 94, 96, 99, 100, 106, 107, 149, 191, 192, 204
BTR 14, 21, 25, 100
BZW 171
Babbage, Charles 69, 70

213